Published by Princeton Architectural Press
37 East Seventh Street
New York, New York 10003

For a free catalog of books, call 1.800.722.6657.
Visit our web site at www.papress.com.

Editor: Lauren Nelson Packard
Designer: Abbott Miller, Pentagram

Special thanks to: Nettie Aljian, Sara Bader,
Dorothy Ball, Nicola Bednarek, Janet Behning,
Becca Casbon, Penny (Yuen Pik) Chu, Russell
Fernandez, Pete Fitzpatrick, Wendy Fuller, Sara
Hart, Jan Haux, Clare Jacobson, John King,
Mark Lamster, Nancy Eklund Later, Linda
Lee, Katharine Myers, Scott Tennent, Jennifer
Thompson, Paul Wagner, Joseph Weston, and
Deb Wood of Princeton Architectural Press
—Kevin C. Lippert, publisher

Library of Congress Cataloging-in-Publication Data
Bierut, Michael.
Seventy-nine short essays on design / Michael Bierut.
p. cm.
Includes bibliographical references and index.
ISBN 978-1-56898-699-9 (alk. paper)
1. Commercial art—United States—History—20th
century. 2. Graphic arts—United States—History—
20th century. I. Title. II. Title: 79 short essays on
design.
NC998.5.A1B52 2007
741.6—dc22
2006101224

Seventy-nine Short Essays on Design

Michael Bierut

Princeton Architectural Press
New York

"Art should be like a good game of baseball—non-monumental, democratic and humble. With no hits, no runs, and no errors at the bottom of the ninth, we know something historical is happening. Good art leaves no residue."

Siah Armajani, 1985

"The cheaper the crook, the gaudier the patter."

Sam Spade (Humphrey Bogart) to Wilmer Cook (Elijah Cook, Jr.) in *The Maltese Falcon*, screenplay by John Huston from the novel by Dashiell Hammett, 1941

Contents

Preface

I consider myself a designer, not a writer.

Over ten years ago, on the basis of very little evidence, three brilliant editors each began giving me modest writing assignments: Steve Heller, Chee Pearlman, and Rick Poynor. Their encouragement and advice taught me how to begin to think as a writer. About four years ago, Rick, Bill Drenttel, Jessica Helfand, and I decided, without any particular game plan, to create a blog. This book is largely the product of that decision, and of that friendship. I go to work every day to be inspired and stimulated by the best designers in the world: Jim Biber, Michael Gericke, Luke Hayman, Abbott Miller, Lisa Strausfeld, and especially Paula Scher, whose own writing was an important model for me. Abbott created the elegant (and funny) design for this book. Sash Fernando heroically saw the design through to completion. I am grateful to all of them. At Princeton Architectural Press, I thank Kevin Lippert, Mark Lamster, Clare Jacobson, and Lauren Nelson Packard; they suggested this book and actually made it happen.

Finally, I send my love and thanks to Dorothy, Elizabeth, Drew, and Martha Marie.

Writing about design has been a valuable way for me to understand the work I do. I hope that reading about design provides some value to others.

Warning: May Contain Non-Design Content

I write for a blog called *Design Observer*. Usually my co-editors and I write about design. Sometimes, we don't. Sometimes, for instance, we write about politics. Whenever this happens, in come the comments: "What does this have to do with design? If you have a political agenda please keep it to other pages. I am not sure of your leaning but I come here for design."

I come here for design. It happens every time the subject strays beyond fonts and layout software. ("Obscure references. . . trying to impress each other. . . please, can we start talking some sense?") In these cases, our visitors react like diners who just got served *penne alla vodka* in a Mexican restaurant: it's not the kind of dish they came for, and they doubt the proprietors have the expertise required to serve it up.

Guys, I know how you feel. I used to feel the same way.

More than twenty years ago, I served on a committee that had been formed to explore the possibilities of setting up a New York chapter of the American Institute of Graphic Arts (AIGA). Almost all of the other committee members were older, well-known—and, in some cases, legendary—designers. I was there to be a worker bee.

I had only been in New York for a year or so. Back in design school in 1970s Cincinnati, I had been starved for design. It would be hard for a student today to imagine a world so isolated. No email, no blogs. Only one (fairly inaccessible) design conference that no one I knew had ever attended. Because there were no

AGIA chapters, there were no AGIA student groups. Few of us could afford subscriptions to the only design magazines I knew about, *CA*, *Print*, and *Graphis*. Those few copies we got our hands on were passed around with the fervor of girlie magazines after lights-out at a Boy Scout jamboree. No *How*, no *Step*, and of course no *Emigre* or *dot dot dot*. We studied the theory of graphic design day in and day out, but the real practice of graphic design was something mysterious that happened somewhere else. It wasn't even a subject for the history books: Phil Meggs wouldn't publish his monumental *History of Graphic Design* until 1983.

In New York, I was suddenly in—what seemed to me then, at least—the center of the design universe. There was already so much to see and do, but I wanted more. I was ravenous. Establishing a New York chapter for the AIGA would mean more lectures, more events, more graphic design. For the committee's first meeting, I had made a list of all designers I would love to see speak, and I volunteered to share it with the group.

A few names in, one of the well-known designers in the group cut me off with a bored wave. "Oh God, not more show-and-tell portfolio crap." To my surprise, the others began nodding in agreement. "Yeah, instead of wallowing in graphic design stuff, we should have something like... a Betty Boop film festival." A Betty Boop film festival? I wanted to hear a lecture from Josef Müller-Brockmann, not watch cartoons. I assumed my senior committee members were pretentious and jaded, considering themselves—bizarrely—too sophisticated to admit they cared about the one thing I cared about most: design. I was confused and crestfallen. Please, I wanted to say, can we start talking some sense?

I thought I was a pretty darned good designer back then. A few years before, in my senior year, I had designed something I was still quite proud of: a catalog for Cincinnati's Contemporary Arts Center on the work of visionary theater designer Robert Wilson. The CAC didn't hire me because I knew anything about Robert Wilson. I had never heard of him. More likely they liked my price: $1,000, all in, for a 112-page book, cheap even by 1980 standards.

The CAC's director, Robert Stearns, invited me to his house one evening to see the material that needed to be included in the catalog: about 75 photographs, captions, and a major essay by the *New York Times* critic John Rockwell. I had never heard of John Rockwell. To get us in the mood, Stearns put on some music that he said had been composed by Wilson's latest collaborator. It was called *Einstein on the Beach* and it was weird and repetitive. The composer was Philip Glass. I had never heard of *Einstein on the Beach* or Philip Glass. Stearns gave me the album cover to look at. I noticed with almost tearful relief that it had been designed by Milton Glaser. I had heard of Milton Glaser.

I was completely unfazed by the fact that I knew nothing about Robert Wilson, John Rockwell, *Einstein on the Beach*, or Philip Glass. In my mind, they were all tangential to the real work ahead, which would simply be to lay out 75 photographs and 8,000 words of text over 112 pages in a way that would impress the likes of Milton Glaser. With single-minded obliviousness, I plunged ahead, got the job done, and was quite pleased with the results.

About a year after my disappointing meeting with the planners of the AIGA New York chapter, I finally saw my first Robert Wilson production. It was the Brooklyn Academy of Music's 1984 revival of *Einstein on the Beach*. And sitting there in the audience, utterly transported, it came crashing down on me: I had completely screwed up that catalog. Seen live, Wilson's work was epic, miraculous, hypnotic, transcendent. My stupid layouts were none of those things. They weren't even pale, dim echoes of any of those things. They were simply no more and no less than a whole lot of empty-headed graphic design. And graphic design wasn't enough. It never is.

Over the years, I came to realize that my best work has always involved subjects that interested me, or—even better—subjects about which I've become interested, and even passionate about, through the very process of doing design work. I believe I'm still passionate about graphic design. But the great thing about graphic design is that it is almost always about something else. Corporate law. Professional football. Art. Politics. Robert Wilson. And if I can't get excited about whatever that something else is, I really have trouble doing good work as a designer. To me, the conclusion is inescapable: the more things you're interested in, the better your work will be.

In that spirit, I like to think that this book might be a place for people to read about graphic design. But I also like to think that it's a place where someone might accidentally discover some other things, things that seem to have nothing to do with design: screenwriting, soul singers, 50-year-old experimental novels, cold war diplomacy. You might even find something about Betty Boop.

Not everything is design. But design is about everything. So do yourself a favor: be ready for anything.

WHY DESIGNERS CAN'T THINK

Graphic designers are lucky. As the people who structure much of the world's communications, we get to vicariously partake of as many fields of interest as we have clients. In a single day, a designer can talk about real estate with one client, cancer cures with another, and forklift trucks with a third. Imagine how tedious it must be for a dentist who has nothing to do all day but worry about teeth.

The men and women who invented graphic design in America were largely self-taught; they didn't have the opportunity to go to fully developed specialized design schools, because none existed. Yet somehow these people managed to prosper without four years of Typography, Visual Problem Solving, and Advanced Aesthetics. What they lacked in formal training they made up for with insatiable curiosity not only about art and design, but culture, science, politics, and history.

Today, most professionals will admit to alarm about the huge and ever-growing number of programs in graphic design. Each year, more and more high school seniors decide that they have a bright future in "graphics," often without much of an idea of what graphics is. This swelling tide of eighteen-year-old, would-be designers is swallowed up thirstily by more and more programs in graphic design at art schools, community colleges, and universities. A few years later, out they come, ready to take their places as professional designers, working for what everybody cheerfully hopes will be an infinitely expanding pool of clients.

There are many ways to teach graphic design, and almost any curriculum will defy neat cubbyholing. Nevertheless, American programs seem to fall into two broad categories: process schools and portfolio schools. Or, if you prefer, "Swiss" schools and "slick" schools.

Process schools favor a form-driven problem-solving approach. The first assignments are simple exercises: drawing letterforms, "translating" three-dimensional objects into idealized high-contrast images, and basic still-life photography. In the intermediate stages, the formal exercises are combined in different ways: relate the drawing of a flute to the hand-drawn letter *N*, combine the letter *N* with a photograph of a ballet slipper. In the final stage, these combinations are turned into "real" graphic design: Letter *N* plus flute drawing plus ballet slipper photo plus 42 pt. Univers equals, voilà, a poster for Rudolf Nureyev. Of course, if the advanced student gets an assignment to design a poster for, say, an exhibition on Thomas Edison, he or she is tempted to (literally) revert to form: combine the letter E, drawing of a movie camera, photo of a light bulb, etc. One way or another, the process schools trace their lineage back to the advanced program of the *Kunstgewerbeschule* in Basel, Switzerland. Sometimes the instructors experienced the program only second or third hand, having themselves studied with someone who studied with someone in Basel.

The Swiss-style process schools seem to have thrived largely as a reaction against the perceived "slickness" of the portfolio schools. While the former have been around in force for only the past fifteen years or so, the latter are home-grown institutions with roots in the 1950s.

While the unspoken goal of the process school is to duplicate the ideal-ized black-and-white boot camp regimen of far-off Switzerland, the portfolio school has a completely different, admittedly more mercenary, aim: to provide students with polished "books" that will get them good jobs upon graduation. The problem-solving mode is conceptual, with a bias for appealing, memorable, populist imagery. The product, not process, is king. Now, portfolio schools will rebut this by pointing to the copious tissue layouts that often supplement the awesomely slick work in their graduates' portfolios. Nonetheless, at the end of the line of tissues is always a beautifully propped photograph of an immaculate mock-up of a perfume bottle. Seldom will portfolio schools encourage students to spend six months on a twenty-part structural analysis of, say, the semiotics of a Campbell's soup label as an end in itself. Unlike the full-time teachers of process schools, the portfolio schools are staffed largely by working profession-als who teach part time, who are impatient with idle exercises that don't relate to the "real world."

However politely the two camps behave in discussions on design education, the fact is, they hate each other. To the portfolio schools, the "Swiss" method is hermetic, arcane, and meaningless to the general public. To the process schools, the "slick" method is distastefully commercial, shallow, and derivative.

Oddly, though, the best-trained graduates of either camp are equally sought after by employers. East Coast corporate identity firms love the process school graduates; anyone who's spent six months combining a letterform and a ballet shoe won't mind being mired in a fat standards manual for three years. On the other hand, package design firms are happy to get the portfolio school graduates: not only do they have a real passion for tighter-than-tight comps, but they can generate hundreds of stylistically diverse alternatives to show indecisive clients.

What, then, is wrong with graphic design education? If there's a smorgas-bord of pedagogical approaches, and employers who can find use for different kinds of training, who suffers? The answer is not in how schools are different, but how they're the same.

Both process schools and portfolio schools have something in common: whether the project is the esoteric Nureyev poster or the Bloomingdale's-ready perfume bottle comp, what's valued is the way graphic design looks, not what it means. Programs will pay lip service to meaning in design with references to "semiotics" (Swiss) or "conceptual problem solving" (slick), but these nuances are applied in a cultural vacuum. In many programs, if not most, it's possible to study graphic design for four years without any meaningful exposure to the fine arts, literature, science, history, politics, or any of the other disciplines that unite us in a common culture.

Well, so what? What does a graphic designer need with this other stuff? Employers want trained designers, not writers and economists.

Perhaps the deficiencies in the typical design education aren't handicaps at first. The new graduate doesn't need to know economics any more than a plumber does; like a tradesman, he or she needs skills that are, for the most part, technical.

But five or ten years down the road, how can a designer plan an annual report without some knowledge of economics? Lay out a book without an inter-est in, if not a passion for, literature? Design a logo for a high-tech company without some familiarity with science?

Obviously, they can and do. Some designers fill in their educational gaps as they go along; some just fake it. But most of the mediocre design today comes from designers who are faithfully doing as they were taught in school: they worship at the altar of the visual.

The pioneering design work of the 1940s and 1950s continues to interest and excite us while work from the intervening years looks more and more dated and irrelevant. Without the benefit of intensive specialized programs, the pioneers of our profession, by necessity, became well-rounded intellectually. Their work draws its power from deep in the culture of their times.

Modern design education, on the other hand, is essentially value-free: every problem has a purely visual solution that exists outside any cultural context. Some of the most tragic victims of this attitude hail not from the world of high culture, but from the low. Witness the case of a soft-drink manufacturer that pays a respected design firm a lot of money to "update" a classic logo. The product of American design education responds: "Clean up an old logo? You bet," and goes right to it. In a vacuum that excludes popular as well as high culture, the meaning of the mark in its culture is disregarded. Why not just say no? The option isn't considered.

Our clients usually are not other designers; they sell real estate, cure cancer, make forklift trucks. Nor are there many designers in the audiences our work eventually finds. They must be touched with communication that is genuinely resonant, not self-referential. To find the language for that, one must look beyond Manfred Maier's *Principles of Design* or the last *Communication Arts Design Annual*.

Nowadays, the passion of design educators seems to be technology; they fear that computer illiteracy will handicap their graduates. But it's the broader kind of illiteracy that's more profoundly troubling. Until educators find a way to expose their students to a meaningful range of culture, graduates will continue to speak in languages that only their classmates understand. And designers, more and more, will end up talking to themselves.

Waiting for Permission

It almost seems like a dream now. Big budgets. Fat, happy, suggestible clients cruising happily along, with fat, happy design firms feeding greedily in their wake. Lavish corporate identity manuals. Hardcover brochures promoting office space in shiny buildings by brand-name architects. Annual reports for non-profit clients—non-profit!—with a little picture on the cover, a flyleaf with nothing printed on it, then another page, new paper stock, with just one or two words in 8-point type, then another page, another paper stock—with nothing on it—then a piece of coated paper with another little picture on it, and then—maybe—the thing would finally start, after the atmosphere had been properly created...

I began my career as a graphic designer in the 1980s. That decade seems far away now, so far away, so much farther than the calendar tells us. To young designers entering the field today, those days will surely seem like an impossibly golden age, one of almost unimaginable excess and bravura. Even to those of us who lived through it, it takes the incontrovertible evidence of a flashy portfolio piece—circa, say, 1986—to remind us how much things have changed.

And they have changed. Design today sees a renewed awareness of environmental issues, much of it lip service abounding with soy-based images of squirrels and pine cones, but for the most part deeply felt. It doesn't necessarily mean that graphic designers have ceased to trade in excess for its own sake, but the examples of that excess are just as likely to provoke embarrassment as envy.

Designers also demonstrate a new social consciousness as well. The voice this consciousness takes is sometimes cracked and halting (perhaps due to years of disuse) but genuine nonetheless. Ten years ago, it seemed as though a typical pro-bono piece was a lavish six-color production of a clever visual pun: today it's just as likely to be something down-and-dirty that at least looks as though it was designed to truly help the client's cause rather than add awards to the designer's trophy cases.

All in all, designers now seem to want more than ever to create work that's appropriate, that's relevant, that challenges the client's brief, that's aimed at more than the next design competition. In short, the spirit is willing. But the flesh, for the most part, remains weak. While these issues dominate designers' consciences, they still remain peripheral to most of our practices. Designers continue to work dutifully (probably, in fact, more urgently than ever these days), wishing that they could do what they think is right, rather than what they're told to do, all in the name of "professionalism." The fundamental idea of truly challenging the client's expectations, of getting outside the grinding process of filling the orders and shipping the goods, of "being bad," (as Tibor Kalman exhorted us at the 1989 American Institute of Graphic Arts Conference in San Antonio) still seems an elusive goal for most designers.

Is it hard to see why? As Milton Glaser said at that same conference, "Friends are friends, but a guy's gotta eat." Most of us would say that our ideals, whether newfound or long held, give way at the end of the day to the pressures of running our businesses; that the sanest course of action is to push environmental activism or social consciousness as far as you can and then back off to fight another day; and that a client's a client and an invoice is an invoice. In the end it's all about money, isn't it?

Well, maybe not. Maybe it's about something else, something that hasn't changed, something to do not with money but with the very structure of the relationship between designers and their clients.

Most relationships in daily life are defined, at least in part, by hierarchy. Someone is in charge and someone is following orders. Often these relationships are immutable: parent and child, student and teacher, employee and employer. Occasionally the roles are more interchangeable, as in the case of marriages or partnerships.

If you believe what you read in most designer's promotional literature, that's what the designer-client relationship is meant to be: a partnership. Sometimes even clients themselves (at least new clients) enthuse about this idea as well. But privately, most designers would concede that most of their client relationships are anything but partnerships, a fact that's seen as both frustrating and basically unchangeable.

In the early sixties, a psychologist at Yale University named Stanley Milgram did a series of notorious experiments that explored the dynamics of hierarchical relationships, ones where someone was in charge and someone else was following orders. He wanted to find out how far someone would follow the orders of another person if he perceived that person's authority as legitimate.

The experiments had many variations, but they all basically went like this. Milgram asked people to volunteer for an experiment they were told was about the relationship of learning and punishment. The volunteers, who came from all walks of life, were each paid $4.50 and were shown the same setup when they arrived in Milgram's lab.

They were introduced to another person they were told was a fellow volunteer. The second person was to serve as the "learner" and the subject was to act as "teacher." The teacher would be directed by the experimenter to read a series of word pairs to the learner, and then test the learner on his memory. For each answer the learner got wrong, the teacher was to administer to him an electric shock. This was done with a control panel with thirty switches ranging from 15 to 450 volts, labeled in increments "slight shock," "moderate shock," "strong shock," and on up to "extreme intensity shock," "danger: severe shock," and finally the cryptic and presumably frightening label "XXX." For each wrong answer, the volunteer teacher was to increase the shock level by one notch.

Of course, the whole setup was an illusion. The shock panel was a convincing-looking but harmless prop; the fellow volunteer, the "learner," was an employee of Milgram's who was particularly good at screaming in agony when receiving the imaginary shocks. The purpose of the exercise was not to study learning, but to study obedience: Milgram wanted to find out how far people would go up the scale, how much pain they would inflict on a fellow human being, just because someone else told them to.

Before he began, Milgram asked his students and fellow psychologists to predict how many people would administer the highest shock. The answers were always the same: at the most, one or two out of the hundred. Milgram himself, then, was surprised when almost two-thirds, 64% of the subjects, did as they were told and went all the way to the top of the scale.

Milgram did a lot of variations in the experiment to try to drive the number down. He moved the setting from Yale to a tawdry-looking storefront; he had the learner complain of a possibly fatal heart condition; he fixed it so the subject actually had to hold the learner's hand down on a "shock plate." None of it made much of a difference. No matter what, about half of the volunteers administered all the shocks to the helpless learner.

These experiments are fairly well known to the general public, and the most common moral drawn from them is something like, "People are capable of anything if they're given an excuse to do it." However, this is a misinterpretation: most of the subjects, even the fully obedient ones, were anything but cheerful as they followed the experimenter's commands. In fact, it was common for subjects to protest, weep, or beg to break off the experiment. Still, the obedient majority, prodded calmly by the experimenter, would pull themselves together, do what had to be done, and administer the shocks.

Of course, designers are regularly paid a lot more than $4.50 to do things a lot less overtly heinous than administering a 450-volt shock to a fellow human being. Occasionally they help promote a cause or product they truly don't believe in or design something to intentionally deceive the public. But these dilemmas are fairly rare.

Most commonly, what most of us have done at one time or another is make something a little stupider or a little uglier than we really thought it ought to be. We've had good reasons: we need the money, we need the experience, we don't want to jeopardize the relationship, we know it's wrong, we have no choice. This would sound familiar to Dr. Milgram. "Some subjects were totally convinced of the wrongness of what they were doing," he observed, "but could not bring themselves to make an open break with authority. Some derived satisfaction from their thoughts and felt that—within themselves, at least—they had been on the side of the angels. What they had failed to realize is that subjective feelings are largely irrelevant to the moral issue at hand so long as they are not transformed into action." We too somehow remain on the side of the angels.

So is it all about money? Probably not. The subjects in Milgram's experiments often wanted desperately to quit, but they just couldn't get up and walk away. What kept them at the shock panel wasn't the $4.50 they were being paid but their idea that the experimenter, and not they, and certainly not the helpless subject at the receiving end of the wire, was in charge. Designers, even in a climate that finds us more and more driven to question the social and ethical underpinnings of our work, cede the same authority to our clients.

Most of us enter the field of design filled with individual passions and unrealized visions, and learn quickly that the other people know better: first teachers, then bosses, finally even the judges of design competitions and editors of design annuals. We put aside our doubts—none of us want to be prima donnas anyway—and become comfortable professionals in just another service industry. And when we're roused to our feet by a call to action, second thoughts set in. "That's easy for him (Tibor, Milton, fill in the blank) to say, "but my clients won't let me do that." But of course that's not true. In fact, we don't know what would happen if we tried. We take too much pride in the quality of our "service" to find out. So business as usual remains business as usual.

Who's in charge here, anyway?

The designer-client relationship can and should be a partnership. It's time to stop blaming the client when it's not. Our work can and should serve society. It should serve an audience beyond ourselves, beyond our clients, and beyond the next design annual. Otherwise, the member of that audience, the users of the products and messages that we produce, will remain wired to their seats, awaiting the next shock.

And we designers, wanting to do what's right but afraid to make trouble, will keep sitting, maybe just a little more nervously, our fingers on our control panels, waiting for permission.

How to Become Famous

Fame, of course, is relative. Madonna and David Letterman are famous. Most normal people, on the other hand, have never heard of Milton Glaser or Paul Rand. In the context of this little guide, fame refers to something very specific: a famous graphic designer is famous among other graphic designers. My mother, for instance, knows that I'm famous because my sister-in-law, who's a dental hygienist, used to clean the teeth of a graphic designer in my home town back in Ohio. Nothing could have astonished my sister-in-law more than when her patient asked her if she was related to me. Other than that, I can't say for sure that being famous counts for anything.

I was asked once to prepare a presentation with the title "Lifestyles of the Rich and Famous Graphic Designers." Rich I know nothing about. It was surprisingly easy to calculate fame, however. I took out the Membership Directory of the American Institute of Graphic Arts. I went through the list and ticked off anyone who had a name I even vaguely recognized from awards books or the lecture circuit. The result was 185 or so names. With further thought I even could have put them in order, from most to least famous.

That was in 1989. Now, there are even more famous graphic designers. Yet, I sense that most people feel there really aren't enough famous graphic designers. A lot of women designers don't feel there are enough famous women designers, a lot of African-American designers don't feel there are enough famous African-American designers, a lot of designers from Ohio don't feel there are enough famous Buckeye designers, and so forth. And, of course, a lot of individual designers don't feel that they themselves are sufficiently famous.

This is too bad, because I feel that becoming famous isn't really all that difficult. Most kinds of fame are based, to a certain extent, on individual merit. But there are a lot of trivial things involved as well. These have to do with things like speeches and competitions. You can only do so much with the talent you were born with. On the other hand, these trivial things are sometimes amusingly simple to manipulate. But remember, there's no guarantee that being famous counts for anything.

How to Win Graphic Design Competitions

People who enter design competitions, particularly people who enter and lose design competitions, comfort themselves by imagining that something sinister goes on in the tomblike confines of the judges' chambers.

When you judge a competition yourself, you learn that nothing could be farther from the truth. Behind the closed doors are table after table covered with pieces of graphic design. Like most things in life, only a few of these are really good. Each judge moves along the tables, looking at each piece just long enough to ascertain whether he or she likes it. It takes a long time and a lot of people to produce even a modest piece of graphic design. The judging process takes less than a second.

The predictability of this ritual, which has all the glamour and sinister aspects of digging a ditch, makes it easy to devise some simple rules that will increase your chances of winning.

1. Enter only the kind of pieces that win in design competitions. For the record, the kinds of things that win in design competitions are cool-looking projects that solve easily understandable problems. Things that are brilliant responses to intricate marketing briefs but that can't be understood by another designer in less than a second will not win. Exception: if something is sufficiently cool-looking, it may not need to be understandable. In fact, being incomprehensible may be part of its allure. (Negotiating your way through the ever-shifting sands of "cool-looking" is your problem.) Note: don't be tempted by competitions that invite you to fill out long forms describing the problem, the client, the market situation, the strategy, and so forth. Very few of the judges read them.

2. Don't enter things that rely on complicated unfolding or unwrapping operations. The first few judges won't bother opening it. The one that does won't bother putting it back together. Also, don't enter things that involve confetti or other supposedly festive materials spilling unexpectedly out of envelopes.

3. Try to enter so your thing is the biggest thing on the table. The pieces to be judged are almost always separated into categories so like is judged with like. Having your piece be one of the largest in its category gives it a tremendous advantage. For instance, your 17" x 22" season schedule poster for the local symphony orchestra that looks nice over your desk will look pathetic next to a gargantuan Ivan Chermayeff Masterpiece Theatre bus shelter poster. Enter it as an "announcement" instead. It will compete—much more successfully, trust me—against things like wedding invitations.

4. Don't enter slides unless you're sure they're going to be projected. See number 3, above. Nothing is smaller than a 35mm slide with a big old entry form hanging off it.

How to Give a Speech

Graphic designers are lucky in that when speaking before a group they can show slides almost the whole time. This obviates most of the advice on speech-making you get in airport bookstores about eye contact and forceful gestures. The only thing left to remember is the reason that the audience is there: they want to see what you're like. The rules:

1. When in doubt, show two trays of 80 slides each, first one, then the other. Dissolve units break down. Side-by-side images get out of sequence. More than 160 slides make people's butts hurt. Don't worry, plenty can still go wrong.

2. Never describe the slide people are looking at. A slide presentation should follow the same dramatic rhythm of an Alfred Hitchcock movie: tension followed by release, tension followed by release. Describe the design problem you were asked to solve. Give the audience a moment to think what they would do. Then, show them what you did. Done properly, this acquires the cadence, and ultimately the effect, of telling a joke. It's boring to be told what you're looking at: you already know what you're looking at. Instead, try to make the audience guess the next thing they're going to see.

3. Never read your speech. It's tempting, but it tends to make an audience dislike you. If you must, use really comprehensive notes instead.

4. If possible, avoid showing slides of annual report spreads or slides created with presentation software. It's very difficult to say anything funny or interesting about projected images of spreads from even well-designed annual reports. And presentation software slides—with all those gradated backgrounds and rules and bullets and Times Roman with crisp little drop shadows—will make your audience afraid you're going to bore them. At the very least, they will question your choice of typeface.

5. Choose the last slide of the first tray with special care. It should be really great or really surprising or really funny. Why? To ensure a satisfied buzz in the audience during the endless amount of time it takes to change to the second tray. For that reason, never change trays in the middle of a thought: the sense of deflation in the audience is palpable when the second tray goes on and you're still talking about that same old damn project.

How to Do Great Design Work

It should be obvious by now that great work, in this context, is work that gets published and wins design awards. Work that communicates effectively and solves marketing problems for actual clients will make you rich, not famous, and consequently is not discussed here.

1. Do lots of work. You only need to do about three really great pieces a year to become famous. Depending on how much talent you have, you may have to design a lot of good things on the off chance that a few of them might turn out to be great. Design anything you can get your hands on. Stationery makes a nice gift; design some for every member of your family and all your friends, particularly those with funny names that permit visual puns. Brewing beer is complicated and messy, but it provides a pretext for designing beer labels. Avoid, however, designing clever wedding and birth announcements, which are sacred events that shouldn't be cheapened with clever design concepts unless the design concept is really, really clever.

2. Do lots of posters. In America, posters are not as relevant a part of the cultural landscape as they are in Europe, but they look good reproduced at a fraction of their original size on the pages of a design annual.

3. Do lots of freebies. It's a cliché, but it's easier to do great free work than great paying work. Be careful, however, about working for charitable causes or large cultural institutions that can be even more cumbersome and bureaucratic than corporate clients. Also, even in the shallow, craven context of this article, there is something particularly distasteful about trying to leverage a worthy cause like fighting HIV or breast cancer in your own personal quest for fame. Do those projects for their own merits, not to win prizes. Instead, find a local theater group. This will permit you to solve easily understandable problems with posters.

4. Make your paying work as good as it can be. While a lot of famous designers make compromises to pay the bills, I don't know any that actually do really bad work just for the money. It seems to be really bad for morale and consequently makes it harder to do great theater posters.

5. Have something cool-looking you can always do when you can't come up with any other solutions. Every really famous designer I know has a visual strategy he or she can fall back on when all else fails. One makes lovely Matisse-like torn paper collages, another makes a complicated three-dimensional model and takes a picture of it, and still another puts big black horizontal stripes on everything. This fallback position, if chosen carefully enough, will eventually become identified as your signature style, another hallmark of a famous designer. Reluctance to develop a surefire fallback position will only mean that you will waste a lot of time trying to invent exciting new solutions that probably don't exist for problems that probably don't deserve them.

6. When in doubt, make it big. If still in doubt, make it red. This rule of thumb, a slight but crucial improvement on "If it's big and ugly, it isn't big enough," is embraced by a surprisingly wide range of contemporary famous graphic designers. It appears to be, like the typeface Garamond, one of the few things that everybody agrees on.

7. Finally, remember what my Mom always says. My mom says: "It's nice to be important, but it's important to be nice." She's not just the smartest woman in the world but the mother of a famous graphic designer. Trust her.

In Search of the Perfect Client

When the business executive Thomas J. Watson, Jr., died in 1994, there was no shortage of obituaries extolling his extraordinary career. The man transformed his father's business—a successful manufacturer of adding machines and time clocks—into the world's largest computer company, IBM; built, in fifteen years, a $7.5 billion-a-year corporation that came to define American business in the postwar world; and was named by *Fortune* "the most successful capitalist in history."

No one, though, seemed to mention the thing that made Thomas Watson, Jr., a heroic figure among designers everywhere, five little words attributed to him that have been repeated endlessly in articles, speeches, design seminars, and slick presentations to hesitant clients, over and over again, like a mantra: "Good design is good business."

The Corporate Design Foundation was established in 1985 to "communicate the significance and importance of design to American Business." At the 1991 AIGA National Conference in Chicago, CDF chairman Peter Lawrence helped organize a presentation to discuss the Foundation's efforts to introduce design into business school curricula. Now, designers claim to be desperately interested in matters of business. Conference organizers, however, have learned to their chagrin that given a choice between a thoughtful discussion on one hand and a show-and-tell by some hot young thing with groovy slides on the other, conferees stampede to the latter. To remedy this imbalance, it was suggested that Lawrence and his organizers give the event a hot title: "Creating the Perfect Client." Thomas J. Watson, Jr., in the mythology of our profession, was the Perfect Client.

Even his great awakening was the stuff of myth, right out of St. Paul on the road to Damascus. "The inspiration for the design program came to me during a stroll I took down Fifth Avenue in the early 1950s," Watson wrote in his autobiography. "I found myself attracted to a shop that had typewriters on sidewalk stands for passersby to try. The machines were done in different colors and had sleek designs. I went inside and saw modern furniture and bright colors. . . .The name over the door was Olivetti." Later a Dutch friend sent him a bundle of Olivetti graphics, which Watson laid side by side with similar IBM material. "The Olivetti material was filled with color and excitement and fit together like a beautiful picture puzzle. Ours looked like directions on how to make bicarbonate of soda."

What happened next was simple. Watson found Eliot Noyes and appointed him IBM's consultant director of design. Noyes in turn brought in Charles and Ray Eames, Eero Saarinen, and, of course, Paul Rand. The rest, as they say, is design history.

Funny thing, though. "Business people often have the impression that design is only about styling," Peter Lawrence once observed regretfully. And certainly few things are as irritating to today's informed and well-intentioned designer as being dismissed as a mere stylist. Yet go back and reread what the real issue was for Watson: beautiful picture puzzle versus bicarbonate of soda. Good design is good business? Maybe. More like, good design just . . . well, looks better, for God's sake. In other words, styling.

So what's so bad about styling, anyway? If styling, mere styling, is so dismissively easy, why does everything look so horrible? Not horrible in terms of "Cranbrook: Bold and Experimental or Ugly and Illegible?" or "Modernism: Utopian Functionalism or European Phallicentricism?" but horrible like what you see on the shelves of any convenience store in America. In other words, Duffy and Tibor and Massimo and Emigre can go on about good and bad and right and wrong for years, but you can be sure their arguments are absolutely inaudible in the aisles of 7-Eleven. Forget about trying to "communicate the value of design to American Business"; can't we just get a few more of these clients interested in this styling thing?

Historically, it seems as though Perfect Clients have been born, not made. Again and again, for each great corporate design patron, a single person can be identified as the prime mover that enabled all that followed: Watson at IBM, Irwin Miller at Cummins, Walter Paepcke at Container Corporation, Frank Stanton at CBS. Designers desperately summon up this pantheon as evidence that good design is good business. It's certainly comforting to assume that these Perfect Clients were driven by something as rational as the profit motive, that it was just good old-fashioned hard-headed business sense that led to all these buildings by Saarinen, and products by Emilio Ambasz, and displays by Rudy deHarak, and ads by Herbert Bayer and Cassandre, and McKnight Kauffer, and Alvin Lustig.

But any designer that's been lucky enough to work with their own version of a Perfect Client knows firsthand that something else is at work here, something less rational than the simple good design/good business equation would admit. Meryl Streep was once asked why she devoted so much time to perfecting aspects of her performances that would never be visible to a movie audience. She sheepishly replied, "I guess I'm just the kind of person who likes to clean behind the refrigerator." The disquieting truth is that the factors that motivate good clients may be genetic rather than strategic. Simply and bafflingly, they may just be the kind of persons who like good design, the same way they might be interested in music or wine or motorcycles or porcelain figurines.

Disquieting also has been the occasional selectivity of good taste. It's been observed that while Walter Paepcke was commissioning world-class designers to create those extraordinary "Great Ideas" ads, Container Corporation was manufacturing vast quantities of truly hideous packaging and point-of-purchase materials untouched by good design by any defini-tion of the word. Even more startling to contemplate is that the exquisite CBS headquarters building by Eero Saarinen was brought to you, at least in part, through advertising revenues generated by *The Beverly Hillbillies*. In other words, good design is good business, but good business may not always be good design.

The whole idea of "good design" must have seemed easier to iso-late in days when there was more of a consensus about what constituted "good." Taken as a class, the pantheon of great clients now seems like a pretty insular world, with the same names—Noyes, Saarinen, Rand, and so on—showing up on everyone's Rolodex. And with the idea of styling held in such low regard these days, the modern Perfect Client seems to be held to a higher standard in non-visual realms; the many designers who admire the Body Shop's Anita Roddick, or Paul Hawken, founder of Smith & Hawken, for instance, obviously do so for more than the way the packag-ing and catalogs look.

Then as now, the design character of each of these companies seem completely tied up with a specific human being. In an Op-Ed piece in the *New York Times*, Paul Rand once noted how many vaunted design programs collapsed with the departure of their idiosyncratic champions, adding reassuringly, "That so many programs for large corporations have had a short life span is no evidence that design is impotent." Perhaps design isn't impotent, but what about designers?

For it seems that so much time and effort is devoted to solving one basic problem: can truly brilliant design—whatever way you want to define it these days—happen without a Perfect Client, some person who, for mysterious reasons, cares desperately about "mere styling" and everything else, and is willing to devote time and intelligence and money to getting it right? We designers have tried lots of different things as substitutes: big thick corporate identity standards manuals, desktop publishing templates, strategic design planning documents with lots of charts, and now design-flavored case histories to sneak under the noses of MBAs-in-training, all intended to counter the sense of impotence that comes with sitting and waiting for a Perfect Client to magically come along.

Of course, there is another approach, one borrowed from the world of counterintelligence. Why not canvass America's schools, find an artisically inclined ten-year-old who might otherwise choose a design career, divert them with CDF and AIGA money to the finest business education available, establish them on the corporate fast track, and wait for this "mole" to become CEO of a major corporation? An anonymous gift subscription to *I.D.* would be all it would take to "activate" the nascent design interests of this influential agent-in-place.

We would then sit back, our lips soundlessly repeating five little words, waiting for the commissions to roll in.

Histories in the Making

If I say "graphic design history," you probably get a pretty clear picture in your mind: an orderly progression of images, a little vague at the beginning (maybe cave paintings, maybe Guttenberg), but clearer in the middle (Art Nouveau, Dada, The Bauhaus), and trailing off in the end to the last thing you saw on the newsstand.

Andrew Blauvelt aimed to change all that with one monumental project: *New Perspectives: Critical Histories of Graphic Design*, three successive issues of the quarterly journal *Visible Language*, which he as guest editor reconfigured as a tripartite meditation on graphic design history, or, as I gather he would prefer, "the history of graphic design," or, better still, "histories of graphic design." Readers temperamentally disinclined to savor linguistic distinctions like this last one should be warned away at the outset. Blauvelt, an influential educator and accomplished designer in his own right, marshaled a veritable army of collaborators who find subtle linguistic distinctions, rather than full-color reproductions of Hohlwein posters, the very stuff from which histories of graphic design should be made.

Blauvelt's argument may be roughly summarized thusly, our traditional conception of graphic design history reduces what is actually a complex and ever-shifting melange of incident and influence to a falsely organized canon of images, indelibly associated with separate histories of (mainly) great men. Fundamental to graphic design is the relationship between word and image, and as Derrida and others have shown us, no territory is more beset by ambiguity and disconnection; attempts to invent fixed relationships are thereby doomed. Consequently, traditional design history can be attacked from every angle. It focuses too much on the product (the full-color plate) rather than the means of production; it "privileges" certain kinds of work above others to serve faintly sinister ends; it fails to acknowledge the social sciences, Marxism, feminism, linguistics, semiotics, and anything else that a lecturer can't make a slide out of; and, finally, it's just plain too reductively simple-minded. Blauvelt calls instead for a plurality of histories to fill out the picture.

Whether or not you buy the argument in its entirety, most thoughtful designers would agree that the more points of view, the better. Teasing those points of view out of *New Perspectives*, on the other hand, takes real dedication. Readers unused to the locutions of academic writing will try in vain to gain purchase on page after slippery page of phrases like "reciprocal subject/object positions," "history's patriarchal privileging of time over space," "the power of speaking as a transgressive act... while writing is seen as the privileged space for intervention," "the reflexive gaze," "gendered priorities," "graphic design's discursive spaces," and so forth. But press on.

Of the three volumes, the first, "Critiques," is the hardest to get through. Anne Bush's essay, "Through the Looking Glass: Territories of the Historiographic Gaze," makes the basic case for diverse vantage points in graphic design history. Along the way, Bush swerves briefly off the argument to make the obligatory swipe at Beatrice Warde's "Crystal Goblet," belief in the supposed objectivity of which is said to have stunted the minds of most designers and made them unreceptive to the essential "multiperspectival" nature of graphic design. The volume's other contributors more or less make the same point, least bafflingly in the case of Victor Margolin, who persuasively argues the limitations of traditional design history as practiced by the likes of Philip Meggs and Richard Hollis.

Readers who make it through Part One will be rewarded with more accessible fare in Part Two, "Practices," which addresses graphic design in its larger social context. It is emblematic of the suspicion with which Blauvelt and his contributors view traditional design history's "limited focus on the design object" that no actual picture of any piece of graphic design appears until well after Part Two's halfway point; when it does—talk about your reflexive gazes!—it's none other than a spread from a seventeen-year-old issue of good old *Visible Language*. Given the vastness of the windy "discursive spaces" Blauvelt has claimed as his purview, the inadvertent irony of this kind of tautological navel-gazing is hard to ignore.

Nonetheless, the image in question, appearing in a smart essay on deconstruction and typography by J. Abbott Miller and Ellen Lupton, serves as an inadvertent watershed, for it is around that point when *New Perspectives* starts getting more concrete. Essays like those by Stuart McKee in Part Two and by Susan Sellars, Jack Williamson, and Teal Triggs in Part Three ("Interpretations") deliver some much-needed specificity to the proceedings. Indeed, when Scotford's "Messy History vs. Neat History: Toward an Expanded View of Women in Graphic Design," introduces names of human beings like Valerie Richardson, Louise Fili, Lorraine Louie, and Dixie Manwaring into a mise-en-scène peopled to that point by the likes of Foucault, de Saussure, Barthes, and Cixous, it seems almost shockingly profane.

If there is a model for the kind of critical analysis that a more open view of design history might invite, it is found in "How Long Has This Been Going On? *Harper's Bazaar, Funny Face* and the Construction of the Modernist Woman." In it, Susan Sellers recasts the 1956 Audrey Hepburn vehicle *Funny Face* as a simulacrum of the postwar American design scene, engaging issues like modernism, consumerism, and feminism along the way. The essay does exactly what good design history should do. It takes something we thought we were familiar with—in this case, the milieu of Alexey Brodovitch, Carmel Snow, and Richard Avedon—and not only adds telling detail but enlarges our view beyond the iconic design object to the big world outside. For me, at least, a Brodovitch layout will never quite look the same.

Sellars manages this feat while avoiding something I grew to dread while reading the three volumes of *New Perspectives*: that moment when the author reaches into the wings and brings in a guest star or two from the world of academia to bolster an already difficult-to-fathom argument. The margins of the essays are crowded with these ringers, from turn-of-the-century art historians to French feminist writers to cultural studies experts, each waiting their turn to step in and do their best to elevate our benighted field. "The complex nature of the design process necessitates an understanding of that which integrates knowledge from many different disciplines," Blauvelt observes in his introduction, adding, "... and in the process develops its own particular account."

This last is the value of this project. By turns challenging and exasperating, *New Perspectives: Critical Histories of Graphic Design* will no doubt be looked back on as a landmark. At its most frustrating, it can be forgiven as an understandable phase in the process of our field's maturation, a symptom of our yearning for the legitimacy that incomprehensibility sometimes confers. At its most lucid, it points the way to the unique "particular accounts" that will fill in the spaces between, above, and below those color reproductions that have passed for graphic design history up until now.

Playing by Mr. Rand's Rules

Most American graphic designers become irrelevant far before they reach Paul Rand's age. No doubt he confounded many onlookers who had him slated for dormant *éminence grise*-hood in the mid-eighties by responding with the one-two punch of the publication of *A Designer's Art* in 1985 (complete with a page-one notice in the *New York Times Book Review*) and, a year later, the design of the NeXT logo for Steve Jobs (the presentation of which was incorporated into a television special on Jobs, along with a notorious reference to the logo's $100,000 price tag). Since then, Mr. Rand has ruled virtually unchallenged as the King of American Graphic Design.

Mr. Rand, or perhaps the mythology that has been attached to him, has also served as the dominant role model for how many of us think design should be practiced in this country. The legendary relationship between Mr. Rand and IBM's Thomas J. Watson, Jr., for instance, has served to define what almost all designers hold as a prerequisite of "getting good work done," that is, Svengali-like access to a Chief Executive Officer genetically predisposed to liking "good design." Whether or not the Rand-Watson relationship is a plausible model for corporate practice is meaningless in the face of our vast collective fantasy about it, a fantasy shared by designers as different from Rand as Rick Valicenti and Tibor Kalman. In the same way, many commonly held beliefs about how to do design reflect Mr. Rand's example: the idea that the smaller the office the better, that a logo is the crucial starting point in corporate identity, and—crucially—that the formal interpretation of visual ideas is the designer's primary mission.

It was indeed from Olympus, then, that Mr. Rand unleashed a thunderbolt in the form of "From Cassandre to Chaos," an essay that appeared last year in the *Journal of the American Institute of Graphic Arts*. Just at the moment when the forces of "deconstructivism" seemed about to overturn the verities of modernism at last, Mr. Rand put his foot down. Much contemporary graphic design, he said, is degrading the world as we know it, "no less than drugs or pollution." No names, of course, but one could easily identify the culprits Rand had in mind from his litany of their modi operandi: "squiggles, pixels, doodles" (Greiman, et al.), "corny woodcuts on moody browns and russets" (Duffy, Anderson, et al.), "indecipherable, zany typography" (Valicenti, et al.), "peach, pea green, and lavender" (anyone from California named Michael, et al.), and even "tiny color photos surrounded by acres of white space" (which obviously only sounds harmless).

Predictably, the essay was received with almost tearful relief in some quarters, and with exasperation in others. Insiders read Rand's statement that "To make the classroom a perpetual forum for political and social issues, for instance, is wrong; and to see aesthetics as sociology is grossly misleading," as a not-so-thinly veiled repudiation of Sheila de Bretteville's newly minted regime at Yale, Rand's distaste for which, it was said, had led him to resign his teaching position there. It was also said that the essay was only a hint of what was to come in Rand's new book, *Design Form and Chaos.*

Now comes the thing itself, and the book, somewhat disappointingly, is less a manifesto than an illustrated anthology not unlike its predecessors. The title (which is variously punctuated throughout, appearing here with no commas, there with two) is nowhere explained, unless it serves to underline the importance Rand obviously places on "From Cassandre to Chaos," which closes the book. About half the book consists of essays, all but one previously published, and illustrated, like those in *A Designer's Art,* that are the author's own work. Subjects include Eric Gill's *An Essay on Typography* (which he feels is great but the original jacket was better), computers (okay but not character building like using a ruling pen), design's role in the business community (not so hot, with much crowd-pleasing condemnation of market research and more longing for genetically predisposed CEOs). But make no mistake, even someone who disagreed with Rand's premises would admit that, nearly without exception, the essays are thoughtful, well reasoned, and gracefully written. For the undecided, a veritable army of names is enlisted to press the cause, including Arp, da Vinci, Kant, Le Corbusier, Kandinsky, Leger,

Malevich, Malraux, Rembrandt, Skinner, Schwitters, Tschichold, and Mies van der Rohe, not to mention Abraham Lincoln and Alistair Cooke.

The book's real appeal, though, probably won't be the essays, but the nearly 100 pages Rand devotes to reprinting brochures about six different logos, which include IBM, IDEO, and NeXT. These were originally created as presentations of identity projects commissioned by these companies, and each is a model of step-by-step clarity and elegance, with no small appeal for the voyeurs among us.

Equally striking, though, especially in the context of the surrounding essays, is the obsession with minute formal issues that recur throughout the presentations. Nearly every example shown has passages that reduce the design process to the lengthy examination of the juxtaposition of round letters and square letters, of too many vertical letters in a row, of adjacent round letters that jumble together, of letters that cluster and separate from the whole. A valid part of the design process to be sure, but oddly emphasized by a designer who quotes approvingly Philip Kotler's claim that "design is a potent strategy tool that companies can use to gain a sustainable competitive advantage." One wonders how skeptical CEOs react when confronted by the mysterious God in these endless details; probably as they do on Sunday mornings, with the proper mixture of awe and reverence, and in the comfort that on Monday it's back to the real world of business as usual. Mr. Rand complains that most businesspeople "see the designer as a set of hands—a supplier—not as a strategic part of business." Can they be blamed?

For when it's all said and done, Mr. Rand sees the design process not as strategy but as an intuitive search for an absolute ideal: "unity, harmony, grace, and rhythm." Content is important, insofar as it provides as starting point for the formal ends that "ultimately distinguish art from non-art, good design from bad design." In this way, he is scarcely different from the culprits he criticizes so passionately.

Mr. Rand himself is aware of this inherent contradiction but doesn't seem to grasp its full implications. "To poke fun at form or formalism is to poke fun at...the philosophy called aesthetics. Ironically, it also belittles trendy design, since the devices that characterize this style of 'decoration' are primarily formal." Having banished social and political issues to the sidelines, the game is reduced to the Good Formalists against the Bad Formalists. There seems to be more than enough irony in this to go around.

Mr. Rand rails against the state of graphic design today, leaving unmentioned the fact that this young profession has been invented very much in his own image. He taught many of today's most influential practitioners; he taught the teachers of countless others. His book goes out into a world where half of us are single-mindedly pursuing our own essentially formal notions of beauty and anti-beauty, and the other half are earnestly trying to solve someone's business problems with an attractive logo. To Mr. Rand's everlasting dismay, all of us keep playing the game by the rules he helped invent.

Certainly there's no denying that Paul Rand is a living legend with an astonishing body of accomplishment. Nonetheless, it's telling and more than a little sad that of the dozens and dozens of names invoked in *Design Form and Chaos*, the only living designer mentioned is that of the author. Perhaps the profession of graphic design is truly in the state of crisis that Mr. Rand says it is. If our respected elders care as much as they say they do, the least one could hope for is a bit less crankiness and a bit more generosity of spirit.

David Carson and the End of Print

Is everyone destined to succumb to David Carson? For me, the moment of capitulation arrived at last when I saw a reproduction of a page from *Ray Gun* that appears a little more than halfway through *The End of Print: The Graphic Design of David Carson.* The page in question, the opener for an article on a band called Mecca Normal, is a note-for-note steal of a page from *Rolling Stone*, circa 1982. It is rendered with the deadly, mocking accuracy of the young Mozart executing a parody of Antonio Salieri. In the midst of so many frighteningly cool layouts, it is in its own deadpan way the most frightening of all.

For someone who obviously yearns to be scary, Carson's near-universal appeal is somewhat startling. Predictably lionized by legions of twenty-something Mac jockeys, his Dennis the Menace antics are privately viewed—to a surprising degree—with affectionate tolerance by the curmudgeonly Mister Wilsons who populate the senior ranks of our profession. The very definition of anti-commercialism, he not only accepts invitations to speak at art directors' club receptions from Cincinnati to Jacksonville, but actually shows up at many of them. Likewise he is a sought-after visitor to academia despite his conspicuous lack of formal training.

This last may be no small key to Carson's popularity. As graduate programs in graphic design multiply and the drive for professional status grows, the field threatens to settle into a comfortable but disconcertingly premature middle age. Into this enervated milieu strides Carson with no more than a few months of commercial art classes to his name, in fact not just untutored but a former surfer, of all things, and not just any surfer but the eighth-ranked surfer in the world! Who better to redefine the practice of graphic design than this innocent man-boy? Could any fictional persona be better suited to such astonishingly original work?

And so much of the work, as this book reconfirms, is astonishing. Although many of the reproduced pages, spreads, and covers are now familiar from relentless exposure in design magazines and awards annuals, they still retain their capacity to surprise with their freshness and daring. Nonetheless, most purchasers of *The End of Print*, given the familiarity of the images therein, will be looking for something more: an explanation, perhaps, or the outline of an ideology, or the explication of the apocalyptic worldview suggested by the book's title. They will be disappointed.

Seekers of Carson's philosophy will no doubt turn first to the interview with the book's author, Lewis Blackwell, that is found at the book's center and titled "The Venice Conversation." While the title's dim echo of "The Geneva Conventions " or "The Helsinki Accords " suggests historic import, in truth it resembles Carson's now-notorious interview with Rudy VanderLans in *Emigre #27* in that the interviewer's questions at times seem longer than the subject's responses. One learns in time that Carson's ideology boils down to two simple convictions.

First, never do the same thing twice. "My big training," says Carson, "was on *Transworld Skateboarding* magazine: 200 pages full-color every month, and I had this personal thing that told me that if I was going to get something out of it, grow in myself, then I couldn't repeat myself. I always had to do something different. I never used the same approach for any two openers." Indeed, the captions in *The End of Print* (which, on the whole, are the best part of the book) find Carson marking milestones with the pride of a parent recording an infant's early steps: "First use of forced justification." "This was the issue that first dropped page numbers." "The first time in magazine history that an inside story jumped to continue on the front cover." While the quest for novelty may constitute a questionable design approach, executed with Carson's virtuosity, it succeeds as an end in itself.

On the other hand, the second component of Carson's approach would be reassuringly familiar to any designer from the "big idea" school: "Things are only done," he says, "when they seem appropriate." Surveyed as a whole, it's surprising how many of the spreads have old-fashioned visual puns as their starting points: from the early all-black spread that opened the story "Surfing Blind " in *Beach Culture* to the three-point body copy used in *Ray Gun* for a story on the band Extra Large. Contrary to the book's title, these are literate strategies that one senses wouldn't seem all that foreign to the likes of Robert Brownjohn.

If the work pictured in *The End of Print* provides testimony to Carson's substantial imagination, the form of the book itself demonstrates its limits. The layout of the text, by definition nothing if not self-referential, lapses at times into self-parody. When for example one discovers the opening must be read, line by line, from the bottom up, the reaction is not delight or even shock but weariness. Moreover, a David Carson layout incorporating blurry pictures of grubby rock musicians is one thing; a David Carson layout incorporating reproductions of still other smaller David Carson layouts is quite another. Carson also enlisted a cast of collaborators to submit visual musings on the book's title; these appear seemingly at random throughout the book, often at moments just when that old devil coherency is threatening to rear its ugly face. One wonders if the shock value would have been greater if the entire thing had been designed to ape, say, *The Graphic Artist and His Design Problems* by Josef Muller-Brockmann. At least it would have been funnier.

Although it wasn't planned, the publication of *The End of Print* marked the end of something else: David Carson's tenure at *Ray Gun*. This will leave him free to continue to do what the book charmingly calls "Selling Out": exporting his approach to other clients, particularly in the world of advertising. While both Blackwell and Carson make preemptive protests to the contrary, it's clear that most of the advertising clients are mindlessly buying style, design as illustration, rather than design as idea. Nonetheless, Carson derives understandable satisfaction from the transaction, saying, "There's a small part of me that uses this to help validate the work against those critics who say it is weird and unreadable: maybe having Pepsi or Nike or Levi's as clients suggests it's not so inaccessible."

It's somewhat disingenuous for the incorrigible who set an entire article in the "typeface" Zapf Dingbat to enlist soft drink companies to confirm his conventionality, but disingenuity is at the center of the Carson worldview. Master of the disarmingly laconic response when faced with a hostile audience, Carson is no more revealing in the book that presumably is meant to serve as his manifesto. But perhaps that explains his appeal, at least in part. The work comes to us free of all those burdensome ideas you so often find attached to avant-garde graphic design these days; you don't need to know anything about French literary criticism or post-McLuhanite communications theory—much less agree with it—to admire what amounts to no more and no less than a bunch of frighteningly cool layouts.

Given a choice between ideology and cool layouts, graphic designers usually surrender to the latter. And the music fans among us will note that no less an authority than ex–Talking Head David Byrne has joined the legions of those who have succumbed, having enthusiastically contributed an introduction to *The End of Print.* Byrne, in fact, makes the only convincing attempt to justify the book's title, suggesting that Carson's work communicates "on a level that bypasses the logical, rational centers of the brain and goes straight to the part that understands without thinking." And, indeed, the brain seems to be where all that doomed print stuff seems to work its fading magic. The end of print, the end of thinking: I'm not sure about the first, but the graphic design of David Carson has got me pretty convinced about the second.

Rob Roy Kelly's Old, Weird America

Rob Roy Kelly died on January 22, 2004, at the age of seventy-eight. A designer, educator, and writer for nearly fifty years, he was best known for a single book: *American Wood Type, 1828–1900: Notes on the Evolution of Decorated and Large Types and Comments on Related Trades of the Period*, published by Van Nostrand Reinhold in 1969. To a national profession well on the way to succumbing to Nixon-era Helvetica, Kelly's book, a loving history and analysis based on his own vast collection of fonts, was nothing more than a Whitmanesque barbaric yawp.

I must have been in my second or third year of design school at the University of Cincinnati when I first saw a copy of *American Wood Type*. Our program was unabashedly modernist, with instructors from New Haven and Basel, under whom we spent endless hours carefully modulating different weights of Univers and painstakingly rendering exquisite letterforms in black and white Plaka paint, imported from Switzerland for that sole purpose. But our department head, Yale-educated Gordon Salchow, knew Rob Roy Kelly from the Kansas City Art Institute, and a first edition of *American Wood Type* quickly found its way to our studio.

It occurred to me while I was reading his obituary by Steven Heller in the *New York Times* that Kelly was not unlike another passionate eccentric, Harry Smith. Like Rob Roy Kelly, Smith was a relentless collector, but instead of wooden typefaces he amassed homegrown field recordings: ballads from

Appalachia, gospel from the Deep South, square-dance music from the Ozarks. Released on Folkways Records in 1952, *The Anthology of American Folk Music* introduced rough, authentic voices into a culture under the spell of crooners like Sinatra and influenced generations of musicians around the world. As Greil Marcus said in his seminal essay on Smith, "The Old, Weird America," the recordings represented "a declaration of a weird but clearly recognizable America within the America of the exercise of institutional majoritarian power."

Having worked so long and so hard to refine my design palette, I was unprepared for the crude vitality of the letterforms that Kelly jammed into his book. Balance, taste, consistency, all the skills I had worked to develop were blown away by page after page of vulgar, monstrous, intoxicatingly bold letterforms. Shockingly, the book today is out of print, but if you can get your hands on a copy you won't let go. Years of digitization and manipulation make it hard to see today how original those hundreds of typefaces are. But—and please forgive me for pushing the metaphor—like the digitally sampled, nearly forgotten voices on Moby's *Play*, even after all these years, their power still comes through.

My Phone Call to Arnold Newman

About twenty-five years ago—about eighteen months into my first job—I was working on the design of a brochure with my boss, Massimo Vignelli. It was some kind of corporate brochure. I don't remember what company. In fact, I mainly remember one thing about it: it was to include a black-and-white photograph of the company's chief executive on one of the first few pages.

The client had approved the design, and I was sitting with Massimo, attentively taking notes as he talked about how we would go about getting it done. On this page, he said, we'd have a series of line drawings of the company's product. *Line drawings*, I wrote in my notebook. This divider page should be a bright color, like PMS Warm Red.
PMS Warm Red, I wrote. And for the portrait? Oh, that should be something special, said Massimo. We should get someone really good to do it. Someone like Arnold Newman. *Arnold Newman*, I wrote.

I went back to my desk, got out a Manhattan telephone book, and looked up Arnold Newman. Oddly, I found the right number right away. I dialed it. A man's voice answered the phone.

"Hello, I'd like to speak to Arnold Newman," I said.

"This is Arnold Newman."

"Arnold Newman, the photographer?"

"Yes," came back the voice.

I wasn't expecting to get him on the phone this quickly, so I switched to a new manner that I had been trying out recently: brisk, businesslike.

"Ah, Mr. Newman. My name is Michael Bierut and I'm a designer"— actually more like a production artist, but no need to get into details—"at Vignelli Associates. We're looking for a photographer to work on a new brochure we've designed, and we thought you could be someone we might consider." I loved this kind of thing: we're considering people. "May I ask you a few questions?"

"Yes?"

"First, do you do portraits?"

There was a long pause. Finally: "Er...yes, I do portraits."

"Great!" Mr. Newman was sounding a little unsure of himself, so I tried to sound peppy and encouraging. "Okay, can I ask if you do *black-and-white* portraits?" An even longer pause. "Yes, black-and-white. Color, and black-and-white. But mostly black-and-white." "Well, that sounds perfect! Would you mind sending us over your portfolio so we could take a look?"

Today I cringe as I write this, wondering what could have been going through Arnold Newman's mind as he submitted himself to some little twerp's inane interrogation. But the voice, though hesitant, was formal, polite, almost pleasant. Arnold Newman agreed to send me his portfolio.

I like to think that he put it together himself, with extra care, just to teach a young punk a lesson. And by the end of the day, it was delivered to our office with my name on it. I opened it up, and there they were, all original black-and-white prints: Igor Stravinsky. Pablo Picasso. Max Ernst. Marilyn Monroe. Eugene O'Neill. Martha Graham. Andy Warhol. It must have been with special relish that he selected the photograph on the very top: his famous picture of John F. Kennedy in front of the White House.

We didn't hire Arnold Newman for the job; he was, of course, too expensive. I never spoke to him again. But in that one short—and needlessly polite—conversation, he taught me a lesson about humility, patience, and elegance that I've never forgotten. He died at the age of eighty-eight in 2006.

Howard Roark Lives

A non-designer who was curious about our field asked me what served as the fundamental textbook in design school. The question so confused me I had to ask what she meant. "You know," it was explained, "like Janson's *History of Art* or Samuelson's *Economics*. The book everyone has to read."

I thought for a long time about my education, and the education of my roommates who had studied architecture and industrial design. While there were books around, it always seemed that design was about doing, not reading. I was about to concede that as a class we were a rather illiterate lot, and we didn't really have a textbook.

Then I remembered *The Fountainhead*. We had all read *The Fountainhead*, by Ayn Rand. Some of us would admit the book was the only thing that had inspired us to go into the design professions. I had read it earlier than most: tenth grade, I think. Like all Ayn Rand books, the central theme of *The Fountainhead* is how individuals of creative genius, the source of all human productivity, are misunderstood and persecuted by the great unwashed. The books usually end with the heroic genius vanquishing his lessers and going on to have great sex with another heroic genius of the opposite sex. As a bookworm with good grades, bad acne, and no social life to speak of, this central theme had considerable appeal for me. I ended up reading it eight times before my junior year of college.

The *Fountainhead*, as most people reading this surely know, is about a heroic, red-headed architect named Howard Roark. The book begins with Howard being kicked out of architecture school for doing single-mindedly modern work for class assignments that called for Renaissance villas. His story is contrasted with that of his classmate Peter Keating, a teacher's pet who graduates at the head of the class and goes to work for a firm not unlike McKim, Mead and White, where he ultimately becomes partner. Roark instead goes to work briefly for a fictionalized version of Louis Sullivan and then works on his own. (Although it seems obvious to anyone reading the book, Rand always denied that Roark was based on Frank Lloyd Wright. Nonetheless, Wright later told Rand that in his opinion Roark should have had white hair instead of red.)

In the rest of the book, Roark never compromises and suffers horribly but without complaint. Keating is a duplicitous second-rater who never has an original idea and consequently enjoys much success. Roark meets a woman who recognizes his genius but is perversely determined to destroy him before the great unwashed can get around to it. He ends up more or less raping her near a stone quarry he's forced to work in. (The tone of this romantic interlude in the novel is admirably crystallized in the 1949 movie version starring Gary Cooper as Roark and Patricia Neal as his love interest. Neal's first glimpse of Cooper is as he drills the rigid shaft of his jackhammer into hard but ultimately yielding marble.) There are complications and reversals, and in the end Keating asks Roark to allow him to take credit for Roark's work in the design of a public housing project. Roark agrees on the condition that the project be built as designed. When changes are made to the design—these include adding blue metal balconies and omitting closet doors—Roark enforces his agreement by dynamiting the project. Amidst great public outcry, Roark makes a passionate speech at his trial that underlines the Randian philosophy and gets him acquitted. He is united at last with his love interest and the book ends with the image of them atop Roark's latest skyscraper.

I just reread *The Fountainhead*, and I was curious to see how fifteen years of work in the real world would change my take on it. The book is viewed with, at best, kindly derision by most practicing architects and designers I know. But Roark's view toward clients still seems to describe the secret yearning harbored by most of my fellow professionals whether they care to admit it or not; they too might declare, "I don't intend to build in order to have clients. I intend to have clients in order to build."

I was also reminded again how simple the world of design was in 1943, when the book was published. In the tenth grade, when I read Roark's declaration that "A house can have integrity, just like a person, and just as seldom," I could clearly imagine the kind of house he was talking about; it looked like the pictures I had seen of Fallingwater. I had yet to read *Complexity and Contradiction in Modern Architecture*, which would confuse things a bit by making a fairly persuasive case for things like blue metal balconies.

What surprised me most were the descriptions of the compromises Roark was asked to make. When I read these at twenty, they seemed like impossibly grotesque caricatures: surely simpering clients didn't actually babble nonsense like, "Our conservatives simply refused to accept a queer stark building like yours. And they claim that the public won't accept it either. So we hit on a middle course. In this way, though it's not traditional architecture of course, it will give the public the impression of what they're accustomed to. It adds a certain air of sound, stable dignity...." Today this sounds exactly like the kind of quite reasonable stuff I listen thoughtfully to and—God help me—acquiesce to, every day. And at this I began to feel a little depressed.

Most of us enter the field with an inexhaustible store of passion and dogged ideological convictions, natural Howard Roarks. It takes years of training to master the arts of compromise and apple polishing, to become a good Peter Keating. Those of us who would claim *The Fountainhead* is overblown nonsense might be surprised by how faithfully we follow its playbook, at least in parts, and surprised by how inexhaustible its power is, despite the passage of the years. I was on the subway last week rereading my dog-eared copy—the same one I had in tenth grade—when I felt some eyes upon me. "Great book!" an enthusiastic kid said. Yup, I nodded. "Are you an architect?" Not really, I said. "That's what I'm going to be," came the assured response.

I took a good look at him for the first time, his eyes burning with the light of all those housing projects to be built and, if necessary, dynamited, and wished him luck.

The Real and the Fake

On one of my first visits to New York City, in the late seventies, I was taken to what I was told was the newest, hippest part of town: SoHo. My college friends and I wandered around the nighttime streets for a few hours; we couldn't find a party that we were invited to, and the one bar we did get into seemed a little boring. The dingy, industrial mise-en-scène reminded me of the corner of 30th and Superior in Cleveland, a place no one in their right mind would visit at any time of day unless they needed plastic tubing or a gross of light bulbs. I came all the way from Ohio for this? But all was not lost. The next day I found myself on a corner that seemed to sum up everything that had thrilled me in my fantasies about Gotham: broad streets, rushing taxis, majestic skyscrapers, important-looking people. I decided then and there that I would never live anywhere else.

Where I was standing was the corner of 50th Street and Sixth Avenue, in front of the Exxon Building, in the midst of a group of brand-new towers built in the '70s to extend the Rockefeller Center complex. Imagine my surprise when, upon moving to New York a few years later, I chanced upon this description of my beloved corner in *The City Observed* by Paul Goldberger: "four ponderous towers...three of which are almost identical...with none of the life and joy of the original buildings."

Context is everything. The context of 50th and Sixth Avenue was not just the surrounding streets, but an idea about New York that a lot of people my age carried in their heads. Mine was derived from television sitcoms set in New York and movies like *North by Northwest*, which featured a brilliant opening-credit sequence by Saul Bass set dynamically against the kind of facades that Goldberger found so oppressively bland. That was the real New York for me back then, not SoHo (despite Goldberger's enthusiastic assessment that it was "far and away one of the most beautiful neighborhoods in New York").

Each person understands a built environment differently, and much of the difference has to do with mental images we bring to an experience. Many of these images are, by necessity, secondhand. For instance, midwestern hotels in the thirties often had spaces "themed," to use the current word, on New York, or rather the idea of New York: the Manhattan Bar, the Empire Ballroom. The robust streamlined glamour of these spaces was derived, naturally, not from the real New York, but from the idea of New York that people got from screwball comedies like *My Man Godfrey or Twentieth Century.*

Compare this with a place like the new Las Vegas hotel and casino complex New York, New York. There the old-fashioned glamour is evoked as always, but with a surprising new layer of graffiti, gum stains, and soot, all simulated with a dazzling degree of stagecraft. This painstaking detail has been made necessary, I suspect, not by any dedication to verisimilitude for its own sake, but to satisfy the expectations of visitors who have never been to the place but know it well not from Carole Lombard movies but from cop shows like *NYPD Blue.* They know what the "real" New York looks like, and it's a little bit dirty.

This sort of simulation appears to drive Ada Louise Huxtable crazy in her book, *The Unreal America: Architecture and Illusion.* She is alarmed and dismayed by shopping malls, amusement parks, theme restaurants, Las Vegas, Colonial Williamsburg, the restoration of Ellis Island, and the pasta primavera at Disneyland. "The replacement of reality with selective fantasy is a phenomenon," Huxtable observes with distaste, "of that most successful and staggeringly profitable American phenomenon, the reinvention of the environment as themed entertainment."

But, one wonders, when has the taste for fantasy ever gone unsated? From high culture to low, from nearly every plate in Janson's *History of Art* to every fast-food stand up and down the American commercial strip, it's difficult to find anything that doesn't revel in a certain degree of simulation. As an architectural critic, Huxtable is particularly unhappy that new faux buildings are making it harder for us to appreciate good new architecture when we see it: "With both patrons and public weighing in for the fast fake, serious architecture is having a particularly heavy going." Yet even architects who attempt to create ex nihilo, without reference to any imagination but their own, find themselves subsumed sooner or later, whether it's Richard Meier's High Museum standing in for a glitzy insane asylum in the movie *Manhunter* or the other-worldy evocation of Eero Saarinen's TWA Terminal in the summer's sci-fi spectacle *Men in Black*. Inevitably, even "abstract" spaces become very powerful, and very specific, signifiers of common ideas. The public imposes their imagination whether they are invited to or not.

"I don't know just when we lost our sense of reality or our interest in it," Huxtable says, "but at some point it was decided that reality was not the only option, that it was possible, permissible, and even desirable to improve on it."

I'm no architectural critic or art historian, but I would guess that we decided the issue back in 15,000 B.C., when one of our ancestors decided to improve on the reality of an ibex with some smudges on a cave wall in Lascaux. And the human race, to its everlasting credit, has never looked back.

Ten Footnotes to a Manifesto

First Things First Manifesto 2000[1]

We, the undersigned, are graphic designers, art directors, and visual communicators[2] who have been raised in a world in which the techniques and apparatus of advertising[3] have persistently been presented to us as the most lucrative, effective, and desirable use of our talents. Many design teachers and mentors promote this belief; the market rewards it; a tide of books and publications reinforces it.

Encouraged in this direction, designers then apply their skill and imagination to sell dog biscuits, designer coffee, diamonds, detergents, hair gel, cigarettes, credit cards, sneakers, butt toners, light beer, and heavy-duty recreational vehicles.[4] Commercial work has always paid the bills, but many graphic designers have now let it become, in large measure, what graphic designers do. This, in turn, is how the world perceives design. The profession's time and energy is used up manufacturing demand[5] for things that are inessential at best.

Many of us have grown increasingly uncomfortable with this view of design. Designers who devote their efforts primarily to advertising, marketing, and brand development are supporting, and implicitly endorsing, a mental environment so saturated with commercial messages that it is changing the very way citizen-consumers speak, think, feel, respond, and interact. To some extent we are all helping draft a reductive and immeasurably harmful code of public discourse.[6]

There are pursuits more worthy of our problem-solving skills. Unprecedented environmental, social, and cultural crises demand our attention. Many cultural interventions, social marketing campaigns, books, magazines, exhibitions, educational tools, television programs, films, charitable causes, and other information design projects[7] urgently require our expertise and help.

We propose a reversal of priorities[8] in favor of more useful, lasting, and democratic forms of communication—a mindshift away from product marketing and toward the exploration and production of a new kind of meaning.[9] The scope of debate is shrinking; it must expand. Consumerism is running uncontested; it must be challenged by other perspectives expressed, in part, through the visual languages and resources of design.

In 1964, 22 visual communicators signed the original call for our skills to be put to worthwhile use. With the explosive growth of global commercial culture, their message has only grown more urgent. Today, we renew their manifesto in expectation that no more decades will pass before it is taken to heart.[10]

Jonathan Barnbrook
Nick Bell
Andrew Blauvelt
Hans Bockting
Irma Boom
Sheila Levrant de Bretteville
Max Bruinsma
Siân Cook
Linda van Deursen
Chris Dixon
William Drenttel
Gert Dumbar
Simon Esterson
Vince Frost
Ken Garland
Milton Glaser
Jessica Helfand

Steven Heller
Andrew Howard
Tibor Kalman
Jeffery Keedy
Zuzana Licko
Ellen Lupton
Katherine McCoy
Armand Mevis
J. Abbott Miller
Rick Poynor
Lucienne Roberts
Erik Spiekermann
Jan van Toorn
Teal Triggs
Rudy VanderLans
Bob Wilkinson

The Footnotes

1

First Things First Manifesto 2000

In 1963, British designer Ken Garland wrote a 324-word manifesto titled "First Things First." It condemned the still-nascent graphic design profession for its obsession with the production of inconsequential commercial work and suggested instead an emphasis on more worthy projects of benefit to humanity. It was signed by twenty-two designers and other visual artists, acquired some notoriety, and then dropped from view.

In fall 1998, Kalle Lasn and Chris Dixon reprinted the thirty-five-year-old document in their admirable and provocative self-described "journal of the mental environment," *Adbusters*. They had an opportunity to show it to Tibor Kalman, who was seriously ill with the cancer that would kill him within a year. "You know, we should do this again," Kalman said.

Adbusters, with help from journalist Rick Poynor, rewrote the statement, updating the references and sharpening the argument but otherwise leaving the spirit intact, and it was circulated by Lasn, Dixon, and *Emigre*'s Rudy VanderLans to an international group of designers, many of whom signed it.

And who wouldn't? Published in the Autumn 1999 "Graphic Agitation" issue of *Adbusters*, bearing Kalman's now-ghostly imprimatur, the revamped manifesto was preceded by a historical overview of thoughtfully captioned political posters and other cause-related graphics. These in turn were contrasted with examples of contemporary commercial work, including packaging for the Gillette Mach 3 razor, Kellogg's Smart Start cereal, and Winston cigarettes. Each of these examples was presented without comment, no doubt with the assumption that its surpassing vileness spoke for itself. Given all this, could someone seriously be against "more useful, lasting, and democratic forms of communication" and in favor of the "reductive and immeasurably harmful code of public discourse," represented by Smart Start cereal?

Good question. As for me, I wasn't asked to sign it.

2

We, the undersigned, are graphic designers, art directors,
and visual communicators.

Most of the thirty-three signatories are names that will be unfamiliar to the average rank-and-file American graphic designer. Many of them built their reputations by doing "cultural work" on the fringes of commercial graphic design practice as critics, curators, and academics. As designers, their clients generally have been institutions like museums and publishers, rather than manufacturers of nasty things like triple-edged razors, cigarettes, and cereal. So it's likely your mom's probably never seen anything ever designed by these people, unless your mom is a tenured professor of cultural studies at a state university somewhere.

In short, with some exceptions (including a glaring one, the prolific and populist Milton Glaser, who sticks out here like a sore thumb) the First Things First thirty-three have specialized in extraordinarily beautiful things for the cultural elite. They've resisted manipulating the proles who trudge the aisles of your local 7-Eleven for the simple reason that they haven't been invited to. A cynic, then, might dismiss the impact of the manifesto as no more than that of witnessing a group of eunuchs take a vow of chastity.

3
techniques and apparatuses of advertising

The phrases in the opening sentence have a tone of urgency that suits the ambitions of a millennial manifesto. But they have been lifted almost verbatim from the thirty-five-year-old original. In effect, the invidious influence of advertising has been haunting the graphic design profession since before most of the signatories were born.

It's hard to say exactly what's meant by this particular phrase. The most obvious interpretation is that graphic designers do work that informs, and that advertising agencies do work that persuades. In the First Things First universe the former is good and the latter is bad. But some of the most effective work on behalf of social causes has appropriated nothing more and nothing less than these same "techniques and apparatuses": think of Gran Fury's work in the fight against HIV, or the Guerilla Girls' agitation for gender equality in the fine arts.

Graphic designers, in truth, view the advertising world with a measure of envy. Whereas the effect of design is secretly feared to be cosmetic, vague, and unmeasurable, the impact of advertising on a client's bottom line has a ruthless clarity to it. At the same time, ad agencies have treated designers as stylists for hire, ready to put the latest gloss on the sales pitch. Revolutions often begin with the politicizing of the most oppressed. And in the ecosystem of the design disciplines, graphic designers have long dwelled at the bottom of the pond.

4
dog biscuits, designer coffee, diamonds, detergents, hair gel, cigarettes, credit cards, sneakers, butt toners, light beer, and heavy-duty recreational vehicles

This litany of gruesome products has one thing in common: they are all things with which normal people are likely to be familiar. Yet haven't such common products comprised the subject matter that graphic designers have tackled throughout history? What is our design canon but a record of how messages about humble things like shoes, fountain pens, rubber flooring, booze, and cigars have been transformed by designers like Bernhard, Lissitzky, Zwart, Cassandre, and Rand? What makes dog biscuit packaging an unworthy object of our attention, as opposed to, say, a museum catalog or some other cultural project? Don't dachshund owners deserve the same measure of beauty, wit, or intelligence in their lives?

If today's principled designers truly believe the role of commercial work is simply to "pay the bills," it should be pointed out it was not "always" so. "In the monotony and drudgery of our work-a-day world there is to be found a new beauty and a new aesthetic," declared Alexey Brodovitch in 1930, summing up what was for him the essence of the modern condition. Graphic designers in mid-century America were passionately committed to the idea that good design was not simply an esoteric ideal, but could be used as a tool to ennoble the activities of everyday life, including commercial life.

This vision of design making the world a better place by marrying art and commerce is no longer a compelling vision for many designers. Tibor Kalman's quote "consumer culture is an oxymoron" is one of those aphorisms so pleasing one accepts it unthinkingly. Yet a centerpiece of his valedictory exhibition, Tiborocity, was a "shop" stocked with selections from his vast collection of unabashedly commercial detritus: packaging for Chinese gum, Mexican soda pop, Indian cigarettes. Is there a contradiction here? Or is this kind of work okay as long as it's performed anonymously and, if possible, in a third-world country?

5
manufacturing demand

Many downtrodden graphic designers will read these damning words with a secret thrill. After countless years of attempting to persuade skeptical clients that "design is good business," or, failing that, that it has any measurable effect on sales whatsoever, here we stand accused of something no less delicious than manufacturing demand for otherwise useless products! If it were but so.

The First Things First vision of consumer capitalism is a stark one. Human beings have little or no critical faculties. They embrace the products of Disney, GM, Calvin Klein, and Philip Morris not because they like them or because the products have any intrinsic merit, but because their designer puppetmasters have hypnotized them with things like colors and typefaces. Judging by the published response, First Things First has been received most gratefully by under-paid toilers in the boiler rooms of the twenty-first-century communications revo-lution. In the manifesto they discover that in deciding between circles or lozenges for the design of those goddamned homepage navigation buttons, they are in fact participants in a titanic struggle for the very future of humanity. When it comes to graphic designers, flattery will get you everywhere.

6

To some extent we are all helping draft a reductive and immeasurably harmful code of public discourse.

To another extent, however, human beings have always used the marketplace as a forum for communication and culturization. "As we enter the twenty-first century, the urban condition is defined more and more by tourism, leisure, and consumption, the hallmark of an evolved capitalist society wherein economic affluence allows personal freedom to seek pleasure," wrote architects Susan Nigra Snyder and Steven Izenour on the (re)commercialization of Times Square. They concluded, "If your model is the cultural mish-mash of the everyday landscape, then commerce is the very glue—visually, socially, and economically—of American civic space." What will happen when the best designers withdraw from that space, as First Things First demands? If they decline to fill it with passion, intelligence, and talent, who will fill the vacuum? Who benefits? And what exactly are we sup-posed to do instead?

7

Many cultural interventions, social marketing campaigns, books, magazines, exhibitions, educational tools, television programs, films, charitable causes, and other information design projects

Finally, here the prescription is delivered, and note the contrast. Gone is the bracing specificity of butt toners and heavy-duty recreational vehicles, replaced by vague "tools," "campaigns," and "causes." The puzzling construction "cultural interventions" will be less baffling to readers of *Adbusters*, who will recognize it as code for the kind of subversive "culture jamming" activities the magazine has long advocated. From other contextual clues we can infer by this point that the books advocated here will deal with subjects other than the Backstreet Boys, that the magazines will feature models less appealing than Laetitia Casta on their cov-ers, and that the television shows will not involve Regis Philbin.

The issue of *Adbusters* that introduced the First Things First Manifesto included a range of classic examples of design as a tool of protest. Almost all of these were historical antecedents to that glamorous old stand-by beloved by right-thinking graphic designers everywhere, the dramatic poster for the pro bono cause. Although Lasn and Dixon in that same issue paint a vivid, knowing picture of the awards and fame that accrue to the creator of "a stunning package design for a killer product," any seasoned designer can tell you that it's a hell of a lot easier to win a prize for a pro bono poster than for a butt toner brochure. What designers can't figure out is whether any of our worthy posters really work.

Illustrated nowhere are examples of some things that absolutely do work, those otherwise unexplained "information design projects." Too bad: designers actually can change the world for the better by making the complicated simple and finding beauty in truth. But things like the FDA Nutrition Facts label, probably the most useful and widely reproduced piece of graphic design of the twentieth century, generally receive neither awards nor accolades from the likes of *Adbusters* or Rick Poynor: too humble, too accessible, too unshocking, too boring.

8
We propose a reversal of priorities

Manifestos are simple; life is complicated. One of my favorite personal clients is the Brooklyn Academy of Music, a fantastic nonprofit organization that courageously supports forward-looking performers and is a first-class citizen of its decidedly heterogeneous urban neighborhood. Yet, like many cultural institutions, they are supported by philanthropy from many large corporations, including the generous Philip Morris Companies. So am I supporting an admirable effort to bring the arts to new audiences? Am I helping to buff the public image of a corporation that sells things that cause cancer? And come to think of it, don't I know a lot of graphic designers who smoke?

9
a new kind of meaning

"Designers: stay away from corporations that want you to lie for them," exhorted Tibor Kalman. But that High Noon moment when we're asked to consciously misrepresent the truth comes only rarely for most designers. We're seldom asked to lie. Instead, every day, we're asked to make something a little more stupid, or a little more blithely contemptuous of its audience. Is the failure of contemporary graphic design rooted in the kind of clients we work for, or in our inability to do our jobs as well, as persuasively, as we should?

The greatest designers have always found ways to align the aims of their corporate clients with their own personal interests and, ultimately, with the public good. Think of Charles and Ray Eames, who created a lifetime of extraordinary exhibitions and films that informed, entertained, and educated millions of people while advancing the commercial aims of the IBM Corporation. Or Kalman himself, who struggled firsthand with the contradictions—and lies, perhaps?—inherent in the ongoing marketing challenge of portraying a sweater company, Benetton, as an ethically engaged global citizen.

What would happen if instead of "a new kind of meaning," the single most ambiguous phrase in the manifesto, we substituted "meaning," period? For injecting meaning to every part of their work is what Kalman and Eames and designers like them have always done best.

10
Today, we renew their manifesto in expectation that no more decades will pass before it is taken to heart.

The creators of *Adbusters* have a dream. "We wait for that inevitable day of reckoning when the stock market crashes, or the world is otherwise destabilized," Lasn declares in the Autumn 1999 issue of *Adbusters*. "On that day we storm the TV and radio stations and the Internet with our accumulated mindbombs. We take control of the streets, the billboards, the bus stops and the whole urban environment. Out of the despair and anarchy that follows, we crystallize a new vision of the future—a new style and way of being—a sustainable agenda for Planet Earth." What a disappointment to learn that this revolution is aimed at replacing mass manipulation for commercial ends with mass manipulation for cultural and political ends.

I have a dream as well. I am the president of a national association of graphic designers and a principal in a large firm that works on occasion for the Disneys and Nikes of the world, so you can dismiss me as someone hopelessly invested in the status quo, and no fit person to lead us into the endless promise of the new millennium. Yet I take inspiration from something designer Bill Golden, the creator of the CBS eye, wrote over forty years ago. You can consider it a twenty-one-word-manifesto: "I happen to believe that the visual environment... improves each time a designer produces a good design—and in no other way."

Golden's manifesto, unlike First Things First, is easy to understand. Yet, if anything, it's harder to execute. As any working designer can tell you, commercial work is a bitch. If you do it for the awards, it's a hard way to get them. If you do it for the money, you've got to earn every penny twice over. Make no mistake, there is much to be alarmed about in the contemporary world, from the continuing establishment of the corporation as global superstate, to the idiotic claims of marketing mavens seeking to elevate brand loyalty to the status of world religions.

Lasn, Dixon, Poynor, and the signers of First Things First are right that graphic design can be a potent tool to battle these trends. But it can be something else, something more. For in the end, the promise of design is about a simple thing: common decency.

About four years after the original First Things First, Ken Garland wrote "What I am suggesting . . . is that we make some attempt to identify, and to identify with, our real clients: the public. They may not be the ones who pay us, nor the ones who give us our diplomas and degrees. But if they are to be the final recipients of our work, they're the ones who matter." And, I would submit, they deserve at the very least the simple, civic-minded gift of a well-designed dog biscuit package.

If you think that's so easy, just try.

The *New York Times:*
Apocalypse Now, Page A1

If you pick up the *New York Times* every day, you may have been as disoriented as I was on Tuesday, October 21st, 2003. The front page looked basically the same, but slightly different, like the replacement husband on "Bewitched." Your increasingly panicked, darting eyes may have finally discovered, down in the very left-hand corner, a teasing note: "Notice Anything? More than the news is new today on the front page and in the main news sections." The full (curiously un-bylined) story was found deep inside on the upper half of page C8. *The Times* had administered to itself what it called "a gentle typographic facelift."

Pay attention, this is a little complicated. Or maybe not! The typeface used for the familiar one-column "A" headline, good old spiky Latin Extra Condensed, is replaced by Cheltenham Bold Extra Condensed. The "decks" beneath the "A" head, previously deadpan and all-business News Gothic, are replaced by Cheltenham Bold Condensed and Cheltenham Medium. For those big multi-column MAN WALKS ON MOON headlines, previously expressing barely controlled hysteria in Century Bold Italic, think Cheltenham Extrabold Italic. Sober and measured Bookman Antique, used for the more analytical stories, is replaced by...well, you get the idea. Only a single headline style from the previous design will be retained under the new regime. You can guess what it is. That's right, the *New York Times* is going all Cheltenham, all the time. And just like any proud cosmetic surgeon, the newspaper displays before-and-after examples of the improvements as part of its note to readers.

As one who has often been asked to describe a rationale for a design change to resistant audiences, I found the explanatory note as masterful as the new design itself, which has been years in the making under the stewardship of longtime art director Tom Bodkin. Lest anyone accuse the *Times* of unbecoming hubris, the redesign is characterized not just as "gentle" but "modest." Enhancing legibility is invoked as a goal (as well as adding a little dramatic heft to the poor "spindly" "A" head) but the clear aim, above all, is consistency. Clients understand (and love) consistency, and the Cheltenham family drawn by Matthew Carter is well suited to this purpose. And to give consistency the air of manifest destiny, the motley ruling coalition of Latin/News Gothic/Century/Bookman is linked to the creaky old "Victorian-era" past, when newspaper typography was composed "on keyboard-operated machines that cast lines of molten metal." Jesus, molten metal? That sounds dangerous! The *Times* manages to make Cheltenham—designed in 1898!—actually sound bracingly progressive. Thus the paper successfully fulfills that most frustrating common of client briefs: to simultaneously signal modernity and heritage.

And, of course, then follow claims that neither goal is satisfied. A few days later, the paper published two letters; whether they were the only ones received or instead plucked from brimming bins labeled "love it" and "hate it" is anyone's guess. Patrick O'Carroll from Seattle falls hook, line, and sinker, congratulating the *Times* on its "subtly cleaner and sharper look." Martin Beiser from Montclair is grumpier. "You have made bland the quirky persona that made the *Times* special and given us the typographic equivalent of New Coke," he says, going on to add, "It's the end of the world as we know it."

I don't share the apocalyptic views of Mr. Beiser from Montclair, but I too felt the loss keenly. The peculiar combination of Bookman and Century, Latin Condensed and News Gothic, made for a kind of typographic counterpoint, giving the *Times's* front page the complexity of a Bach fugue. The logic—unassailable, really—of using a single typeface family takes us back to unison plainsong. But like the Emperor in *Amadeus*, someone at the *Times* must have thought there were too many notes.

Graphic Design and the New Certainties

Graphic designers claim to want total freedom, but even in this intuitive, arbitrary, "creative" profession, many of us secretly crave limitations, standards, certainties. And certainties are a hard thing to come by these days.

I was reminded of this by several presentations at the AIGA's "Power of Design" conference in Vancouver a few weeks ago. Katherine McCoy's talk began with images of one of her own early projects, a corporation's rulebook for their janitorial crew. McCoy worked at Unimark at the time, and the piece was a classic example of High Modernism: sans serif typography on a three-column grid, subheads flush left in the first column hung beneath one-point rules, geometric icons, and diagrams. Emil Ruder would have been proud. McCoy showed it to set the stage for a thoughtful presentation that urged designers to be more sensitive to the vernacular of the subcultures with which we communicate, to not force Ulm and Basel down the unwilling throats of people we would never bother getting to know personally. The implication was: can you believe we used to believe this kind of stuff?

God only knows what all those janitors made of all that Swiss modernism. Moreover, Swiss modernism is so dead that I'm not even sure what those twenty-somethings in the Vancouver audience thirty years later made of it: probably they were wondering "Who is Emil Ruder and why is he ripping off Experimental Jetset?" As for me, I was remembering—with no small amount of longing—those days when everything seemed so clear. Working for Massimo Vignelli in 1980, I had no doubt whatsoever that the purpose of graphic design was to improve the life of every person on earth beyond measure by exposing him or her to Helvetica on a three-column grid. That was certainty, and it made design into a crusade.

But that certainty wasn't long for this world, and it was replaced by a series of others with ever-shorter shelf lives. For instance: the purpose of graphic design is to provide graphic designers with a medium of self-expression (great for designers with something to express, not-so-great for designers with access to a lot of Photoshop filters). Or, the purpose of graphic design is to change the world by subverting the goals of its corporate patrons (Tibor Kalman, we hardly knew ye). Or, the purpose of graphic design is to provide a medium for designers to act as "authors" (see the previous two certainties). For what was great about Swiss modernism was that anyone could do it. You didn't have to have an authorial point of view, political conviction, or even be particularly talented.

But at another presentation, I glimpsed what perhaps will be a starting point for a new certainty, perhaps the ultimate one. Michael Braungart, author with William McDonough of *Cradle to Cradle: Remaking the Way We Make Things*, talked about how graphic designers are contributing to the destruction of the environment. Braungart is not a designer. He's a chemist. At one point in his presentation, he displayed a chart that described the precise amount of toxic elements in a single ink color. You felt the audience, two thousand–plus strong, draw a collective breath. Here, at last, was true certainty: the promise that every piece of graphic design, each an amalgam of dozens of arbitrary, intuitive, "gee, this looks right to me" decisions, could be put into a centrifuge, broken down into its constituent parts, and analyzed for the harm it could do to our environment.

Of course, with certainty comes responsibility, and with responsibility comes power, which, after all, is what those two thousand attendees had come to Vancouver to find out about. And what greater power than to discover forensic proof that even this seemingly harmless profession has the capacity to inflict damage, as well as to do good? Now we can think, as did J. Robert Oppenheimer upon seeing that his atomic bomb really worked, "I am become death, the destroyer of worlds," each time we specify PMS 032. And, like Oppenheimer, we may find that power isn't all it's cracked up to be.

Mark Lombardi and
the Ecstasy of Conspiracy

With the 40th anniversary of the assassination of JFK behind us, our abiding romance with conspiracy theories seems more ardent than ever. And around the time of that anniversary, I happened to see a remarkable expression of that romance at The Drawing Center in New York: "Global Networks," an exhibition of the work of Mark Lombardi. In an age where we all dimly sense that The Truth Is Out There, Lombardi's extraordinary drawings aim to provide all the answers.

Although Lombardi's work has combined the mesmerizing detail of the engineering diagram and the obsessive annotation of the outsider artist, the man was neither scientist nor madman. Armed with a BA in art history, he began as a researcher and archivist in the Houston fine arts community with a passing interest in corporate scandal, financial malfeasance, and the hidden web of connections that seemed to connect, for instance, the Mafia, the Vatican bank, and the 1980s savings and loan debacle. His initial explorations were narrative, but in 1993 he made the discovery that some kinds of information are best expressed diagrammatically.

The resulting body of work must be seen to be believed—an admittedly oxymoronic endorsement of subject matter of such supreme skepticism. Lombardi's delicate tracings, mostly in black pencil with the occasional red accent, cover enormous sheets of paper (many over four feet high and eight feet long), mapping the deliriously Byzantine relationships of, say, Oliver North, Lake Resources of Panama, and the Iran-Contra operation, or Global

International Airways and the Indian Springs State Bank of Kansas City. Because the work visualizes connections rather than causality, Lombardi was able to take the same liberties as Harry Beck's 1933 map for the London Underground, freely arranging the players to create gorgeous patterns: swirling spheres, hopscotching arcs, wheels within wheels.

Lombardi was indeed an enthusiastic student of information design, a reader of Edward Tufte and a collector of the charts of Nigel Holmes. But if the goal of information design is to make things clear, Lombardi's drawings, in fact, do the opposite. The hypnotic miasma of names, institutions, corporations, and locations that envelop each drawing demonstrates nothing if not the inherent—the intentional—unknowability of each of these networks. Like Rube Goldberg devices, their only meaning is their ecstatic complexity; like Hitchcockian McGuffins, understanding them is less important than simply knowing they exist.

Lombardi, who was born in 1951 and died in 2000, did not live to see today's historical moment, where his worldview seems not eccentric but positively prescient. His drawing BCCI-ICIC & FAB, 1972–91 (4th version) was studied in situ at the Whitney Museum by FBI agents in the days after 9/11; reportedly, consultants to the U.S. Department of Homeland Security previewed the show at the Drawing Center. One wonders whether he would have felt vindicated or alarmed by this kind of attention.

The catalog for the exhibition, which was organized by Robert Hobbs and Independent Curators International, cannot possibly do the drawings justice. But it may be worth it for the extended captions alone, each one of which could serve as an outline for a pretty decent John le Carré novel. And in what other art catalog could you find an index where (under the Cs alone) one finds Canadian Armament and Research Development Establishment; capitalism; Capone, Al; Castro, Fidel; and conceptual art? And it is in the catalog that one finds, tossed away almost casually in a footnote, the following fact: "The police report cited suicide by hanging as the reason for Mark Lombardi's death. The door to his studio was locked from the inside." That last detail is an all-too-common device in mystery novels, where it inevitably raises the same question: yes, that's how it seems, but what really happened? Mark Lombardi's work tries, valiantly, to answer that very question.

George Kennan and the Cold War
Between Form and Content

The graphic designer's role is largely one of giving form
to content. Often—perhaps even nearly always—this process
is a cosmetic exercise. Only rarely does the form of a
message become a signal of meaning in and of itself.

Several years ago at Princeton University's Firestone
Library, I saw an example of the power that form can give
content: George F. Kennan's legendary "Telegraphic Message
from Moscow of February 22, 1946," or, as it is better known
to students of twentieth-century foreign policy,
"The Long Telegram."

The curriculum vitae of George F. Kennan, who turned
100 this year, makes him sound a bit like the Acciden-
tal Diplomat. After graduating from Princeton, he entered
the foreign service with "the feeling that I did not know
what else to do." Yet time and time again he found himself present at moments of global crisis: in Moscow during
Stalin's show trials, in Prague for the Nazi invasion of
Czechoslovakia, in Berlin when Hitler declared war on the
United States.

In the aftermath of World War II, Kennan was posted
again to Moscow, where he viewed the intentions of our

wartime ally, the Soviet Union, with progressively deeper despair, and with increasing concern that Washington was failing to understand the changing postwar landscape. As he wrote in his memoirs, "For eighteen long months I had done little else but pluck at people's sleeves, trying to make them understand the nature of the phenomenon with which we in Moscow were daily confronted....So far as official Washington was concerned, it had been to all intents and purposes like talking to a stone."

So when Kennan received a rather routine question about why the Russians seemed unwilling to join the World Bank, he decided to unburden himself once and for all. As he put it: "Here was a case where nothing but the whole truth would do. They had asked for it. Now, by God, they would have it." The resulting dispatch was an eight-thousand-word telegram that ran for seventeen pages. It provided a detailed analysis of postwar Soviet aims and precise recommendations of how the United States should respond.

It's possible a document this long sent by courier would have been delivered, forwarded, read, and filed. But Kennan, who took pains to "apologize in advance for this burdening of the telegraphic channel," must have been hoping for a more dramatic effect. And he got it: as he put it, the effect was "nothing less than sensational." The document quickly became known as "The Long Telegram." Hundreds of copies circulated, including, Kennan suspected, to President Truman. "My reputation was made. My voice now carried." Less than two weeks later, Winston Churchill delivered his "Iron Curtain" speech and the Cold War was officially underway.

I am fascinated by The Long Telegram. Like its ideological opposite, Mao Zedong's *Little Red Book*, it seems to be a case where, indeed, the merger of content and form has created an icon. At Princeton, where it was on view for the first time ever as part of a Kennan exhibition in the Spring of 2004, it sat in a custom-made, climate-controlled eighteen-foot glass case. I confess I was disappointed that it wasn't printed on a single roll (like that other icon of postwar American literature, the original manuscript of Jack Kerouac's *On The Road*), but in all its

Courier-besotted glory (now disavowed as a sanctioned font by the State Department, alas, in favor of Times Roman), it has its own unique power.

This was not the last time the seemingly discreet Kennan would prove himself to be a (perhaps inadvertent) master of public relations. A year later, asked to expand on his analysis for the journal *Foreign Affairs*, he asked that his article be published anonymously due to his sensitive position at the State Department. Attributed to the mysterious "X," his piece caused a sensation in no small part because of speculation as to its author. This was revealed in short order, adding further to Kennan's fame.

I have always known that graphic design requires a degree of tact, especially when dealing with clients. But I would not have expected to get useful advice from a diplomat, as I did in Kennan's *Memoirs*: "It is axiomatic in the world of diplomacy that methodology and tactics assume an importance by no means inferior to concept and strategy." That's as useful a description of the interplay of the forces we designers grapple with as any.

Errol Morris Blows Up Spreadsheet, Thousands Killed

Errol Morris's brilliant new documentary, *The Fog of War: Eleven Lessons from the Life of Robert McNamara*, is a design achievement of high order. Morris has long been obsessed with the question of how ordinary people can do evil things. In Robert McNamara, he has his ideal subject. Harvard Business School professor, WWII efficiency expert, head of Ford Motor Company, McNamara was tapped by John F. Kennedy to serve as his Secretary of Defense. Serving under Kennedy and then Lyndon Johnson, he supervised the escalation of America's involvement in southeast Asia, or, as it was often called then, "Mr. McNamara's War."

The recurring—make that relentless—motif in *The Fog of War* is McNamara's attempt to reconcile the messy, bloody loss of human life with the sterile world of the accountant's ledger. Morris's film combines his contemporary interviews with McNamara with a remarkable collection of archival footage and, finally, pictures of documents in extreme closeup. The interviews with McNamara feel more like merciless interrogations. The archival footage includes images you'd expect (bombers in flight, McNamara in press conferences) with images that are revelations (the long, slow-motion footage of Kennedy at a desk before a speech, seemingly unaware of the camera, that serves as the visual counterpoint to McNamara's account of learning of his assassination).

But, fittingly, it's the documents that steal the show. Time after time, McNamara describes the data that led him to make his decisions. And over and over, Morris fills the screen with words, diagrams, and—especially—numbers.

Not since Reid Miles designed for Blue Note has so much Courier been blown up to such seductive effect. Newspapers, magazines, textbooks, military reports, maps, every kind of information is enlarged to the point of abstraction—which to McNamara it all seems to be.

At one point, McNamara describes with admiration the statistical techniques used by his first commander, General Curtis LeMay. Others used to count missions flown or bombs dropped, he says. But LeMay was the only one he knew that measured success by the number of targets destroyed. It's typical of McNamara that he is more impressed by the method of tabulation than by the act itself. And no wonder: some of those numbers represented the women and children killed during the Allied firebombing of Tokyo and other Japanese cities, a campaign that McNamara concedes would have gotten them convicted as war criminals had the Allies lost.

McNamara takes pains to separate the statistics from the carnage. Morris does the opposite. In the film's most audacious visual invention, after alternating shot after shot of sixty-year-old spreadsheets with ruined Japanese cities, he slams the two together with an image of airplanes dropping actual numbers onto their targets. It sounds corny. It is corny. That it works to such devastating effect is a tribute to Errol Morris. He is our most poetic information designer.

Catharsis, Salesmanship,
and the Limits of Empire

In the Spring of 2003, I got a note from Nicholas Blechman, the talented designer at the New York City firm Knickerbocker, inviting me to contribute to the next issue of his magazine *Nozone*. With the United States beginning its invasion of Iraq, Blechman had decided to create a special issue with the theme "Empire." As I prepared my contribution, a reproduction of a proclamation by British troops on the occasion of their own invasion of Iraq eighty-six years ago (not "as conquerors or enemies," they took pains to point out in 1917, "but as liberators") I remember worrying that the ironies would no longer be relevant by the time the book was published.

Sadly, I needn't have worried. The occupation was still in full swing by the time *Nozone #9* made its debut, with America and its nominal coalition under increasing attack with no light at the end of the tunnel. And *Empire* turned out to be great, filled with passionate expressions of alarm by artists and designers as various as Stefan Sagmeister, Luba Lukova, Christoph Niemann, Robbie Conal, Ward Sutton, Seymour Chwast, and Edward Sorel. All this and a promising distribution plan: Princeton Architectural Press was supporting a first printing of 10,000. "The result," wrote Dan Nadel in *Eye*, "besides solid, often cathartic, political criticism and satire, is a glance at what today's designers and illustrators can do outside the bounds of commercial gigs."

As satisfying as catharsis can be, the project felt a little bittersweet to me. I was reminded once again how irresistible it is for sincerely committed designers to preach to the choir. What effect would those 10,000 copies of left-wing artistry have on the world at large, those millions of otherwise normal people who don't make a habit of buying left-leaning 'zines at Barnes and Noble?

I was astonished, and then heartened, one morning about a month later to find the main subway station at New York's Grand Central Terminal transformed into a veritable hotbed of anti-Bush propaganda. Surrounding us sleepy commuters on all sides were large—and well-designed—posters sporting much the same messages as could be found in *Empire*: the words "Because he doesn't read" plastered over the face of George W. Bush; "Fighting the axis of Enron" over Cheney; "The war on error" over Rumsfeld; and the Homeric "What if one man owned all the media. 'D'oh!'" over Rupert Murdoch. But this was no abstract exercise in graphics-as-political-engagement by the students of the School of Visual Arts or the members of the AIGA. Instead, in the old-fashioned capitalist way, these posters were selling us something. They were, in fact, tune-in ads for a new left-leaning radio network, Air America. The posters were created by the New York studio Number Seventeen, and they would be seen by about 10,000 people every day, if not every hour. In short, we were witnessing the results of nothing more and nothing less than a "commercial gig."

This is not to diminish the considerable accomplishment represented by *Empire*. It's a historic document and everyone should buy one. But I wonder whether the best way to affect public opinion in a free-market economy is not to disavow the market, but to embrace it. In the days after 9/11, marketers in New York were hesitant to stoop to anything so crass as advertising. Times Square billboards were filled with images of billowing flags and empty, eerily unattributed exhortations: "United We Stand!" The effect was Orwellian. I found myself yearning for some Calvin Klein underwear ads: at least with those you knew where you stood.

So why can't we sell the anti-imperialist agenda like a pair of jockey shorts? Recent history has some lessons here. Anti-AIDS activists like Gran Fury understood the power of the market: their most effective messages took the form of commercial communication. The "Silence = Death" logo was deployed with the consistency of a corporate brand; the best Act Up ads looked exactly like the corporate P.R. that they viciously critiqued. Gran Fury's Marlene McCarty, a classically trained graphic designer, put it well. She talked about "the authority of the media," and explained, "Our idea was to use that authority to sell a different agenda."

There will always be room—no, a necessity—for impassioned individual voices like those represented in *Empire*. But what we need right now is salesmanship. Those posters in Grand Central for Air America represented the intrusion of another voice in the public conversation in an arena of real consequence: the public marketplace. The more of us who can wade right into its murky depths, the better.

Better Nation-Building Through Design

When a new CEO takes charge, often at the top of the agenda is a new logo. What better way to project the enterprise's newly redirected mission, not to mention the authority of the new regime?

Someone must have been thinking along those lines in Iraq, where, a year after their country's "liberation," the beleaguered interim Governing Council unveiled a new flag design. And a handsome design it is: a pure white field representing the freshly reborn nation, a blue crescent standing for Islam, twin blue bands for the Tigris and Euphrates rivers, and a yellow stripe for the Kurdish population.

Iraqis, however, didn't rush to buy it.

"When I saw it in the newspaper, I felt very sad," said Baghdad supermarket owner Muthana Khalil on MSNBC. "The flags of other Arab countries are red and green and black. Why did they put these colors that are the same as Israel? Why was the public opinion not consulted?" Other Iraqis objected to the deletion of the phrase "God is great," which had been added to the old flag in an admittedly cynical move to shore up religious support for Saddam Hussein.

The design, by Rifat al-Jadirji, was selected out of "more than 30 proposals" according to Al Jazeera. Unfortunately, flag design, like logo design, is one of the most volatile of professional activities and should not be undertaken lightly. Flags, like logos, don't mean anything in and of themselves. The swastika, argu-ably one of the most beautiful symbols from a purely formal point of view, has been irredeemably tainted by its association with the Nazis. On the other hand, the American flag is a fussy affair that would not make it out of a first-year design school critique. Instead, people use flags (and logos) as tabulae rasae, upon which they project their hopes, dreams, fears and, sometimes, nightmares.

In his classic textbook *Corporate Identity: Making Business Strategy Visible Through Design*, Wally Olins describes how the British Empire asserted its control over India after the mutiny of 1857 through the imposition of "a complex set of symbols and a fiendishly complicated hierarchy of ranks," including coats of arms, heraldic symbolism, and uniforms, all presided over by Lockwood Kipling (father of Rudyard) who functioned as de facto "design director" for the effort. It culminated in an Imperial Assemblage in Delhi in 1877 at which the new Indian "identity" was officially "launched" in an affair that involved 85,000 people in its staging. "The whole business," observes Olins, "was contrived to create new loyalties and supplant old ones in the most spectacular way."

Ah, the days when imperialists really knew what they were doing. Today's efforts seem halfhearted by comparison. The leadership in Iraq—like many logo-manipulating management teams before them—committed the common error of mistaking easy symbolism for difficult substance. As a dissenting Governing Council member, Mahmoud Uthman, observed, "I think there are issues more important to concentrate on than the changing of the flag."

Absolutely. But symbolism can be meaningful, as long as it's yoked to a clear idea of what's meant to be symbolized. Toward the end of his book, Olins warns that unless a corporate identity is communicated with consistency and commitment, it has little chance of success: "Where there is hesitation, lack of coordination, disagreement, there will be perpetual confusion in the minds of the audiences, and myths of a destructive kind will reign unbridled." Absent any semblance of consensus, a flag is doomed to become a target.

The T-shirt Competition Republicans Fear Most

When fellow designer Sam Potts first emailed me about DOTWHO, the Designs On The White House Organization, my initial reaction was slightly exasperated bemusement: when the going gets tough, designers have a t-shirt contest. With the 2004 presidential election heating up, a group of celebrity judges, including Milton Glaser, Chip Kidd, and Todd St. John, along with more conventional celebrities like Margaret Cho, Al Franken, and Moby, were slated to help select the best pro-Kerry t-shirt designs in a number of categories, including "funniest," "most stylish," and "best retro shirt," with proceeds from sales of the winners going to help the Democratic campaign.

This is all fine and good, and certainly the "official" Kerry t-shirt was pretty awful (if there were a Geneva Convention for typography, horizontal scaling would be a capital crime at my tribunal). Yet with the news getting worse every day, I wondered if designing t-shirts was anything near a sufficient response to the crisis in leadership we're facing. But a visit to the DOTWHO website started me thinking: there's more here than meets the eye.

It's natural for designers to respond to an issue they care about by doing what they do best: design. But haven't we all sensed that often our talents are a bit inadequate, that sometimes something more direct is called for? I'm reminded of the scene in the Woody Allen movie *Manhattan* when Allen's character, Isaac Davis, suggests at a cocktail party that they confront some Nazis who are planning to march in New Jersey:

Party Guest: There is this devastating satirical piece on that on the
Op-Ed page of the *Times*. It's devastating.
Isaac Davis: Well, a satirical piece in the *Times* is one thing, but
bricks and baseball bats really get right to the point.

DOTWHO's site didn't include bricks and baseball bats, but it was about more
than t-shirts. There were news updates on liberal issues, links to other Democratic
sites, a weblog attracted substantial participation, and a light, lively tone, epitomized by the slogan "We're the T-Shirt Competition that the GOP Fears Most!"
DOTWHO's President, Andrea Moed, was the original web editor for the American
Institute of Graphic Arts, and she clearly knows what it takes to engage her audience.
Designers can go along with theories, principles, and ideologies, but if you really
want to get them energized, you need to give them a project.

Social psychologist Muzafer Sherif demonstrated the "power of the project"
forty years ago. An expert on intergroup relations, he conducted a famous series
of experiments that proved that disparate, even hostile, groups could be coalesced
around tasks requiring cooperative participation, even tasks as trivial as pulling a
truck out of the mud. DOTWHO's t-shirt project, as trivial as it was, was the pretext
around which a politically committed design community—and its ever-increasing
audience of design sympathizers—could rally. In short, the contest is just an
excuse to bring together a community of like-minded people. And who knows
where that may lead.

Even to me, this sounds a little like wishful thinking. But history provides
examples from which we can derive some hope. Late on a Thursday evening
in December, 1955, a group of black teachers in Montgomery, Alabama, met
to discuss what to do to protest the arrest of a black woman who had refused to
relinquish her bus seat to a white passenger. They came up with a project: a bus
boycott. The project became a cause, the cause became a movement, and fewer
than eight years later, a quarter-million people marched on Washington and heard
Martin Luther King's "I Have a Dream" speech. Designing a t-shirt is a humble
act, but humble acts are how revolutions begin.

India Switches Brands

Like many other insular Americans, I was only vaguely aware when India was holding elections in 2004. Listening to an account of the historic upset via BBC World Service on my car radio the morning after, I found myself a bit confused by an interviewer's question: What role did India Shining play in the election? Did India Shining have more appeal in progressive urban areas? Did India Shining alienate less-affluent people?

What? India Shining? Was this some kind of political movement? A new party? Some kind of special government program? Some kind of insurgent group? I had never heard of it before.

This was not true for the citizens of the world's biggest democracy, who had not only heard of India Shining, but had found it an inescapable part of their lives for the weeks leading up to the election. Until, that is, when the voters decided to escape it.

India Shining, I now know, is not a movement or political party, but that even more important holy grail sought after by institutions around the world: a brand. Created by Grey Advertising's India division for the ruling Bharatiya Janata Party (BJP), "India Shining" was the tagline for a $100 million media campaign intended to emphasize the role the popular BJP had played in India's economic upswing. The campaign was so dominant, according to the *Wall Street Journal*, that it "worked its way into daily life, headlines, and even other ads." The BJP, in effect, attempted to consolidate its power in

India by rebranding the country itself, and it seems to have come pretty close. The ubiquitous slogan made its way to Indians not only through television, radio, and print ads, but through screensavers, cellphone ring tones, unsolicited mass text messages, and, of course, a (now shut down) website.

Rebranding a country can be seen as the ultimate challenge for design consultants. (Landor, for instance, takes credit for Jordan, as well as Hong Kong and Pittsburgh.) And what some marketers excitedly call "360-degree branding"—integrated messages that come at you from all directions—must seem truly relentless when the subject is your nation rather than a mere beverage or a lowly sneaker.

These kinds of efforts invariably evoke, for me at least, the tragic huckster in Michael Moore's documentary *Roger and Me* who, given the charge to sex up the image of bleak, post-industrial Flint, Michigan, comes up with a goofy logo and maniacally cheerful slogan ("Flint: You'll Love Our New Spark!"). These delusional communication tools, predictably, have as much effect on the city's sagging fortunes as would sacrificing a goat. I watched that sequence in the film with a queasy sense of self-recognition: how many times have we designers been asked to reposition the image of a reality whose substance had proven impervious to change?

As it turned out, the heavily favored BJP made some key miscalculations. India Shining was designed to appeal to an urban, affluent constituency. But television ads—never mind websites—don't count for much in a country of over one billion where not even 90 million households own television sets. And, according to the *New York Times*, India is a country where the voting pattern of the United States is reversed. In the U.S., the more rich and educated you are, the more likely you are to vote; in India it's the opposite.

Sonia Gandhi's underdog Congress Party seems to have taken advantage of the BJP's hubris, carefully crafting appeals to India's "common man," complete with gritty, cinema verité–style testimonials. And, lest brandmongers lose heart, Congress's victory was achieved with the active assistance of their own consultants: a wholly owned local subsidiary of Leo Burnett, the agency best remembered for concocting, in simpler times, the Jolly Green Giant and the Marlboro Man.

Perhaps, in the end, the voters of India were not rejecting a brand but picking one more to their liking.

Graphic Designers, Flush Left?

David Brooks, cultural observer and author of *Bobos in Paradise: The New Upper Class and How They Got There*, once proposed an alternative analysis of the American political scene in his engaging *New York Times* column. "There are two sorts of people in the information-age elite, spreadsheet people and paragraph people," wrote Brooks. "Spreadsheet people work with numbers, wear loafers, and support Republicans. Paragraph people work with prose, don't shine their shoes as often as they should, and back Democrats." He went on to point out that "CEO's are classic spreadsheet people," five times more likely to donate to Bush than Kerry, and "Professors, on the other hand, are classic paragraph people," with Kerry donors outnumbering Bush donors eleven to one.

Are graphic designers spreadsheet people, paragraph people, or something else altogether? Where do we fall on the political spectrum? Do we even have to ask?

Paragraph people or number people, most of the designers I know lean left. My perspective may be skewed: I practice, after all, in a city where Democrats outnumber Republicans five to one. Yet judged by their poster projects, manifestos, and t-shirt contests, there is plenty of evidence that this is more than a local anomaly. Brooks posits an "intellectual affiliation theory." Number people, reassured by the "false clarity that numbers imply," respond to Bush's simple (minded?) decisiveness; paragraph people like the "postmodern, post-Cartesian, deconstructionist, co-directional ambiguity of Kerry's Iraq policy."

This makes sense. Graphic designers largely operate in a world of ambiguity and, with their antipathy to focus group testing and double-entry bookkeeping, most are definitely not number people.

This left-wing bias has deep historic roots. So much modern graphic design traces its roots back to the typographic innovations of the avant-garde work of early Soviet designers like Lissitzky, Rodchenko, Stepanova, and the Stenberg Brothers. Pioneering American graphic designers like Paul Rand, Charles Coiner, and Lester Beall were nurtured in the crucible of FDR's New Deal and the anti-Fascist fervor of the late thirties.

On the other hand, the most devastatingly effective design program of the twentieth century was commissioned by Adolf Hitler. A rigorously applied graphic identity, potent event planning, single-minded architectural design: no design detail was too petty for the Third Reich, even (in a weird echo of this moment's obsession with the political uses of vintage office equipment) the customization of typewriters, each one of which was fitted out with a key that would render the twin lightning bolt logo of the SS. Based on the historical record, might Brooks be tempted to further sort out corporate identity designers on the right, and poster designers on the left?

Some professionals feel that design and politics shouldn't mix. After the publication of an unashamedly partisan article on our blog, reader Adrian Hanft wrote, "Time after time this blog pushes its political agenda and I am tired of it...I am baffled as to why you can't stick to the issue that you are good at: observing design." On the blog he runs with a group of writers including Bennett Holzworth, Hanft makes his own position clear: "Politics is not off limits, but when the topic comes up, you can be sure we are talking about design, and not pushing an agenda or endorsing a candidate. Doing so can only lessen the impact of our design discussion. We are professional graphic designers who have dedicated our lives to design, not politics. You don't care what our political views are, do you?"

Well, actually, I do. Many subsequent writers seemed to assume that Hanft and Holzworth were writing from a pro-Bush position, but, true to form, they never disclosed their own leanings. I for one would like to hear from more conservative designers, if they truly exist. One of the few is Christian Robertson, who described himself as "one of the few registered Republican typoholics" while posting on Typographica. "The one thing I take from this," he wrote about the typographic controversy that erupted in 2004 around some disputed papers related to George Bush's National Guard Service, "is that you can't underestimate the power of political/cultural identity in shaping thought. In all of the blogs, news stories, newspaper articles, and cable 'shout shows' I've seen in the past couple days (and believe me, I've seen a lot of them), almost never did anyone support a view that crossed their team affiliation. People will sometimes grudgingly change their view, but it takes a true preponderance of evidence."

I would add that you can't underestimate the power of political and cultural identity in shaping design as well. As much as you might like to separate your political beliefs from your professional life, in the end it's folly. Satirist Tom Lehrer put it best in his song about mid-century America's most notorious non-ideological specialist, Werner von Braun, the Nazi weapons expert who joined the postwar space race as a designer for NASA:

Once the rockets are up, who cares where they come down?
That's not my department, says Werner von Braun.

We can try to compartmentalize our lives, but it's impossible. Graphic designers work with messages, and the messages mean something. We may think we're responsible only for launching those messages, and certainly there's some comfort (and profit) in thinking that. But if you care about your work, you have to care not only about how it goes up, but where you come down.

Just Say Yes

I don't get many emails from the Dow Chemical Corporation, so when I get one, I take notice.

The press release from "retractions@dowethics.com" was headlined, "'DOW' STATEMENT A HOAX: 'HISTORIC AID PACKAGE FOR BHOPAL VICTIMS' A LIE." The message that followed took the form of a typical corporate announcement, but it sounded a little...well, strange. "Today on BBC World Television, a fake Dow spokesperson announced fake plans to take full responsibility for the very real Bhopal tragedy of December 3, 1984. Dow Chemical emphatically denies this announcement. Although seemingly humanistic in nature, the fake plans were invented by irresponsible hucksters with no regard for the truth."

The Yes Men had struck again.

Here's what happened. On the twentieth anniversary of the disaster in Bhopal, India, where over 3,500 people died from a toxic gas leak at a Union Carbide plant, a BBC reporter was contacted by a supposed representative of Dow Chemical, the current corporate parent of Union Carbide, and told to expect a "historic announcement" from Paris. And the announcement was historic indeed: after two decades, the company was finally assuming responsibility for the accident and promised to establish a fund of $12 billion to compensate the victims' families.

It took a few hours, and the worldwide dissemination of the story, before the BBC realized it had been hoaxed. An angry Dow representative called the BBC, denying the story outright, and disavowing the spokesman who had appeared hours before. As the *London Times* observed, "There was something odd about the name of this new spokesman: Jude Finisterra—named after the patron saint of lost causes and a Mexican landmark that translates as 'the end of the Earth.'" Dow quickly issued a terse retraction.

That wasn't good enough for the hoax's perpetrators, who issued a second, more elaborate, retraction, available on a convincing-looking corporate website, complete with an elegantly displayed tagline: "This is Dow Corporate Responsibility." It was this release that I discovered in my email box that Friday afternoon.

The website's tagline, like the entire "retraction," had the remarkable quality of being both scrupulously accurate and absolutely damning. And that's exactly how The Yes Men work.

Finisterra, the fake Dow spokesperson, was articulate and well-prepared. "He was incredibly plausible," a helpless BBC executive told the *New York Times*. So was "Andreas Bichlbauer," who gave a Powerpoint presentation to an "intrigued" audience at a World Trade Organization conference in Salzburg; there he recommended that democracy (and capitalism) would be best served if votes were auctioned off to the highest bidder. So was the textile industry expert who suggested at a conference in Finland (again, to a polite and even receptive audience) that the U.S. Civil War might have been averted had the South the foresight to replace slavery with "infinitely more efficient" offshore sweatshop labor. Not to mention the McDonald's spokesman who tried to convince an audience of hostile college students that the solution to Third World famine is to provide the means for starving people to recycle their feces.

These are just some of the guises of The Yes Men, two guys named Andy and Mike who describe themselves on their website as "a couple of semi-employed, middle-class (at best) activists with only thrift-store clothes and no formal economics training." They're dedicated to what they call "identity correction." As opposed to identity theft, where "small-time criminals impersonate honest people in order to steal their money," The Yes Men's brand of identity correction is when "honest people impersonate big-time criminals in order to publicly humiliate them." Their pursuit of their targets—"leaders and big corporations who put profits ahead of everything else"—has been documented in a well-reviewed film named, yes, *The Yes Men*. These are guys that know how to stay on brand.

You might ask, "Is it design?" I remember being struck by Ralph Caplan's famous observation that the segregated lunch counter sit-in was "the most elegant design solution of the fifties." As he put it, "Achieved with a stunning economy of means, and a complete understanding of the function intended and the resources available, it is a form beautifully suited to its purpose." And he's right: civil disobedience at its best is a beautiful kind of problem solving. The Yes Men take the action to the global stage for the benefit of a new digital audience and deploy whatever tool it takes—websites, logos, Powerpoint presentations—to perform their elegant jujitsu on their stunned corporate victims: how devastating that the most effective part of the hoax wasn't the hoax itself but the forced retraction. Sure, it's a con game. But to quote one of the oldest design maxims in the book, you can't con an honest man.

Of course, what they do isn't fair, and some people are going to protest. One of them was George W. Bush, who was flummoxed by Andy and Mike's design of his wildly popular illegitimate website, www.gwbush.com. "There ought to be limits to freedom," he complained.

Maybe so. But until there are, we'll have to deal with The Yes Men.

Regrets Only

The Cooper-Hewitt National Design Museum began the National Design Awards in 2000 to honor the best in American design. In the museum's words, the program "celebrates design in various disciplines as a vital humanistic tool in shaping the world, and seeks to increase national awareness of design by educating the public and promoting excellence, innovation, and lasting achievement."

If design has an Oscar, the National Design Award is it. The honor is taken seriously. Nominations are solicited from advisors in every state of the union. The submissions of entrants are reviewed with great care over a two-day period by a panel of judges (which included me this year). Three individuals or firms are announced as finalists in each of six categories: architecture, landscape architecture, interior design, product design, fashion design, and communication design. Finally, the winners in those categories are announced, along with special awards that include honors for "Design Mind" and Lifetime Achievement.

Because the Awards program was originally conceived as an official project of the White House Millennium Council, the First Lady serves as the honorary chair of the gala at which the winners are celebrated. She also traditionally hosts a breakfast at the White House to which all the nominees and winners are invited.

In 2006, however, five Communication Design honorees decided to decline the invitation. Here is the letter that Michael Rock, Susan Sellers, and Georgie Stout, from that year's winning firm, 2x4, and Paula Scher and Stefan Sagmeister, respectively finalist and winner for 2005, sent to the White House:

Dear Mrs. Bush:

As American designers, we strongly believe our government should support the design profession and applaud the White House sponsorship of the Cooper-Hewitt National Design Museum. And as finalists and recipients of the National Design Award in Communication Design we are deeply honored to be selected for this recognition. However, we find ourselves compelled to respectfully decline your invitation to visit the White House on July 10th.

Graphic designers are intimately engaged in the construction of language, both visual and verbal. And while our work often dissects, rearranges, rethinks, questions, and plays with language, it is our fundamental belief, and a central tenet of "good" design, that words and images must be used responsibly, especially when the matters articulated are of vital importance to the life of our nation.

We understand that politics often involves high rhetoric and the shading of language for political ends. However it is our belief that the current administration of George W. Bush has used the mass communication of words and images in ways that have seriously harmed the political discourse in America. We therefore feel it would be inconsistent with those values previously stated to accept an award celebrating language and communication, from a representative of an administration that has engaged in a prolonged assault on meaning.

While we have diverse political beliefs, we are united in our rejection of these policies. Through the wide-scale distortion of words (from "Healthy Forests" to "Mission Accomplished") and both the manipulation of media (the photo op) and its suppression (the hidden war casualties), the Bush administration has demonstrated disdain for the responsible use of mass media, language, and the intelligence of the American people.

While it may be an insignificant gesture, we stand against these distortions and for the restoration of a civil political dialogue.

2006 finalist Chip Kidd was also asked to sign. But Kidd questioned the appropriateness of the gesture, and said so in an email to the group.

"The real issue here is that we were not invited to a rally in support of the war in Iraq. We were invited to recognize the National Design Awards, in our nation's capital, in an extraordinary building that is a cornerstone of our history." He added that, like them, he was opposed to the Bush administration's policies and pointed out that, also like them, he had created and published work that had expressed those views in no uncertain terms. But, he added, "it is that ability (hey, the freedom!) to make and send meaningful messages that we are supposed to be celebrating." Kidd concluded, "Of course I respect your decisions, as I hope you all know how much I respect you and your extraordinary talents. But as graphic designers, we rightly complain that those talents are too often uncredited and taken for granted. Personally, in this case, I think it accomplishes more to stand up and be counted than to stay away."

Accomplishment, as defined here, is nothing if not relative. Hosting a breakfast to honor the National Design Awards is hardly a public relations coup for the White House, and the attention that design gets from such a gesture is pleasant but not exactly transformative. Likewise, the erosion of George Bush's approval ratings are unlikely to accelerate just because a handful of graphic designers take a stand, no matter how principled. What we have here, then, is a symbolic protest to a symbolic event.

The commitment of the Bush administration to design has been negligible, unless one considers made-for-television stagecraft and obsessive typographic sloganeering worthy additions to the design canon. Mrs. Bush's remarks at the 2002 White House brunch are gracious and polite, but don't go much beyond saying that, well, design is nice. Speaking of the grandeur of the White House itself, she said, "Thanks to the dedicated work of design experts, we have landmarks like this one, places that are so well-loved, lived-in, and preserved that many generations are able to experience its stories and offerings. Design, in all its disciplines, is the world's greatest facilitator—it allows us to enjoy life and all of its pursuits."

To find real commitment to design, you have to go back: not to the Clintons, who helped initiate the Awards, but nearly thirty years earlier, to a time when that commitment was clear and unequivocal. Here's a quote from the President of the United States, circa 1973: "There should be no doubt that the federal government has an appropriate role to play in encouraging better design."

That was none other than Richard Nixon, launching the first Federal Design Assembly in 1973. Under the theme "The Design Necessity," it was the first of four conferences to bring together over 1,000 architects, product designers, interior designers, graphic designers, and public sector managers to discuss how design could be used more effectively by government on every level. Part of the NEA-sponsored Federal Design Improvement Program, it remains a high-water mark in government commitment to design in this country, creating legacies that include the conversion of the Pensioners Building into the National Building Museum and the enduring graphic program for the National Parks Service. What does it mean that we gained a design advocate in the man who many considered—until recently, at least—the worst president in the last 100 years?

In the days leading up to the breakfast, emails flew and tempers were raised. Interestingly, the controversy appeared to be confined to those of us who practice what the Cooper-Hewitt calls communication design; if any architects, product designers, interior designers, or landscape architects had any qualms about attending this event, they've remained silent. This may be our collective professional guilt: after all, George W. Bush owes his election, at least in part, to one inept amateur graphic designer in Palm Beach County, Florida. But there may be something more.

At their best, architects create buildings that outlive the patrons that commissioned them: the grandeur of the White House, invoked by both Chip Kidd and Laura Bush, can be experienced by contemporary visitors who need not know or care about George Washington or James Hoban. Similarly, the creations of fashion and product designers are perceived on their own terms once they're out in the world. But a piece of graphic design is more than an arrangement of lettering and images. It's also a message. And graphic designers, "intimately engaged in the construction of language, both visual and verbal," cannot escape the fact that—no matter how slippery—language, in the end, means something, or at least it's supposed to.

The Cooper-Hewitt is an extraordinary institution, and every designer in this country should be grateful to the role it plays as an advocate for design. And although it's part of the Washington-based Smithsonian, its future is never as secure as it ought to be. But isn't it appropriate that the museum be, as it has been here, a focal point for dissent as well as celebration?

Laura Bush was right about one thing, and no one knows it better than graphic designers: design *is* a facilitator. Now, more than ever, we should be aware of what we choose to facilitate.

The Forgotten Design Legacy
of the *National Lampoon*

I recently came across a new edition of something I had thought I would never see again: the legendary *National Lampoon* 1964 High School Yearbook. Originally published in 1971, the publication has, at its heart, what purports to be the yearbook of the fictional C. Estes Kefauver Memorial High School in tragically woebegone Dacron, Ohio. What struck me anew was the astonishing level of graphic detail that the *Lampoon* design staff brought to the task: every aspect of the yearbook (plus a basketball program, literary magazine, and history textbook) is rendered with awful, pitch-perfect fidelity, from each badly spaced typeface to every amateurish illustration. I would suggest that the *Lampoon's* designers, Michael Gross and David Kaestle, anticipated our profession's obsession with vernacular graphic languages by almost fifteen years.

Tony Hendra's book *Going Too Far* documents the rise and fall of postwar American humor, with a special emphasis on his years as an editor at the *Lampoon*. Perceptively, he sees the hiring of art director Michael Gross in October 1970 as a turning point in the magazine's fortunes. Originally, the founders of the *Lampoon* had sought to project an anti-establishment image and hired a "hippie" firm called Cloud Studios to evoke the look and feel of the underground press. This was a mistake: the writers were creating sophisticated, deadpan parodies, while the artists at Cloud Studios were making the magazine look self-consciously "funny"; as Hendra says, this was "the print equivalent of a comedian laughing while delivering a joke."

Enter Michael Gross, no graphic radical but a Pratt Institute–educated art director with experience at, among other magazines, *Cosmopolitan*. The publisher wanted a professional-looking magazine, which Gross was ready to provide. But the editors were worried he would play it too straight.

Gross had to explain to them that this was exactly what the content needed. As he told Hendra years later, "I flipped through the magazine and there was an article about postage stamps [a piece called 'America as a Second-Rate Power,' a new issue of stamps commemorating modern American failures], and there were all silly underground comic drawings. I said, 'What you've done here is no different than what *Mad* magazine would do. You're doing a parody of postage stamps. They would have Jack Davis do funny drawings of postage stamps. You've got an underground cartoonist doing funny drawings of postage stamps. What you need is postage stamps that look like postage stamps. The level of satire you've written here isn't being graphically translated."

Thereafter, Gross and his partner David Kaestle crafted each monthly issue of the *Lampoon* with a degree of care that would put a master forger to shame. As Hendra observes, "Any graphic form, and indeed any print form, had to look like the original on which it was based, whether it was a postage stamp or a Michelangelo or a menu. Only thus could the satirical intent come through with crystal clarity." In effect, Gross and Kaestle more resembled movie production designers than traditional art directors, creating convincing backgrounds before which the action could unfold. Unlike the knowing graphic quotations that we would come to associate in years to come with designers like Paula Scher and Tibor Kalman (or, to cite someone who has probably never even heard of the magazine, Jonathan Barnbrook, particularly in his work with Damien Hirst), there is no trace of irony in the work, just an obsessive determination to get every detail exactly right.

Gross and Kaestle do not show up in graphic design history books today, but there was a moment when they were riding high. Asked to create a special humor issue for *Print* magazine in the late seventies, they proved to be incisive commentators on their own profession. I remember in particular an article purporting to explore replacements for the seven-headed cobra emblem of the radical Symbionese Liberation Army, kidnappers of heiress Patty Hearst. The entries they created on behalf of Ivan Chermayeff, Rudolph de Harak, and Herb Lubalin all reduced the identity, through various elaborate pretexts, to the same Helvetica Medium solution.

The yearbook parody was a special project based on a ten-page piece by the late Doug Kenney, who would in turn use it as the seed for his screenplay for the 1978 movie *Animal House*. Thirty-five years later the precision of Kaestle and Gross's work still shines through, and deserves to be rediscovered.

McSweeney's No. 13 and the Revenge of the Nerds

The *McSweeney's* phenomenon is a force to be reckoned with in American graphic design. It began as—and still is—an online journal with an admirably understated visual presentation: while website designers worked themselves into grand mal seizures of hyperactivity in the late twentieth century, McSweeneys.net never abandoned its plain vanilla format. But it was when founder Dave Eggers moved into the world of conventional publishing with *McSweeney's Quarterly Concern* that the design world took notice. Simultaneously intricate and restrained, the densely packed all-Garamond pages of the *Quarterly* refracted Victorian foppishness through a prism of ironic cool and provoked Andrew Blauvelt to take to the pages of *Eye* to proclaim the arrival of a new movement: Complex Simplicity.

Eggers's brand of simplicity got ever more complex with successive issues: issue 4 was fourteen saddle-stitched books in a cardboard box; issue 7, nine perfect-bound books held in a case with a massive rubber band; issue 11, ersatz-elegant brown leatherette with gold foil stamping. Issue 13, guest edited and designed by Chris Ware, goes far beyond anything *McSweeney's* had previously done. It is extraordinary.

Eggers is a self-taught designer who famously writes his best-selling books in QuarkXPress rather than Microsoft Word; the cover of *McSweeney's* No. 2 included the aphorism: "If words are to be used as design elements then let designers write them." But thinking of him as a designer required quite a leap when Blauvelt did it. He became the perennial flavor of the month. He was featured in the Cooper-Hewitt design biennial. At the AIGA Voice conference, he entertained the crowd by evaluating his pages in terms of the frequency of their paragraph breaks, and noted that the most recent IBM annual report had a more-than-suspicious resemblance to the design (and editorial tone) of the most recent *McSweeney's Quarterly*. Perhaps he began to sense that when corporate America starts appropriating you, it's time for a change. Enter Chris Ware.

The theme of *McSweeney's* No. 13, not surprising to anyone who knows Ware's amazing work, is the comics. The 264-page hardcover book is bound with a giant, folded, comic-festooned dustjacket ("an enormous dust jacket that does much more than guard against dust," as it says on the website). It took me right back to the way the Sunday paper used to arrive on my childhood doorstep, and it conjured up that same sense of excitement. Inside is a feast of work: beautifully wrought pages by R. Crumb, Art Spiegelman, Julie Doucet, Chester Brown, Daniel Clowes, Charles Burns, Richard McGuire, and of course Ware himself, to name a few. These are complemented by thoughtful essays from Michael Chabon, John Updike, Chip Kidd, and others. Finally, there are appreciations of cartoonists of the past, including Rodolphe Topffer, George Harriman, Milt Gross, and—perhaps most tellingly—Charles Schulz, the creator of *Peanuts*.

Ira Glass, the eloquent host of Public Radio International's *This American Life*, describing his childhood obsession with *Peanuts*, nails the essentially tragic tone of *McSweeney's* No. 13 in particular and the world of cartoons in general. He read Schulz's strip not for amusement ("I don't remember ever thinking they were funny") but for reassurance ("I thought of myself as a loser and a loner and *Peanuts* helped me take comfort in that"). Charles Schulz himself understood the worldview he was setting forth. Glass quotes from a 1985 interview: "All the loves in the strip are unrequited. All the baseball games are lost, all the test scores are D-minuses, the Great Pumpkin never comes, and the football is always pulled away."

The artists that Ware brought together for *McSweeney's* No. 13 do not seem to lead enviable lives. They are, as Glass says, loners and losers, inept at human relationships, tormented by the popular kids, given to swearing, hostility, and compulsive masturbation: in short, like Charlie Brown, nerds. But drawing and storytelling is their way to connect with the world, and with us. Lynda Barry's painfully revelatory contribution, my favorite, describes the moral quandary faced by the cartoonist (and perhaps by the designer as well): "Is this good? Does this suck? I'm not sure when these two questions became the only two questions I had about my work, or when making pictures and stories turned into something I called 'my work'—I just know I'd stopped enjoying it and instead began to dread it."

In the four short pages that follow, Barry seems to overcome her dread to find a place of solace. So do the other artists in the book, and, somehow, so do we. In a hostile, uncaring world filled with senseless wrongs, *McSweeney's* No. 13 provides a moment of exquisite, gorgeous revenge.

The Book (Cover) That Changed My Life

It's a strange, even ugly, color combination. Solid maroon with lemon-yellow type: it looks like PMS 194 and PMS 116. One of the most generic typefaces in the world, Times Roman, set in all capitals, two slightly different sizes, with no particular finesse. The back looks just like the front. Nothing else.

Yet, using nothing more than these peculiar—dare I say crumby?—ingredients, the cover of the old Bantam paperback edition of *The Catcher in the Rye* has the power to move me like few other pieces of graphic design.

I can still remember the first time I saw it. It was in the "Young Adult" section of my local library, on a rotating wire rack. I must have been in the seventh grade. The other books on the rack—*It's Like This, Cat; The Outsiders; Go Ask Alice; Irving and Me*—all had illustrations on the front, usually peculiarly out-of-date, although perhaps only by months in the fast-moving time continuum of teenage fashion. Punks in leather jackets, preppies in checked button-down shirts and khakis. Handlettered titles for that "youthful" feel.

Catcher in the Rye was different. I think the only other book I knew at that point that had a type-only cover was the Bible. Was this book making the same claim to authority? And that title: what did it mean? I had heard, somehow, that Catcher in the Rye was transgressive and quirky, although I couldn't have known then of all the local school boards that had sought to ban it (as they do to this day), or of the self-imposed isolation of its author,

J. D. Salinger (which continues to this day). I took it home, brought it to my room, began reading, and didn't move a muscle until I was done.

Of course, I'm not alone in this. College admissions officers are resigned to the fact that, if asked to write an essay on "The Book That Changed My Life," the majority of students will pick The Catcher in the Rye. Or read the 2,260(!) customer reviews on Amazon if you doubt its enduring appeal.

The book does not have that cover now, and it did not have it when it was first published. The dustjacket on the original 1951 edition, designed by Michael Mitchell, had a Ben Shahn–style drawing of a carousel horse dwarfing the skyline of uptown Manhattan, an image clearly inspired by the book's "so damn nice" final scene. Early in its paperback life, I recall it had an incarnation I hated: a drawing of protagonist Holden Caulfield wearing the Sherlock Holmes–style hat described in the book (but looking much dorkier, somehow, than I had pictured him in my mind).

Then somewhere along the way (was it the mid-sixties? My attempts to find a chronology have been unavailing), Catcher acquired the cover it bore when I checked it out for the first time. I've heard rumors, but have not yet found any proof, that Salinger so hated the earlier illustrations that he insisted that the covers of all his books be type-only. Certainly this was borne out by the U.S. paperback editions of his other three books then in circulation. Nine Stories had its grid of colored squares (courtesy of Pushpin); the two Zen-themed books about the Glass family, Franny and Zooey and Raise High the Roofbeam, Carpenters both bore someone's idea of Asian-flavored lettering.

But for me, the maroon cover of Catcher has a special place. Blank, enigmatic, vaguely dangerous, it was the perfect tabula rasa upon which I could project all my adolescent loneliness, insecurity, anger, and sentimentality. It was as if possessing it provided a password into an exclusive club, even if that club existed only in my own mind. I wonder if a different cover, a more "designed" cover, could have been able to contain quite so much emotion and meaning.

Well, Catcher in the Rye has a different cover now. More than ten years ago, its publisher did what any intelligent marketer would do. They created a unified look and feel for the Salinger brand. Now all four of the paperbacks have identical white covers, identical black typography, and—here my heart sinks—a little sash of rainbow-colored stripes up in the corner. No horrible pictures of Holden and his hat, thank God, but those happy little lines just seem to be...what? I guess they're trying a little too hard for my taste. As Holden Caulfield might say, the new covers just look phony. The old one was just so goddam nice, if you know what I mean.

Vladimir Nabokov: Father of Hypertext

It was too cold to even think about going out in the sunshine, and I had spent about two hours at my computer, following links from blog to blog. Moving irresistibly from gawker.com to kottke.org to adrants.com to liberaloasis.com to moveon.org and on and on, it's easy to lose track of time. Finally, fatigue set in, as well as a bit of disgust that I was wasting an afternoon meandering through a lot of barely connected ideas.

I turned to my chores for the weekend, which included putting away a bunch of books that my wife had been piling up. One was *Pale Fire*, by Vladimir Nabokov. I opened it up, and immediately found myself back in that same world, but this time in the hands of a master. In 1962, Nabokov not only anticipated the linked world of hypertext, but also created that genre's first—and only?—undisputed literary masterpiece.

I would claim *Pale Fire* as one of my favorite books, except it has so many rabid fans that I'm not sure I qualify to join their number. If you aren't familiar with it, it's one of the few pieces of literature that I would argue is essentially "designed" in its conception and execution. The book consists of four parts: a foreword by "Dr. Charles Kinbote"; the eponymous 999-line poem by "John Shade"; more than 200 pages of commentary on the poem by Kinbote, and an index, again by Kinbote. The names are in quotes above because the entire book was actually written, of course, by Nabokov, who uses the fictional authors and interlocking elements to tell many stories at once—some, all, or none of which may be "true."

An analysis by Nabokov scholar Brian Boyd, *Nabokov's* Pale Fire*: The Magic of Artistic Discovery*, exposes the protohypertextual quality of the narrative in his description of the book's opening pages. At the end of the foreword's fifth paragraph—three pages into the book—a parenthetical aside refers the reader to Kinbote's note to line 991 of the poem. If one turns forward to the note, one finds midway through it further instruction to turn to the note to lines 47–48, which in turn contains a reference to the note on line 691. Returning back to the note on lines 47–48, one encounters a second reference to the note to line 62. And on and on. The whole book works that way, and we're only three pages in. Sound familiar?

Of course, Nabokov's genius is not simply that, in contrast to the multiple voices of the blog world, he's the author behind all the different parts that make up *Pale Fire*'s universe. It's that the elaborate structure of the book is so perfectly conceived that regardless of what path you follow, you can have an endlessly stimulating literary experience. In fact, I hesitate to raise this one again, but might I suggest that *Pale Fire* is design and, say, *Lolita* is art? (Sorry, let's not get into that.)

A check on Google reveals that my *Pale-Fire*-as-protohypertext revelation is far from original. Entering "pale fire" + Nabokov + hypertext + links turns up over 200 hits. One of these includes the interesting fact that as early as 1969, IBM had obtained permission from Nabokov's publisher, Putnam, to use *Pale Fire* for a demo of an early version of a hypertext-like system by Brown University's Theodor Nelson. (IBM did not go through with the proposal.)

My copy of *Pale Fire*—I have a first edition in not-so-hot condition—has that old book smell. There is nothing interesting about the interior layout. The cover is the same format that Putnam seems to have used for all their Nabokovs: a condensed sans serif with a bit of color behind it. When I recommend it to students, I can tell that at first glance it disappoints: this wordy old thing has something to do with design?

Trust me, it does.

The Final Decline and Total Collapse
of the American Magazine Cover

One Saturday morning I turned on the Public Radio International program *Studio 360* and was pleased to hear the unmistakable Bronx accent
of legendary adman George Lois, who was host Kurt Andersen's guest that
day. The talk inevitably turned to Lois's covers for *Esquire* in the sixties,
the high point of his career and probably one of the high points in twentieth-century American graphic design, period. Why, wondered Andersen,
didn't anybody do covers like these any more? "They're all infatuated with
the idea that celebrity, pure celebrity, sells magazines," growled Lois.

One week later, I served as a judge for the annual competition of the
Society of Publication Designers. Seeing table after table groaning under
the weight of glossy magazines festooned with photographs of celebrities
(or "celebrities") Jessica Simpson, Ashton Kutcher, and Justin Timberlake,
it was hard to deny that Lois was right.

George Lois's covers for *Esquire* provided my first glimpses into
the world of graphic design thinking. In the suburban Cleveland of my
childhood and early adolescence, Lois's images—Muhammed Ali pierced
with arrows à la St. Sebastian, Richard Nixon in the makeup chair, Andy
Warhol drowning in his own soup—didn't look like anything else in our
house. I realize now they were like messages from another world, a world
of irreverence and daring. Each was so brutally concise, so free of fat and
sentiment. They weren't just pictures, they were ideas. Even before I knew

he existed, I wanted to do what George Lois did. I wanted to come up with those ideas. I suspect I wasn't the only one.

But that was then. Today, you'd search in vain for a magazine that commissions covers like those. The best-designed mass circulation American magazines today—*Details, GQ, Vanity Fair,* and, yes, *Esquire*—usually feature a really good photograph by a really good photographer of someone who has a new movie out, surrounded by handsome, often inventive typography. The worst magazines have a crummy picture of someone who has just been through some kind of scandal surrounded by really awful typography.

The *"Esquire* cover"—a simple, sometimes surreal, image that somehow conceptually summarizes the most provocative point of one of the stories within—never found many imitators outside of *Esquire* even at its peak. Certainly few editors, then or now, were willing to imitate *Esquire's* Harold Hayes, who gave Lois the freedom to devise covers from nothing more than a table of contents.

And it's important to remember that Esquire was famous then not only for its covers but as the place for great writing, a place where Tom Wolfe, Norman Mailer, Gay Talese, and John Sack helped invent the New Journalism. Indeed, it was Sack's profile of Lt. William Calley, accused of leading a massacre of women and children in a Vietnamese village, that inspired one of the magazine's most powerful covers. I doubt that Lois at his peak could do one tenth as much with a vapid puff piece on Cameron Diaz.

But today I also think that there is simply a general distaste for reckless visual ideas. In the sixties, the bracing clarity of the "big idea" school of design was fresh: Lois, like Bob Gill and Robert Brownjohn and their disciples, could rightly claim to have found a position beyond style. But eventually the cadences of the big idea, the visual pun, began to seem not just brazen, but crass, with all the subtlety of an elbow in the ribs.

You can only have your rib poked so many times, and it doesn't seem to put you in the mood to buy things. Today's ideal magazine cover is enticing, not arresting, aiming not for shock, but for seduction. A George Lois *Esquire* on today's newsstand would be as out of place as an angry vegetarian at an all-you-can-eat steak dinner. And whatever function graphic design is supposed to serve these days, ruining your appetite doesn't seem to be one of them.

Information Design and the Placebo Effect

Despite Enron and Martha Stewart, scandal in the Catholic Church, and the failure to uncover weapons of mass destruction in Iraq, I would describe myself as a trusting sort, one who fundamentally still believes in the institutions that govern our public life. That trust was shaken to the very core by a report in the *New York Times* about the buttons that are mounted on poles at over 3,000 street corners in New York City. Despite the fact that they bear official-looking signs that read "To Cross Street/Push Button/Wait for Walk Signal/Dept. of Transportation," it appears that at least 2,500 of them have not worked for the last fifteen years.

Like everyone else, I've trusted those instructions, pressed the buttons, and waited dutifully, fearing—and, indeed, this is the literal interpretation of the sign—that the light would not change, ever, unless one pushed the button. Now I learn that I've been the dupe of what *Times* reporter Michael Luo calls mechanical placebos, where "any benefit from them is only imagined." My eyes newly opened, I wonder: can this possibly be an isolated case?

Now that I think about it, I've always wondered about those "Door Close" buttons on elevators. I mean, the door always eventually closes, but it's hard to tell if there's really any causation involved. Like the crosswalk buttons, all of these buttons may function simply as therapy for the overanxious. And it's significant that even if they seldom work, they still work sometimes. Every behavioral scientist knows that if you reward the rats every time, they take it for granted; if you never reward them, they give up. The most effective approach is to reward them every once in a while. This principal of intermittent reward is well understood by casino owners.

I myself have deployed meaningless information to assuage my own anxiety. We bought our first house from a fairly paranoid owner who had outfitted the (modest) property with an elaborate security system. Its operation was well beyond the ken of my family and, after setting off various alarms at various hours of the early morning, we finally had the whole thing disabled. But we left up all those signs reading "This Home is Protected by the Neverrest Ultra Security System," reasoning that intruders would be as alarmed by the signs as by the (now disarmed) alarms.

In post 9/11 Manhattan, this exchange of meaningless information has become part of daily life. Visit any office building over four stories in height and you're likely to run a gauntlet of inquisitors. The truly diligent ones subject visitors to x-ray examination and require tenant escorts. It's an inconvenient procedure, but at least you can understand its efficacy. More often, you're merely asked to sign a log and, sometimes, present your driver's license. How this is supposed to deter cunning terrorists, who presumably can acquire cheap fake IDs as easily as anthrax or dirty bombs, I've never understood.

And of course, to move from the personal to the political, no one is exploring the frontiers of information as placebo like our own Department of Homeland Security. What exactly are we expected to make of Tom Ridge's color-coded terrorism alert levels? When the level is raised, are we supposed to hide under the bed or go about our business? Are they trying to reduce anxiety or increase it? Do they mean anything at all? We don't know, and I'm not sure they really know either. But one way or another, they seem to be trying to press our buttons.

Stanley Kubrick and the Future of Graphic Design

Imagining what the future will look like is never easy. Does anything go out of date faster than someone's idea of what decor, fashion, and hairstyles will look like ten, one hundred, or a thousand years from now? But there was one artist who got it perfectly right: Stanley Kubrick.

Intrigued by an article on Kubrick's newly released archives in the Guardian, I went back and watched *2001: A Space Odyssey*. From the moment the prehistoric bone-as-weapon turns into the floating spacecraft (the best jump cut in the history of cinema), you know immediately you're in the hands of a master. Thirty-five years later (plus three years past due), it all looks better than ever.

As a graphic designer, I was interested to learn from the *Guardian* article that Kubrick was obsessed with typography, with a special affection for Futura Extra Bold. This font is so strongly associated with *2001* that I was surprised to realize that it appears only in the promotional material for the movie; the main titles are a kind of cross between Trajan and Optima, and I regret to say this is as horrible as it sounds.

In space, however, all is forgiven. In film after film, Kubrick proved himself to be a poet of the horrors and pleasures of boredom, and I mean that in a good way. The little boy going round and round on the Big Wheels in *The Shining*, the exquisitely slow zooms in the vast landscapes of *Barry Lyndon*: these are some of the most memorable images ever put on film.

In *2001*, the everyday banality of space travel gets its own special treatment that will ring true with any *Wallpaper*-toting frequent flyer. Buck Rogers's histrionics are rejected in favor of the simple pleasures of the low-cost flight to Fort Meyers; my eleven-year-old daughter, seeing the seat back video screens on the film's space shuttle, exclaimed, "Just like JetBlue!" Graphic design provides the grace notes. *2001*'s vast space station is fully colonized by corporate brands, some still with us (Hilton), some still with us but a little more unlikely (the glamorous-sounding Earthlight Room is operated by Howard Johnson) and some, alas, gone forever (Bell Telephone, Pan Am). Each logo is deployed with understated precision, contributing to the sense of place no less than the red Olivier Mourgue "Djinn" chairs and the Saarinen occasional tables.

Kubrick knew well the power of brand name as mot juste. My favorite line in *Dr. Strangelove* is delivered by Keenan Wynn as he grudgingly permits Peter Sellars to shoot off the lock of a soda dispenser to get enough spare change to make a phone call to the president to call off World War III. "If you don't get the President of the United States on that line, you know what's going to happen to you?" he growls as if he's delivering the biggest threat of all. "You're going to have to answer to the Coca-Cola Company." There, in one sentence, you have the DNA from which was to spring both Davos and *Adbusters*.

Kubrick's sense of humor in *2001* is more subdued, but no less evident. In *The Making of Kubrick's 2001*, a great out-of-print paperback edited by Jerome Agel (of The Medium is the Massage fame), the space shuttle's daunting instructions for its Zero Gravity Toilet are identified as the film's "only intentional joke," and in Eurostile to boot. In an age where few of us can access the advanced features of our cell phones, it still gets laughs. Kubrick understood so well that the everyday hallmark of the twenty-first century would not be the wonder of technology, but our day-in, day-out struggle to master it.

I Hear You've Got Script Trouble:
The Designer as Auteur

Once, writing about the obsession of designers with the everyday, Jessica Helfand mentioned the film *All the President's Men*, and the drama that it loaded into mundane activities like the manipulation of an on-hold button, saying "William Goldman's screenplay masterfully lyricizes a plot where the stakes are huge." The movie is great, but one thing you don't know from its title sequence is that Goldman wouldn't claim full credit for its screenplay. In his book *Adventures in the Screen Trade*, Goldman said it was "the most stomach-churning time I've ever had writing anything," with competing scripts offered up by, among others, Carl Bernstein and Nora Ephron. Although he would go on to win an Oscar for it, he was dismissed in favor of another writer before the filming began, and said, after seeing the movie in his local neighborhood theater, only that "it seemed very much to resemble what I'd done." Hardly a confident statement of ownership.

Screenwriting, like graphic design, is a collaborative art. That puts the people who write about it in a tough position. It's always easier to evaluate a creation in terms of its relationship to its creator. So what happens to the idea of authorship when many hands are involved in bringing something to life?

William Goldman is one of the best writers ever on the day-in, day-out struggles faced by anyone attempting to create good work in a hostile environment. His account of writing *All the President's Men* is particularly harrowing. At one point, while writing "God knows how many" versions of the screenplay, he is introduced by a friend to the legendary anchorman Walter Cronkite, who dismisses him with a curt "I hear you've got script trouble" before going on his way. And you thought graphic design was tough.

Goldman has no illusions about what it takes to create a great movie: lots of talented people. After the death of Alan Pakula, director of *All the President's Men,* eulogists were quick to credit him with, among other things, the shadowy paranoia of the movie's parking-garage scenes with Deep Throat. "Sorry," says Goldman, "that is [cinematographer] Gordon Willis you're talking about here." Obviously, the auteur theory—briefly, the critical view (advanced in France by François Truffaut and Jean-Luc Godard and championed in the United States by Andrew Sarris) that a film's sole "author" is its director—finds no fan in William Goldman; his reaction to hearing about it for the first time is a sardonic "What's the punch line?"

The average piece of graphic design is certainly less complicated in its genesis than the average movie. Yet all but the simplest have multiple hands involved in their creation. Nonetheless, those who write about design find it irresistible to evaluate work as expressions of individual vision. And I'd be lying, as one of those individuals, to say that I haven't reaped the benefits of, and enjoyed the attention that goes with, that kind of simplification. Becoming famous, as anyone who watches the Academy Awards knows full well, means being gracious about thanking your many wonderful collaborators while making absolutely sure the spotlight stays focused on you.

On top of that, unlike filmmaking, graphic design is still largely an anonymous art. For anyone at all to get public credit (at a mass-market level, at least) for designing, say, a logo or a sign system is still a novelty. Those gruesome details about who actually did the final digital artwork, who did the illustration, who contributed to the underlying strategy, who influenced whom, who argued with whom, who stole what from whom, not to mention the client, God help us, are mind-numbing details that would tax already-brief attention spans. Easier to stick with This Object Was Designed By This Designer and move on to the next caption.

I do wonder, however, what's being lost here. There seem to be two popular modes of recording design history: either as the product of a succession of visionary creators, as described above, or, more ambitiously, perhaps, as the product of massive but essentially anonymous historical forces. Sometimes we get one, sometimes we get the other, sometimes we get a mix of the two. But what we seldom get is the messy truth in between. I think that's part of what Lorraine Wild is asking for in her essay "Sand Castles" in *Emigre* No. 66: more accounts of "the specific energy and texture, seriousness and rebellion, the orneriness and fun," that goes into producing graphic design in the real world.

This would not be easy, but I suspect it would be worth the trouble if anyone were brave and dogged enough to undertake the challenge. In my mind I see my own favorite scene from *All the President's Men*: Woodward and Bernstein doggedly sifting through records under the rotunda of the Library of Congress . . . played by Robert Redford and Dustin Hoffman, cast by Alan Shayne, filmed by Gordon Willis, scored by David Shire, edited by Robert Wolfe, designed by George Jenkins, produced by Jon Boorstin, Michael Britton, and Walter Coblenz, and directed by Alan Pakula, from a screenplay by—more or less—William Goldman.

The Idealistic Corporation

What kind of work do we do? For whom do we do it? These are the fundamental questions for practicing designers, and it's tempting to reduce the options to a depressingly simple choice: do commercial mainstream work that may have an impact on the mass market, or do what Rick Poynor calls "independent" work, projects of a more personal nature that may never extend beyond a small, specialized audience of connoisseurs. In other words: sell out, or resign yourself to marginalization.

But it wasn't always so.

The years following World War II were giddy ones not only for American designers, but for the corporations that employed them. These were the days of "good design is good business," to quote the emblematic business leader of the age, IBM's Thomas J. Watson, Jr. What is striking today about these postwar design patrons is not just their willingness to use good design to advance their company's commercial aims, but their seeming conviction that design could do more than simply move product, it could make the world a better place. Watson's counterpart at Container Corporation of America (CCA), Walter Paepcke, wrote in 1946:

> Artists and businessmen, today as formerly, fundamentally have
> much in common and can contribute the more to society as they come
> to complement their talents....It should be made easy, remunerative

and agreeable for the artist to "function in society not as a decorator but as a vital participant." The artist and the businessman should cultivate every opportunity to teach and supplement one another, to cooperate with one another, just as the nations of the world must do.

Just as the nations of the world must do! Paepcke put his money where his mouth was, commissioning dozens of artists and designers to create advertising and design for CCA and starting the International Design Conference at Aspen, conceiving it as a summit at which business leaders and designers could meet, share ideas, and, presumably, plan together how to save the world. Herbert Bayer's extraordinary *World Geo-Graphic Atlas*, which Rick would like to see displayed at MoMA, exists thanks to a commission from CCA. In its foreword, titled "Why Container Corporation Publishes an Atlas," Paepcke writes, "We, in Container Corporation, believe that a company may occasionally step outside of its recognized field of operations in an effort to contribute modestly to the realms of education and good taste," and "It is important that we know more about the geography and the conditions of life of our neighbor[s] in the world so that we may have a better understanding of other peoples and nations."

Paepcke was by no means alone. Watson's IBM not only commissioned graphics from Paul Rand, products from Eliot Noyes, and buildings from Eero Saarinen, but extraordinary exhibits by Charles and Ray Eames like Mathematica which could have had only, at best, an indirect influence on the corporation's bottom line. "How much business did a good-looking exhibit attract to the IBM Company?" asked Watson. "These are intangible things that we believe are genuine dividends of a good design program."

Other notable examples include General Dynamics and their long-term relationship with Erik Nitsche, which produced his masterpiece volume *Dynamic America*, as well as the ultimate expression of corporate munificence, Cummins Engine Company's hometown of Columbus, Indiana. There the visionary CEO Irwin Miller transformed a southwestern Indiana city into a virtual demonstration laboratory for design in daily life. A church by Saarinen, a firehouse by Robert Venturi, an elementary school by Richard Meier, and a newspaper printing plant by SOM's Gordon Bunshaft are among dozens of buildings built there in the second half of the twentieth century that tourists can visit with the help of a guide designed by...you guessed it, Paul Rand.

Today, one is hard pressed to find counterparts to Watson, Paepcke, and Miller. After the tumult of the late sixties, Watergate, stagflation, and Reagan-era deregulation, corporations are no longer looked to for civic leadership. Offshore outsourcing makes the Columbus-style company town seem like a paternalistic anachronism. The inefficient realms of education and good taste no longer tempt rigorous CEOs with their eyes on the bottom line. Even Thomas Watson's heir apparent, Steve Jobs, limits his passion for design to stuff that sells product; Apple's dazzling contribution to civic life is the Apple Store, where you can go have a social experience that has solely to do with buying Apple products.

Is all hope lost, then? Here is some optimism, perhaps perverse, from a surprising source. "I offer a modest solution: Find the cracks in the wall," wrote Tibor Kalman in his valedictory monograph. "There are a very few lunatic entrepreneurs who will understand that culture and design are not about fatter wallets, but about creating a future. . . . Believe me, they're there and when you find them, treat them well and use their money to change the world." Wishing will not make it so, but Kalman knew that the search itself was fundamental to the design process. Now more than ever, let's start looking.

Barthes on the Ballpoint

Ballpoint was an exhibition at London's Pentagram Gallery organized by my partner Angus Hyland that featured the work of "artists, illustrators, and designers invited to make an artwork using only ballpoint pen." The participants include Ron Arad, Nicholas Blechman and Christoph Niemann, Paul Davis, Marion Deuchars, Jeff Fisher, Alan Fletcher, Benoît Jacques, Uwe Loesch, and Ian Wright.

The exhibition prompted an interesting note from Dan Hedley. Hedley, who describes himself as having recently completed a PhD on "the strategic use of branding in Renaissance literature," pointed out a passage from a 1973 interview with theorist Roland Barthes. "It would appear from the interview," says Hadley, "that not only is M. Barthes no friend of the ballpoint, but he is rather critical of those who are."

Barthes admits, "I have an almost obsessive relation to writing instruments." As his pronouncement goes on to betray, however, this obsessive relation is itself (in Hedley's words) "obsessively particular, and not a little snooty":

> When felt-tipped pens first appeared in the stores, I bought a lot of them. (The fact that they were originally from Japan was not, I admit, displeasing to me.) Since then I've gotten tired of them, because the point flattens out too quickly. I've also used pen nibs—not the "Serjeant-Major," which is too dry, but softer nibs, like the "J." In short, I've tried everything

except Bics, with which I feel absolutely no affinity. I would even say, a bit nastily, that there is a "Bic style," which is really just for churning out copy, writing that merely transcribes thought.

Writers are notoriously obsessive about the tools of their trade, investing perfectly sharpened pencils, specific brands of writing papers, obsolete manual typewriters and such with nearly magical qualities. Barthes, who readily admitted "as soon as I see a new pen, I start craving it. I cannot keep myself from buying them," was certainly in their number, and his distaste for ballpoints is certainly a precursor to the profoundly conflicted feelings that so many writers have toward their computers.

It is interesting to think how much is lost when a work of literature is converted from messy, quirky, all-too-human manuscript into printed document: authoritative, polished, impersonal, and remote. Designers are certainly complicit in this transformation, and, indeed, take pleasure in it. Might one say that we are undisputed masters of Barthes's smooth, plastic, dependable, throwaway "Bic style," no matter what medium we work in?

The Tyranny of the Tagline

Here are some thoughts from a few magazines on my nightstand right now: This is who we are. This is how we earn it. Solutions for the adaptive enterprise. The right way to invest. We move the world. Life inspiring ideas. Inspiration comes standard. Break through. Make life rewarding. Live famously. Like a rock. Creating essentials. The passionate pursuit of perfection. Born to perform. Beyond petroleum. Pleasure to burn. Your natural source of youth. Get the feeling. Get the good stuff. Win.

Maybe some of these will sound familiar to you. Corporate America certainly hopes so. Millions of dollars are spent contriving these platitudes, exhortations, and non sequiturs, and billions more are spent communicating them to us. Why do ad agencies and their clients love taglines so much?

Taglines used to be called slogans, and in the days of hard sell advertising mavens like Claude Hopkins and Rosser Reeves, they summed up the product and the promise in one viciously efficient little package: Winston tastes good like a cigarette should. Somewhere along the way, though, slogans turned into taglines, vague bits of poetry that sought to transcend the mundane commercial world and commune with the divine. Hence: Get the feeling. (That one's for Toyota.)

Ad agencies put great stock in taglines, hoping that with a simple phrase they can create the indestructible core of an evergreen advertising campaign. There is a holy grail, of course—Just do it—the three words that have anchored Nike's presence in the marketplace for what now seems like eternity. It's a hard act to follow, though. Nike's agency, Wieden and Kennedy, won the Microsoft account in the mid-nineties with a tagline they hoped would surpass Nike's: Where do you want to go today? It came and it went.

Of course, taglines have always had their doubters. "Agencies waste countless hours concocting slogans of incredible fatuity," wrote David Ogilvy. "Notice that all of these bromides are interchangeable—any company could use any of them."

And working with taglines is challenging for a graphic designer. When they're freshly minted, clients tend to invest them with the power of a magician's spell, and insist that they appear everywhere. "Locking up" the logo and tagline is tricky, though, and not just visually: logotypes are meant to have long shelf lives, and taglines...well? There are plenty of warehouses full of three years' worth of business cards bearing taglines for campaigns that were abandoned after three months.

This is a bit of a prelude to a remarkable new corporate identity that was unveiled last month for the YWCA. It is not remarkable because of the way the identity relates to the tagline. It is remarkable because, as far as I can tell, the tagline is itself the identity.

Throughout its 150-year history, the YWCA has been dedicated to two things: eliminating racism and empowering women. I have to admit I did not know this; I just found out on their website. I thought the YWCA was simply the female version of the YMCA. Obviously, I'm not alone in my ignorance, so the YWCA must have decided that their old identity, a stylized Y by Saul Bass, just wasn't getting the job done.

Having designed many identities for non-profit groups, I can imagine what a challenge this must have represented. What kind of typeface communicates the elimination of racism? What kind of pictorial image or abstract shape projects the empowerment of women? One common argument, of course, is the Paul Rand one, the claim that the logo has no inherent significance, and that it gains meaning only through association with the activities of the group it stands for: think of the peace sign or the swastika. But this requires a long-term investment, and for the YWCA, desperate times must have called for desperate measures.

So Landor, the creators of the new YWCA identity, did something so obvious it's amazing it hasn't been done before. They simply set the words "eliminating racism" and "empowering women" on two lines in a bold sans serif typeface. Then underneath, and smaller, is the actual organization's name: YWCA. Voila. You can love it or hate it, but the one thing you can't deny is that it certainly communicates the organization's raison d'être, at least to people who can read.

Corporate identity is a trendy business. In the last twenty years we've gone from logos with horizontal stripes (à la IBM) to swooshes (Nike) to geometric shapes (Target). Brace yourself: the tyranny of the tagline may be just beginning.

Ed Ruscha: When Art Rises to the Level of Graphic Design

Fine artists have been taking inspiration—when not outright stealing—from the world of graphic design for a century. The list is long: Kurt Schwitters and Georges Braque, Stuart Davis and Charles Demuth, Jasper Johns and Andy Warhol, Barbara Kruger, and Jenny Holzer.

But I admire one above all, not just as an artist but as a graphic designer, and I mean that as a compliment: Ed Ruscha. His exhibition, Cotton Puffs, Q-tips ®, Smoke and Mirrors: The Drawings of Ed Ruscha, at the Whitney Museum of Art in New York proves why.

Born in Oklahoma City, as a child Ruscha wanted to be a cartoonist. Moving to Los Angeles, in 1956 he enrolled as a commercial art student at Chouinard Art Institute (now Cal Arts). Ironically, it was seeing a tiny, black-and-white reproduction of Jasper Johns's *Target with Four Faces* in *Print* magazine, of all places, that inspired him to become a painter rather than a graphic designer. But from his earliest days, he exhibited a love for typefaces—perfectly drawn, used with intelligence and passion—with which any graphic designer would sympathize.

Certainly other artists have incorporated the language of advertising, signage, publications, and package design in their work. But where, say, Andy Warhol sought an offhand, almost sloppy, casualness in his mechanically reproduced small-space ads and Brillo boxes, Ruscha's lettering from the early sixties (SPAM in Frankfurter, GAS in Cooper Black, HONK in

Stymie Bold) is lovingly, respectfully precise. And where an artist like Barbara Kruger would seize upon a single signature graphic style (Futura Extra Bold Italic, in her case) and repeat as relentlessly as a corporation seeking a proprietary house style, Ruscha has been restless and endlessly inventive, changing typefaces to suit the messages, and inventing new ones (most notably his calligraphic "ribbon" style) seemingly just for the sheer joy of it. Similarly, he has explored different media with a vengeance; the show includes drawings executed in vegetable juices, gunpowder, blood, and tobacco juice as well as more prosaic ink, tempera, graphite, and pastel.

Unlike other artists of his generation, but with an enthusiasm that, again, would be familiar to any graphic designer, Ruscha began publishing, early and often. Books like *Twentysix Gasoline Stations* and *Every Building on the Sunset Strip* were ways of documenting his deadpan obsessions at a modest cost (four hundred numbered copies for $3.00 each) that, he felt, anyone could afford. "I want to be the Henry Ford of book making," he explained at the time. Obviously, at that price the books would be sold at a loss, but, he confessed, "It is almost worth the money to have the thrill of seeing four hundred exactly identical books stacked in front of you."

A few of Ruscha's notebooks are on view at the Whitney, and it was there, more than anywhere else, that I experienced the shock of recognition. Careful sketches of Hector Guimard's signage for the Paris Metro, studies of how paper folds and curls, layouts of future projects with typefaces effortlessly indicated with a few scribbled lines: if this isn't the way a designer thinks on paper, nothing is. Particularly fascinating are the frequent lists of words that serve as Ruscha's starting point; without clients to provide the messages, he has to invent them himself. "They come about in strange ways," he told *New York* magazine; "There's no formula; they just have to be emotionally loaded. It may be something that I hear on the radio, or a lyric from a song...It's a simple thing."

It's no surprise that one of Ruscha's earliest—and most loaded—subjects is one that he returned to repeatedly: that most iconic of American typographic expressions, the landmark, once-temporary-now-permanent HOLLYWOOD sign that symbolizes his hometown to the rest of the world. Monumental, yet in its way as ephemeral as the celluloid fantasies it indelibly evokes, it's a perfect demonstration of how graphic design can inflame the popular imagination. At the Whitney exhibition, we see evidence that Ed Ruscha has been conducting the same kind of demonstrations for over forty years.

To Hell with the Simple Paper Clip

If there's one design cliché that has come to really irritate me, it's this one: answering the question "What's your favorite design?" with an answer like "The simple paper clip." Or the rubber band. Or the stop sign. Or the Post-It Note. Or any other humble, unauthored object from everyday life.

To me, this is like answering the question "What's your favorite song?" with "You know, is there any song as beautiful as the laughter of a child?" It's corny. It's lazy. It's a cop-out.

I do admit, it's a tempting cop-out. We've all done it at one time or another. In the *New York Times Magazine*'s 1988 annual design issue five years ago, they put the question to a bunch of well-known people, some designers, some not. A few people named objects that were actually designed, although, oddly, the designer was not always named: the Pie Watch (named by Leon Wieseltier, not credited to M&Co.), the Braun Travel Alarm Clock (named by Martha Stewart, not credited to Dieter Rams), and, okay, even I myself went on the record for the Beatles' *White Album* without crediting Richard Hamilton.

But more frequent were the hymns to those damned anonymous objects, sometimes industrial in origin like the Sylvania half-frosted light bulb (chosen by Richard Gluckman), or sometimes humble like chopsticks (chosen by frog design's Hartmut Esslinger). Or how about...beads? That's right, just beads. "Beads focus and concentrate esthetic attention," we learned from *Nest*'s Joseph Holtzman. "One becomes supremely aware of color, shape, and especially surface." Ah, the humble bead! On some level, I do see why designers in particular like to dodge this question. On one hand, you can be honest, select as your favorite something that you yourself designed, and look like an egomaniac, which you probably are. The alternative is to pick something someone else designed, and thus give aid and comfort to a competitor. Tough choice. Wait, how about . . . the humble white t-shirt, designed by absolutely no one? Perfect!

The white t-shirt and 121 other objects were recently on view at New York's Museum of Modern Art, in an exhibition that started a new orgy of paper clip fetishization. Humble Masterpieces was organized by the first-rate curator (and unrepentant Post-It Note fan) Paola Antonelli, and included the Bic pen, the whisk broom, the tennis ball, and bubble wrap. "Although modest in size and price," Antonelli observes, "some of these objects are true masterpieces of the art of design and deserving of our admiration." And now, thanks to MoMA, so are many of their designers: Antonelli and her staff have diligently researched the names of the creators of these seemingly authorless objects. So we learn that Scotch tape was—what, designed? invented? discovered?—in 1930 by Richard G. Drew (American, 1886–1956). And it all sparked a lively discussion on the Speak Up website where people posted their own nominations.

Antonelli points out that MoMA's commitment to finding the sublime in the everyday has a long history. The museum's landmark Machine Art show in 1934 exhibited industrial objects like springs and ball bearings. The undeniable beauty of these objects must have been a revelation to audiences used to Victoriana and ersatz Streamline. The intention, I think, was to create a bracing demonstration of how form following function could lead to enduring, honest solutions, unencumbered by the fussy hand of the stylist. But what is the effect on the twenty-first-century museumgoer who is confronted with a display of Legos, Slinkys, soy sauce dispensers, and M&Ms? I wonder.

At any rate, since MoMA put its imprimatur on the whole idea, perhaps we can finally move on. All these things have now gotten their rightful due, and it's time to turn our attention to other worthy subjects. So if one of these days you're challenged to come up with your own favorite design and you just can't come up with one, take the easy way out: just pick something designed by me.

The Man Who Saved
Jackson Pollock

A few years ago, I opened the newspaper to find a story on the resurrection of a beloved graphic icon. It seems a group of railroad fanatics had come together to restore sixteen locomotives to bear the black-and-red paint scheme of the long-defunct New Haven Railroad. And they were successful: today the trains are running in and out of Grand Central Terminal bearing the striking logo that looks as good now as it did when it was retired in 1968.

I read the article with pleasure at first, and then with mounting exasperation. A half dozen names were invoked in the saga: the conductor who had the original idea to restore the trains; a trainspotter from the Bronx who spearheaded the effort; a couple of transit bureaucrats who moved the effort along; the president of the New Haven Railroad Historical and Technical Association; even "a graphic artist from Queens, James C. Smith Jr." who was "brought in to adapt the New Haven designs." Everyone got some credit, it seems, except the genius who was the original author of those beloved New Haven Railroad designs, Herbert Matter.

These days, however, Herbert Matter is finally in the news. Except this time it's not as a designer, but as a particularly prescient packrat.

Thirty-two previously unknown works attributed to the late Jackson Pollock were revealed to the world by Alex Matter, the sixty-three-year-old son of Herbert and Mercedes Matter. According to the *New York Times*, these early "drip" paintings, "wrapped in brown paper and tied with string, were included with other artworks and letters that the elder Mr. Matter had left with other personal effects after his death in 1984." While their legitimacy has been disputed in some quarters, to many Pollock authorities the paintings appear genuine. If so, some experts suggest they could be worth up to $10 million.

In accounts about the discovery, Herbert Matter has been variously described as a "graphic artist and photographer," "photographer, filmmaker, and Pollock friend," and most frequently the all-purpose "associate." To many, this might suggest a faceless hanger-on, hoarding the castoffs of his famous friends. Herbert Matter was anything but.

Matter was born in Switzerland in 1907 and studied in Paris with Fernand Léger. Working as a designer and photographer inspired by Man Ray and Cassandre, he secured his reputation with his iconic posters for the Swiss Tourist Office and emigrated to the United States in 1936. There, Matter and his wife Mercedes established deep and profound ties to the mid-century art community that were deep and profound. From their studio in Greenwich Village's MacDougal Alley, the Matters maintained friendships with not just Pollock and his wife, Lee Krasner, but Alexander Calder, Franz Kline, Philip Guston, and Willem de Kooning, among others. His immersion in this world led to the design of books, catalogs, exhibitions, and films, all informed by Matter's sympathetic imagination and sure sense of design. His friendship with Pollack began when the painter was largely unknown; there is speculation that the forgotten package of early work was put aside to form the basis of some never-realized publication.

What is striking today is Matter's ability to reconcile this level of cultural engagement with commercial projects of the highest order, which included not only his robust work for the New Haven Railroad, but corporate identities for Knoll and posters for Container Corporation. His friend and fellow Yale faculty member Paul Rand put it well in a poem he wrote for a catalog for a 1977 exhibition of Matter's work. It begins:

Herbert Matter is a magician.
To satisfy the needs of industry, that's what you have to be.
Industry is a tough taskmaster.
Art is tougher.
Industry plus Art, almost impossible.

About twenty years after Matter's death, I nearly discovered my own treasure trove. On a rare trip to the Hamptons, I walked into a bookstore and almost fainted. There on the walls were displayed a striking set of about a dozen large illustration boards, each featuring a variation of an immediately recognizable design scheme, painstakingly rendered in black and red gouache. Composing myself, in my most blasé tone I casually asked the proprietor if he'd consider breaking up the set. Alas, at Glenn Horowitz Booksellers, they know their graphic design. "We would never sell these separately," I was cooly informed. "These are Herbert Matter's original presentation drawings for the New Haven Railroad." Rats. The price was something like $20,000.

That East Hampton bookstore is an exception, of course. Even within the world of art and design, Herbert Matter is relatively unknown, and unfairly so. I would argue that Matter was as important a figure in the field of graphic design as Jackson Pollock was in the world of art. With Pollock's long-lost paintings finally seeing the light of day, it is a perfect occasion to bring some overdue attention to the designer who stored them away.

Homage to the Squares

In 2005, I visited two exhibitions on view at the Cooper-Hewitt National Design Museum. The big one, Design is not Art, seemed to be intended as an ambitious, provocative statement on the relationship of those two sometimes contentious fields. The other, Josef and Anni Albers: Designs for Living, was something I assumed would be more of an *amuse bouche*, a modest survey of some familiar work to be sampled as a counterpoint to the main course.

I was in for a surprise.

It was Design is not Art that I was really looking forward to. The exhibition's name, however, should have provided a faint warning. Not just complex but complicated, it would be more properly expressed here as Design [is not] Art, since the actual title used the mathematical symbol for "not equal to, but not greater than and not less than." The fact that it is so hard to transcribe the title says something about a missed connection between conceptual ingenuity and practical utility. Yet what's not to like about a cornucopia of functional work by some of my favorite artists, including Donald Judd, Scott Burton, Barbara Bloom, Robert Wilson, and Rachel Whiteread?

Josef Albers, on the other hand, had always left me cold. Like many art and design students, I was assigned *Interaction of Color* as a freshman and forced to spend several weeks manipulating sheets of Color-aid, all the while thinking okay, simultaneous contrast, I get it, for God's sake. Later, I read a tossed-off assessment from Tom Wolfe: "Albers had spent the preceding fourteen years of his life investigating the problems, if any, of superimposing squares of color on each other." The viciousness of that little "if any" nailed it for me exactly.

In the excellent catalog for Design is not Art, Cooper-Hewitt director Paul Thompson quotes David Hockney: "Art has to move you and design does not, unless it's a good design for a bus." But the work of the artists left me surprisingly unmoved. It wasn't just that most of the furniture on display (and design, according to artists, mostly means furniture) looked almost sadistically uncomfortable: after all, no reasonable person would expect a Barcalounger from Sol LeWitt. Instead, what I sensed was the chilly insularity of the fine-art world. Most of the artists on display began as their own clients; the only way to avoid the distasteful products of the mass market was to take matters into their own hands. As Donald Judd put it bluntly, "It's impossible to go to the store and buy a chair." This mania for creating a completely self contained world, centered entirely on the artist's vision, may produce objects of extraordinary beauty, but omits one of the fundamental characteristics of great design, respect for the user. The overall effect was one of tense, hermetic constriction, of meanness where one would hope for meaning.

It was with some trepidation then that I went downstairs to view the output of Josef and Anni Albers: surely it was these protominimalists who were partly to blame for all this. So what a delightful surprise to find room after room filled with rich, sensual objects, addressing an almost promiscuously wide range of problem types, from furniture to record covers. I felt like I was discovering an oasis after a parched desert trek.

Josef and Anni Albers: Designs for Living, with essays by Nicholas Fox Weber and Martin Filler, is the only exhibition catalog I've ever read from cover to cover in one sitting. Intimate and engaging, it provides insights into the creative process that will stay with me, and that provide instructive contrasts to those in Design is not Art. Here, for example, is Josef Albers explaining how he approached his famous *Homage to the Square* paintings: "I paint the way I spread butter on pumpernickel." Compare that to Scott Burton: "Art just seems spiritually insufficient in a doomsday climate and it will take an increasingly relative position. It will place itself not in front of but around, behind, underneath (literally) the audience—in an *operational* capacity."

Whose chair would you rather sit in?

For me, the most startling images in Designs for Living were the pictures of the modest suburban raised ranch at 808 Birchwood Drive in Orange, Connecticut, that Josef and Anni Albers lived in since 1970, so prosaic compared to the iconic Masters' Houses at the Dessau Bauhaus that they called home at the beginning of their marriage. While the photographs of the interiors betray the extraordinary taste of its occupants, there is no mistaking that this is where everyday life happened, from the Sears furniture to the Formica tabletops, from the blender on the kitchen counter to the potted palm on the coffee table. Clearly, these artists delighted in the world around them. They were not afraid to be uncool.

It is that sure sense of life, everyday life lived to the fullest, that is the mark of a great designer, and perhaps it is part of what separates the designer from the artist. Establishing his isolated retreat in remote west Texas, Donald Judd wrote, "Most art is fragile and some should be placed and never moved again." I imagine that Josef and Anni Albers would have disagreed.

Eero Saarinen's Forty-Year Layover

On its fortieth anniversary, Broadway revived Arthur Miller's 1964 drama *After the Fall*. The cast included some familiar faces—Peter Krause from *Six Feet Under*, Carla Gugino from *Karen Sisco*—but the most familiar face of all was the set. Richard Hoover's design is not just inspired by, but is a nearly faithful reproduction of, Eero Saarinen's famous landmark. If you fly into JFK, you may see the unmistakable silhouette of the TWA Terminal from the outside. But not the inside: its namesake carrier defunct, the interior spaces have been closed to visitors for years.

This makes its hold on the popular imagination all the more fascinating. As a moviegoer, you may have seen Saarinen's interiors in *Catch Me If You Can*, where Steven Spielberg and production designer Jeannine Oppewall used TWA's concourses to instantly evoke the breezy, sexy spirit that informed the dawn of the jet set era. Sometimes the reference is more indirect. In *Men in Black*, anti-alien operatives Jay and Kay work out of a high-tech headquarters filled with TWA's characteristic sculptural swoops. (The Saarinen influence even provides one of the movie's great sight gags, when Will Smith casually attempts to move one of the master's much-heavier-than-they-look Knoll coffee tables.)

When first staged, Miller's psychodrama *After the Fall* attracted attention for its thinly disguised portrayal of Miller's tumultuous marriage to Marilyn Monroe. The script leaves the setting ambiguous: the action is meant to take place inside the protagonist's head. But in Michael Mayer's staging, instead of a darkened stage, we see Saarinen's voluptuous curves. "The design Richard Hoover and I came up with very specifically situates the play at TWA at Kennedy, which we discovered was built in May of 1962," said director Mayer. "In my mind, the play starts in the fall of that year, a few months after the terminal was built, and it was sleek, brand new, and very beautiful. This design seems to lend itself to the transformational quality you want from the rest of the play." To Hoover's credit, the set is not just respectful but downright adulatory: he even gets the signage right.

More than any other modern monument, Saarinen's TWA seems to capture a lost America of imagination and hope, captured forever in Ezra Stoller's dreamlike black and white photographs. But for a moment, the building itself appeared to be doomed: a plan was afoot to demolish parts of the complex and build an enormous new terminal around it, preserving a token vestige of the original building as a site for retail shops and administrative offices. But thanks to the intervention of preservation groups led by the Municipal Arts Society, a new plan is awaiting Federal Aviation Administration approval. It calls for leaving the building largely intact as an entrance to the gates of its new tenant, popular low-cost carrier JetBlue. The restored, reopened terminal will no doubt create new associations for new generations of travelers.

When it was first built, Saarinen's terminal was criticized by doctrinaire modernists for the crowd-pleasing literalism of its metaphors: the outside looked like a bird in flight, the inside like billowing clouds. It all seemed a bit too easy and specific, not cool and abstract enough for the universal-ist ambitions of modernism. How strange it is that forty years later that same building has come to mean so many different things to so many people.

Michael Mayer has said that his production of *After the Fall* is meant to explore the idea of "borders in the mind being the most lethal borders that exist," and asks, "What is an airport but a border between two places?" In Saarinen's indestructable terminal, we may have found a perfect monument for these uncertain times.

The Rendering and the Reality

The winner of the competition to transform New York City's High
Line—an abandoned elevated freight track that winds among the
buildings of lower Manhattan—was announced in 2004: a team led
by landscape architects Field Operations and architects and planners
Diller Scofidio & Renfro. (The extended team includes my partner Paula
Scher, a long-time consultant to Friends of the High Line.) And with
the announcement came a vision of what, presumably, we can expect.
A rendering of the project viewed from street level at 23rd Street and
Tenth Avenue reveals a dreamlike urban wonderland of skateboarders
and film buffs, suspended above the sidewalks in magical equipoise
beneath the climatic sequence from *Kubrick's 2001: A Space Odyssey.*

Predictably, the team's renderings have come in for their share of
criticism from cynical New Yorkers who claim with absolute assurance
that whatever the finished product looks like, it will never look like this.
But, for architects, the rendering has a completely different purpose
from the blueprint. The latter governs the nitty-gritty of construction,
the former is designed to excite the imagination.

Highlights, that magazine you may remember from your childhood
visits to the dentist, had a feature called "What's Wrong with this
Picture?" A child could play the same game with FO/DS&R's 23rd
Street rendering. The auditorium seats for the outdoor cinema have no

visible means of support. Neither does the movie screen itself. The elevator from street to High Line rises in a transparent glass shaft without the help of machinery. The graceful stairs have no handrails. The cinema has no projection booth. And the whole thing looks incredibly cool, which is undoubtedly the point.

Architects have a real challenge. They have to make people believe in—and accept, and support, and pay for—a reality that lies far in the future. And that reality is built incrementally: all the renderings submitted for the High Line competition, no matter how convincing, are sketches to show general design intent rather than fully developed proposals. Unlike their lucky graphic designer cousins, architects can't show their clients a same-size prototype with every detail in place. That's why so many architects compensate with out-of-scale personalities: it takes real personal magnetism to make a bunch of suspicious people give you a lot of money to remake the world.

The architectural rendering is central to this process. Libeskind and Childs's original design for Ground Zero's Freedom Tower was usually shown from far across New York Harbor, the better to emphasize the relationship of its assymetrical crown and the raised arm of the Statue of Liberty; this exotic viewpoint is clearly the money shot. Philip Johnson's AT&T Building became a postmodern *cause célèbre* because its Chippendale profile was presented, again and again, in point-blank Palladian elevation; no matter that no one has ever seen the real building that way, or ever will. Again and again, architects present their offerings in splendid isolation, editing out anything that inconveniently impedes the view, adding those props that support the rhetorical theme.

In some cases, the renderings themselves have acquired a life of their own. Michael Graves and Zaha Hadid became famous through what has been unfairly dismissed as "paper architecture." Before them loom artists like Claude-Nicolas Ledoux and Hugh Ferris, who created extraordinary—and imaginary—drawn environments that anticipated, influenced, and, in some cases, superceded reality.

"Make no small plans, for they have no magic to stir men's blood." There isn't an architect alive who can't recite Daniel Burnham's famous admonition. It's a long, torturous path from sketchpad to ribbon-cutting. It is the fever dream of the architectural rendering that sustains us on the journey.

What We Talk About When
We Talk About Architecture

The most popular show on American non-commercial radio is *Car Talk*. For an hour, two auto mechanic brothers from Boston ostensibly do just that: they talk about cars. People call in and describe automotive problems, and Tom and Ray Magliozzi offer suggestions on how their cars might be fixed. What makes the show so listenable, even to people like me who don't know or care that much about cars, is the fact that the show isn't really about cars, it's about life. A simple question about an alternator digresses quickly into a discussion of psychology, economics, or geography; the Magliozzis function as marriage counselors, career advisors, and therapists just as often as car mechanics.

Listening to *Car Talk* got me thinking about the pleasures of truly discursive discourse. Does it occur often enough in the world of design? And when it does happen, who gets to hear it? Which brings me to the Yale University School of Architecture.

I have been involved with Yale Architecture's promotions and publications program since Robert A. M. Stern came aboard as dean in 1998. Stern takes his school's publications seriously because he knows their power firsthand: in the sixties, as a student editor of Yale's architecture journal, *Perspecta*, he was the first to print Robert Venturi's seminal manifesto "Complexity and Contradiction in Modern Architecture."

Perspecta, which is published to this day, has a counterpart called *Retrospecta*, the school's annual review of student work. *Retrospecta* is edited by students from the School of Architecture and designed by students from the graphic design program in the School of Art. The designers and editors are different every year; I serve as advisor and "continuity director" for the project. Most of the space of the book is taken up by reproductions of student projects and brief descriptions of the assignments that inspired them.

A critical part of the design school experience is the critique, where student work is reviewed by faculty and outside assessors. Previous issues of *Retrospecta* have included quotes from the visiting critics, sometimes simply to punctuate the layout typographically. In the latest issue, however, the editors (Jason Van Nest, Yen-Rong Chen, and Mathew Ford) and the designers (Willy Wong and Yoon-Seok Yoo) have brought the transcripts of the review sessions front and center. Much of what passes for architectural writing, particularly in academia, is turgid and stilted. In contrast, "the diverse arguments, critiques, and provocations" faithfully recorded here are compulsively readable.

This drama inherent in the design critique has not escaped notice. In fact, Oren Safdie (an architect-turned-playwright and son of the legendary architect Moshe Safdie) used it for the setting of last year's off-off-Broadway play *Private Jokes, Public Places*, in which a young architecture student defends a thesis project against two increasingly combative professors; the *New York Times* praised its "verbal acrobatics." And there are acrobatics of sorts to be had in the pages of *Retrospecta*, where the cast of characters include Peter Eisenman, Leon Krier, Charles Jencks, Frank Gehry, Zaha Hadid, Lise Anne Couture, Greg Lynn, and Rafael Viñoly.

What I find interesting is that when the conversation is lively enough, just as in *Car Talk*, I don't need to understand much about architecture or even the specifics of the problem at hand; I can just enjoy the give-and-take. Some examples:

> Jeffrey Kipnis: Where did this public and private thing come from? Did they assign you to think about public and private? Or did you just assume it was a natural way to think about it? I have seen it all day long. When I think about the Schindler House and I look at the plan, it is labeled in terms of "his" spaces and "her" spaces, not public and private.
> Zaha Hadid: It is definitely not part of our repertoire.
> Kipnis: I didn't think it was.
> Hadid: I think it is a Yalie repertoire.
> Charles Jencks: Yes, it was [Louis] Kahn who...
> Kipnis: And he's dead, right? I asked Nathaniel [Kahn] and he was pretty sure. A lot of the things you take for granted stop you from

making more objective use of your research and that is where you should pause, as soon as you think something too quickly.

Kenneth Frampton: . . . I could tell you to cut six more slots into this thing, and it wouldn't make a difference. It's a negative critique of the project, but it's also a critique of the whole god damn situation. You have to have a principle, otherwise you cannot communicate anything to anybody. Why should I invest my money in this, as opposed to some other project? You have to have a reason, otherwise the architects don't even talk to the society. Don't you see that predicament? These computer renderings produce aesthetic effects very well, seamless, very seductive, but they are not about anything. They are delusions! They are mirages! I'm sorry, it's very aggressive to say this, but aren't we going to start talking? It's just ridiculous to say, "Ok—individual interpretations," "So on and so forth." One has to talk about something fundamental, otherwise we're never going to talk about anything anymore.

Demetri Porphyrios: I'm not sure what you're talking about.

Frampton: I'm talking about the fact that there is a total degeneration. . .

Porphyrios: Do you want some coffee?

Frampton: No, I don't. Sorry, I don't. . .

Porphyrios: Look, look, look. This is a disgusting situation. It's not right to get upset. . .

Frampton: It's something to get upset about. We always have polite discussions; we have to sometimes get upset, because otherwise we just don't talk about the things that matter.

Jorge Hernández: I think this jury, this studio project, brings up this whole question of "history and modernity" and the confidence, or lack of confidence that this age has in its own capacity. There is uncertainty whether one believes in the capacity of this age to build like it intended to build. These are questions the architects have to ask about their own moment of working. . . That's what it is, and yet, the building gesture is not confident in its own epoch, it fiddles around with the past epoch, and doesn't assert its epoch. It is a manifestation of a lack of confidence in its own epoch. It's using the syntax of the epoch, but doesn't want to build at the full capacity of the epoch.

Peter Eisenman: Is that a historicist argument?

Hernández: Why not, why not?

Eisenman: Is that what your argument is, Jorge, the spirit of the age?

Hernández: The problem is this, when society loses confidence in its own capacity to build, it gets completely confused.

Robert A. M. Stern: It's not the spirit of the age argument. Kenneth [Frampton] was saying that the Victorians had a total confidence in their own time, they weren't trying to reflect the time, in the Gideon historicist way. They just had an assignment, they had a problem, and then went out at it full-bore. They used iron and glass and they made it in old forms or new forms—whatever they thought was right. They just did it.

And, finally, this comment on an Advanced Studio project:

Rafael Viñoly: I think it's great! [Long pause.] You know, one always feels obliged to say something past this point, so I hesitate to go on. However, I must say...

Needless to say, Mr. Viñoly goes on. You may hear echoes here, as I did, of dialogue by David Mamet, Michael Frayn, Tom Stoppard, and even (I'll go on) Harold Pinter. But unlike the work of playwrights, these are the kind of conversations that are almost always unrecorded and forgotten. There is real value in having them set down for the record. How many other spirited critiques—some even about graphic design, perhaps—have been lost?

Once I told a radio producer I know about my million-dollar idea: Car Talk, except for design. A few quick-witted experts could take calls from people seeking advice on typefaces and color choice, directional signs and ballot layout, while the rest of us listened in to the supremely diverting proceedings. With a sigh, she said everyone had this idea: Car Talk for Opera, Car Talk for Grammar, Car Talk for Macrame, Car Talk for... well, you fill in the blank. But that was before I had my pilot episode. I'm sending her a copy of Yale Retrospecta: Car Talk for Architecture! The phone lines are open.

Colorama

We moved to the suburbs in 1984. It was my wife's idea. After only four years in Manhattan, I was resistant to the idea of retreating to a place like the subdivision I had grown up in, so I insisted to Dorothy that we move to Westchester County. There were two reasons. First, I had the idea, based mostly on my obsessive reading of John Cheever, that Westchester possessed some kind of literary superiority to, say, New Jersey or Long Island. Second, I wanted desperately to commute every day through Grand Central Terminal.

The main concourse of Grand Central is New York's great public room. When it opened in 1913, architects Warren & Wetmore's building was hailed as an engineering marvel and a "temple to transportation." But by 1984 it was dark, dirty, and marred with advertising. Sticky trash was stuck in every corner. Homeless people slept in its subterranean passages. And looming above it all, blocking the main hall's east windows, presiding over its tumult no less than West Egg's Eyes of Dr. T. J. Eckleburg, was the Colorama, the massive backlit billboard that its creator, Eastman Kodak, trumpeted as the World's Largest Color Photograph.

The first Colorama was installed in 1950. It was eighteen feet high and sixty feet wide. According to *Colorama*, a new book from Aperture, the backlit transparencies required over a mile of cold-cathode tubes to illuminate. The image changed every month; eventually there would be a total of 565 Coloramas deployed in Grand Central. The president was Harry Truman when the first went up, and it was George H. W. Bush when the last one came down. The images, however, did not directly reflect a changing America, but rather gently refracted it through a hazy lens of unironic, idealized nostalgia that today seems absolutely eerie.

The subject, again and again, is the American family at leisure, picnicking, playing, sightseeing. The images are clearly advertisements: for years, in fact, they were pictures of people taking pictures of other people, at golf outings, fishing trips, teen parties, weddings. The Coloramas today remind me of a lot of things: the vast flattened panoramas of Andreas Gursky, the alienated subjects of Tina Barney, the creepy psychodramas of Gregory Crewdson. But at the time, these pictures must have seemed like an epic attempt to merge two great American traditions: the impossibly vast landscapes of Frederic Edwin Church, and the homey tableaus of Norman Rockwell. (Although no Hudson River School painter was on hand to help with 1959's *Camping at Lake Placid*, Rockwell himself is credited as art director for 1954's *Closing on a Summer Cottage*.)

For the six years I commuted past the Colorama in the eighties, the pictures were more generic, not quite as obviously stilted. Only one of them is pictured in the Aperture collection. This was, after all, the decade of David Lynch and *Twin Peaks*: we knew about irony, okay? The forced smiles of happy families frozen in contrived poses would have conjured up questions of what these repressive characters could possibly be concealing. It was not unlike the way my hero John Cheever, writing of a bucolic commuter town pretty much identical to my own, could hint at the undercurrents of adultery, alchoholism, and ennui that festered behind the pretty suburban facades.

"The Colorama format," writes Alison Nordstrom in the book's opening essay, "exaggerated the epic presentation of things in rows: midshipmen, choirboys, babies, fighter jets, gondolas, iceboats, koalas, kittens, and tulips were all graphically displayed in rhythmic and gargantuan display." Indeed, the most memorable Colorama from my early commuting days was a portrait of a dozen babies, lined up like so many top-heavy dolls, snapped at a moment when—impossibly—each had decided to look his or her absolute cutest for the camera. This ridiculously corny but endlessly enthralling image was so popular that it was reprised a few years later. The adorable dozen, now toddlers, were lined up for a reshoot.

In the nineties, Grand Central received a masterful renovation at the hands of architects Beyer Blinder Belle. The Colorama, once a welcome diversion, seemed by then vulgar and obtrusive. It had to go, and it did. Grand Central is splendid now, and I doubt few people long for a corny, sixty-foot-long color picture to block the morning sunlight streaming through the concourse's east windows. I do, however, wonder whatever happened to those babies.

Mr. Vignelli's Map

The New York subway system has been around for more than one hundred years. It reached its high point in 1972, the year of Massimo Vignelli's beautiful subway map.

I still remember the first time I heard the rationale for this extraordinary graphic solution. Up on the sidewalks, New York was a confusing bedlam of sights and sounds. Below ground, however, it was an organized system. Each line had certain stops. Each stop had certain connections. Getting from here to there wasn't the result of a meandering sojourn, but a series of logical steps, one following on the next like a syllogism. What was happening on the streets was meaningless. What happened below ground—that sequence of stops and connections—was supreme. It was as logically self-contained as Marxism. And, like Marxism, it soon ran afoul on the craggy ground of practical reality.

Like many complex urban transportation systems, the New York subways were aggregated over many years, as a variety of competing businesses (the Interborough Rapid Transit, the Independent Subway System, the Brooklyn-Manhattan Transit) were consolidated into a single integrated network. The result was a tangled spaghetti of train lines, a mess of a "system" that was almost comical in its complexity.

In 1968, Unimark International was commissioned to design a sign system for the subways, and out of this chaos came order. Two Unimark designers, Bob Noorda and Massimo Vignelli, developed a signage plan based on a simple principle: deliver the necessary information at the point of decision, never before, never after. The typeface they recommended, the then-exotic, imported-from-Switzerland Helvetica Medium, was unavailable; they settled for something at hand in the New York City Metropolitan Transit Authority train shop called Standard Medium. The designs they proposed assumed that each sign would be held in place at the top with a black horizontal bracket; the sign shop misinterpreted the drawings and simply painted a black horizontal line at the top of each sign. And so the New York City subway signage system was born.

Four years later, Vignelli introduced a new subway map. It was based on principles that would be familiar to anyone who appreciated the legendary London Underground map designed in 1933 by Harry Beck. Out with the complicated tangle of geographically accurate train routes. No more messy angles. Instead, train lines would run at 45- and 90-degree angles only. Each line was represented by a color. Each stop represented by a dot. What could be simpler?

The result was a design solution of extraordinary beauty. Yet it quickly ran into problems. To make the map work graphically meant that a few geographic liberties had to be taken. What about, for instance, the fact that the Vignelli map represented Central Park as a square, when in fact it is three times as long as it is wide? If you're underground, of course, it doesn't matter: there simply aren't as many stops along Central Park as there are in midtown, so it requires less map space. But what if, for whatever reason, you wanted to get out at Fifty-ninth Street and take a walk on a crisp fall evening? Imagine your surprise when you found yourself hiking for hours on a route that looked like it would take minutes on Vignelli's map.

The problem, of course, was that Vignelli's logical system came into conflict with another, equally logical system: the 1811 Commissioners' Plan for Manhattan. In London, Harry Beck's rigorous map brought conceptual clarity to a senseless tangle of streets and neighborhoods that had no underlying order. In New York, however, the orthoginal grid introduced by the Commissioners' Plan set out its own ordered system of streets and avenues that has become second nature to New Yorkers. Londoners may be vague about the physical relationship of the Kennington station to the Vauxhall station: on the London underground map, Vauxhall is positioned to the northwest of Kennington when it's actually to the southwest, and it doesn't seem to bother anyone. On the other hand, because of the simplicity of the Manhattan street grid, every New Yorker knows that the Twenty-eighth Street number 6 train stops exactly six blocks south and four blocks east of Penn Station. As a result, the geographical liberties that Vignelli took with the streets of New York were immediately noticeable, and commuters without a taste for graphic poetry cried foul.

And thus it was that by 1979, the Vignelli map was replaced by a conventional, less elegant, more geographically accurate map that persists in revised form to this day. I remember a presentation at the Cooper-Hewitt Museum at which designer Wilburn Bonnell presented this revision as the graphic design equivalent of the demolition of the Pruitt-Igoe housing development: impractical, elitist Modernism succumbing to the practical, flawed imperfections of everyday life. The Vignelli map is remembered today as "colorful and handsome" but also "incomprehensible," a regrettable lapse from good sense, if not good taste.

But it wasn't to me. My favorite souvenir from my first trip to New York in 1976 was my very own copy of the Vignelli map, straight from the token booth at Times Square: gorgeous, iconic and cerebral, it represented a New York that didn't care if it was understandable to a kid from Ohio. It hung on my wall, in all its mysterious unknowability, for the next three years. That was the city I wanted to live in. It still is.

I Hate ITC Garamond

My daughter Liz called me from college to recommend a book she had been assigned for a political science class: *Mr. Truman's War* by J. Robert Moskin, a non-fiction account of the end of World War II and the dawn of the Cold War. On Amazon, I learned it was out of print, but she was so enthusiastic about it that I tracked down a used copy.

It arrived in the mail a few weeks later, and I opened it to receive a ghastly, devastating shock. The entire book, all 400-plus tightly-packed pages of it, is set in a typeface that I absolutely despise: ITC Garamond.

Sorry, Liz, I just don't think I can do it.

There are lots of typefaces I don't like, but each of them usually has a saving grace. I've always had a distaste for Herman Zapf's Optima, for instance, but I have to admit that there are occasions when it's been used well. Maya Lin's Vietnam Veterans Memorial is an example. But ungainly ITC Garamond repulses me in a visceral way that I have trouble explaining.

ITC Garamond was designed in 1975 by Tony Stan for the International Typeface Corporation. Okay, let's stop right there. I'll admit it: the single phrase "designed in 1975 by Tony Stan" conjures up an entire world for me, a world of leisure suits, harvest-gold refrigerators, and "Fly, Robin, Fly" by Silver Convention on the 8-track. A world where font designers were called "Tony" instead of "Tobias" or "Zuzana." Is that the trouble with ITC Garamond? That it's dated?

Maybe. Typefaces seem to live in the world differently than other designed objects. Take architecture, for example. As Paul Goldberger writes in his book on the rebuilding of lower Manhattan, *Up From Zero*, "There are many phases to the relationships we have with buildings, and almost invariably they come around to acceptance." Typefaces, on the other hand, seem to work the other way: they are enthusiastically embraced on arrival, and then they wear out their welcome. Yet there are fonts from the disco era that have been successively revived by new generations. Think of Pump, Aachen, or even Tony Stan's own American Typewriter. But not ITC Garamond.

The most distinctive element of the typeface is its enormous lower-case x-height. In theory this improves its legibility, but only in the same way that dog poop's creamy consistency in theory should make it more edible. Some people dislike ITC Garamond because it's a desecration of the sacred memory of Claude Garamond. That part doesn't bother me. For one thing, despite its name, Garamond as we know it appears to be based on typefaces developed by Jean Jannon, who lived about a century after Garamond, and Garamond based his designs on those of Aldus Manutius; it's hard to say where you'd locate authenticity in this complicated history. And I've been stimulated by Emigre's revivals like Mrs. Eaves and Filosofia, which take inspiration from—and bigger liberties with—the work of, respectively, John Baskerville and Giambattista Bodoni with great success. But there are good revivals and bad revivals, and ITC Garamond is one of the latter.

There was a moment in time where it seemed that bad type would drive out good type. Reporting on a now-legendary 1987 debate where Paula Scher faced off against Roger Black and denounced ITC Garamond for the simple reason that "it's called Garamond and it's not Garamond," Karrie Jacobs pointed out what was then a cause for widespread alarm: "ITC faces have a way of muscling out the faces from which they were adapted....In the largest of cities, a designer has a great many type suppliers to choose from. If she doesn't want an ITC Garamond, she can get a Berthold or a Linotype version. But in a one-typesetter town, the odds are that the local type shop will offer mainly ITC faces. The distinctions between Garamonds then become moot. ITC Garamond is Garamond." Thanks to the internet and the digital typesetting revolution, there's no such thing as a "one-typesetter town" anymore. Too bad. It sounds nice and peaceful.

ITC Garamond enjoyed its apotheosis when it was adopted as the official corporate typeface of Apple Computer in 1984; adding insult to injury, the font was condensed horizontally eighty percent. Associated with Apple's brilliant packaging and advertising for the next twenty years, the resulting mutation became a part of the global landscape, seeming no less impregnable and unchanging than the Soviet empire. And then, just like global communism, it just went away, replaced overnight with a sleek customized version of Myriad.

Today, ITC Garamond is no longer ubiquitous, but it pops up in unlikely places and still gives me a nasty start, as in my daughter's book recommendation. I've come to realize that I don't hate it for any rational reason; I hate it like I hate fingernails on a blackboard. I hate it because I hate it. Yet I do know one use of it that I would call an unqualified success: it's the classic poster by Jack Summerford from way back when the typeface was shiny and new, where the nastiness of the typeface and the dissonance of the message combine in one deafening clang. To promote ITC Garamond's arrival in Texas, Summerford used it, in all its monstrous glory, to set a single giant word: Helvetica. It's not a good font, but just this once, it made a great punch line.

1989: Roots of Revolution

Two classic pieces of critical design writing from over fifteen years ago foretold the path that design would take in the twenty-first century. One was Neville Brody's collaboration with cultural critic Stuart Ewen, "Design Insurgency." The other was Tibor Kalman's collaboration with writer Karrie Jacobs, "We're Here to Be Bad." Both were scathing analyses of the relationship of the design profession and the forces of corporate commercialism. Both were calls for awareness and resistance.

And both had their roots in a conference that occurred fifteen years ago in San Antonio, Texas, where Brody, Kalman, Ewen, and Jacobs all spoke: 1989's "Dangerous Ideas," the third biennial conference of the American Institute of Graphic Arts. John Emerson, the Design Observer reader who provided a link to his online version of the Ewen/Brody piece, said in an offline exchange, "I had no idea the AIGA was wrestling with (or at least presenting) these ideas back then," and added, "It makes me wonder how far back these ideas go and how the debate has changed."

Each AIGA conference is, to a certain extent, a reaction to the one that immediately precedes it. The 1987 conference in San Francisco was criticized as lifeless and flat; one of the main stage presentations was about what kind of health insurance was right for design studios. At an AIGA board meeting in its aftermath, the two board members who were most critical of it were the renowned Milton Glaser and a younger designer who was more of an unknown quantity, Tibor Kalman. Dared to put up or shut up, they were appointed to co-chair the next conference.

They gave it something the first two conferences didn't have, a theme: "Dangerous Ideas." Milton, who had been interested for some time in questions of personal ethics in our profession, proposed a number of thoughtful explorations of those themes. Tibor shared those concerns but also seemed to have a more-or-less irresistible compulsion to simply disrupt the complacency of the graphic design world by any means necessary. Tibor took the theme seriously, and even literally; when a designer-led boogie band was proposed for the entertainment at the closing party, Tibor objected: not dangerous enough. (He lost.)

The conference itself had its ups and downs, as they all do. But unlike the previous AIGA convocations, which had alternated between the celebratory and the practical, there was a recurring note of self-doubt. Stuart Ewen provided his critical analysis of the social, economic, and political power of the "style industry." Erik Spiekermann's presentation was entitled "Hamburger and Cultural Imperialism: A World View." Karrie Jacobs began her talk on environmentalism by telling the audience, "Everything you do is garbage." And there was one oddly recurring motif.

Earlier in 1989, Minneapolis's Joe Duffy had sold his design firm to the then-high-flying, publicly traded British design firm The Michael Peters Group. In the wake of that sale, the merged entity took out a full-page ad in the Wall Street Journal that simultaneously proffered their services and made a case for the value of design to business, including the claim that "as more and more competitive products become more and more alike, a good package can become a packaged good's best, if not only, point of difference."

The Duffy ad was the talk of the conference. I suspect the rank-and-file was actually rather impressed with it. I certainly was. No other design firm had ever done anything as audacious as taking out a full-page ad in the Wall Street Journal, for God's sake. But to the conference organizers and speakers, who had come to San Antonio with weapons fully loaded, the Duffy ad gave them what they didn't have until that moment: a fat, juicy target. As I recall, Ewen and Brody both mentioned it. Tibor read the passage quoted above from the stage and illustrated it by juxtaposing cans of Diet 7-UP and Diet Sprite. Graphic design never seemed more trivial, and it set up his ringing conclusion: "We're not here to help clients eradicate everything of visual interest from the face of the earth. We're here to make them think about what's dangerous and unpredictable. We're here to inject art into commerce. We're here to be bad."

Joe Duffy, bright, polished, and articulate, was at the conference too. Finally, he had had enough, and asked for equal time. A hastily scrawled sign was posted announcing an unscheduled debate: "TIBOR: YOU AND ME. TODAY. 5:15. BREAKOUT ROOM G. JOE." That afternoon, the room was standing-room only. Tibor had arranged the chairs in a circle. He and Duffy stood in the middle, circling each other like gladiators. It was pure theater, and more memorable for that than for anything that was said. The arguments, like the setting, were circular. As in the Kennedy-Nixon debates, this one seemed to be more about style than substance; unlike Kennedy and Nixon, the swarthy guy in the ill-fitting suit seemed to get the upper hand. At one point, I made my own unconstructive observation: "It seems to me that both of you do the same thing, except Tibor feels guilty about it." Tibor called me when we were back in New York and yelled at me for breaking ranks. (I stand by my comment, except I've come to appreciate the transformative power of guilt—or let's just call it responsibility—more than I did fifteen years ago.)

It all sounds legendary now, but as I remember it, the crowd wasn't as galvanized as you'd think. People were baffled by Stuart Ewen's Marxism and irritated by the fact that he didn't show any slides. Tibor's ringing conclusion failed to get a standing ovation: the audience had been hoping for something funnier. And Brody, the closest thing we had then to a rock star, wore the requisite black but spoke thoughtfully and quietly about our role in society, not about how he did those cool *Face* covers. Ewen's keynote was called "Design Notes for the New Millennium." Like the whole conference, the title was ten years ahead of its time.

The World in Two Footnotes

Are you an Agent of Neutrality? Or are you an Aesthete of Style? *Eye* no. 53 is a landmark in the history of that irreplaceable publication. The theme is "brand madness" and editor John Walters introduces the topic with a tongue-in-cheek essay that cheerfully reveals a new *Eye* slogan ("Love critical writing! Love *Eye*!") but concludes on a queasier note: "Personally I hope never to use the 'B' word again. In the course of editing this issue, I have literally typed it out more times than I have had hot dinners—and that can't be good."

At the core of the issue are a group of essays by Rob Camper, David Thompson, and, in an impressive coup, respected theorist Terry Eagleton, who has been persuaded to turn his attention to Wally Olins's *On Brand*. (He pronounces it "a slick account of a supremely shallow phenomenon.")

But the article I was most intrigued by was "The Steamroller of Branding" by designer, teacher, and *Eye* creative director Nick Bell. In it, Bell mounts a provocative attack on the encroachment of branding into the world of culture, where museums and performing arts centers increasingly present themselves using the same visual tactics as major corporations and consumer goods companies. Most interesting of all were two footnotes that Bell tosses off almost casually discussing the concerns of two types of designers: the "agents of neutrality" and the "aesthetes of style." Bell's descriptions are so acute that I've asked him for permission to reprint them here.

The agents of neutrality

Those graphic designers who see no role for self-expression in design. For them, the graphic designer is a passive mediator of the client's message and is charged with the responsibility of communicating it with clarity and precision. Unfortunately passive often means mute and can lead to an absence of "point of view." Get very excited by regulating systems such as grids, identity guidelines, and manuals. Love following orders. Have a positive view of limitation and are lost without it, which leads them to being dismissed (sometimes unfairly) as "jobbing designers." Theirs tends to be an apolitical stance which makes it easier for them to practice their discipline for all types of clients irrespective of sector without too much soul-searching. Contains a large contingent of neo-Modernists now that Modernism is merely a style. Tend to view content as something that is delivered by others and must not be questioned.

The aesthetes of style

Those graphic designers who are consumed by the formal aspects of design. Tend to practice design for design's sake and see every project as an opportunity to produce beautiful design. Often guilty of underappreciating the client's point of view or at least seeing their involvement as problematic. View visual expression (often their own) as the most important ingredient in design. Harbour a point of view but one which is often meaningless outside their own profession. Complain of being misunderstood or underappreciated. Some hate to be constrained by grids and identity guidelines whereas others amongst them have embraced it and that is when they turn on the style. Get turned on by Pantone flouro' colors, spot varnishes, and foil blocking. Not known for their awareness of ecological or sustainable production methods. Theirs tends to be an apolitical stance which makes it easier for them to practice their discipline for all types of client irrespective of sector without too much soul-searching. Contains a large contingent of neo-Modernists now that Modernism is merely a style. Tend to view content as something that is delivered by others and it will only be questioned if it gets in the way of producing something beautiful.

In two footnotes, Bell has neatly nailed the choice that many designers feel they face. They can choose to become the passive, "objective" voice of their clients, or they can be creative fountainheads, beholden to no one but their own imaginations. These two types of designers are widely viewed as polar opposites and mutually antagonistic: the Aesthetes sneer at the Agents for selling out to big business; the Agents dismiss the Aesthetes for their self-indulgent immaturity.

This divide has been observed and debated for years, if not decades. But Bell's skill is the way he slyly delineates not the differences but the similarities. In his account, both types of designers are willfully apolitical and, tellingly, uninterested in the content of the work they undertake. In short, a pox on both your houses. Designers (and perhaps all of us) resist binary classifications. Yet surely we would all have to concede that Bell's group portrait as diptych has more than a little truth in it.

But the choice is a false choice. Bell has a prescription: "It's quite simple, it's been said before and so many times that it has become a cliché. And that is to design from the inside outwards." He is talking specifically about designing for cultural institutions, but the advice is universal. "The practice of corporate identity design"—and here I would add graphic design in general—"must be inextricably tied to the content it is supposedly serving; make content the issue and resist making design the issue."

I have never met a designer who would deny the importance of content. Yet "making content the issue" takes real humility and self-effacement, qualities that are sometimes in short supply in the ego-driven world of creative production. Designers are more often tempted to serve more urgently demanding gods: their clients on one hand, their inner muses on the other. What the world demands, however, is something more. Call it content, call it substance, call it meaning: it is the too-often-forgotten heart of what we do. It is the way out of the binary world that Nick Bell describes so well. It is the third choice. Choose content.

Logogate in Connecticut

A government agency unveils its new logo. A geometric abstraction, it intrigues some but baffles many. Eventually, the inevitable question: my tax money paid for this? Finally, the handwringing once the exorbitant fee is revealed.

The government agency is the Connecticut Commission on Culture and Tourism. The logo was created by the respected Chester, Connecticut, firm of Cummings & Good. And the fee? Cue that special Dr. Evil voice: *ten...thousand...dollars!*

That's right, $10,000. It is all depressingly familiar, another in a long line of stories that demonstrate the suspicion—if not outright hostility—with which Americans view art and design. Particularly if they're paying for it.

The tourism commission's new logo conjures up a surprisingly broad range of references. The Bridgeport-based *Connecticut Post*, which broke the story ("$10,000 logo prompts head-scratching"), quoted some locals who saw images as various as "a double set of theatre curtains," "a bunch of speakers, very loud speakers," as well as film reels and fountains. Peter Good, the designer, intended to suggest "one entity with four divisions": arts, culture, tourism, and film. I personally assumed that it was a riff on the letter "C."

The *Connecticut Post*, sniffing blood, has been all over this story, which provoked a deluge of angry my-kid-coulda-done-that letters. It followed up with a fire-breathing editorial beginning "We wuz' [sic] robbed!" calling the episode an "evident case of daylight robbery of taxpayers." Even the *New York Times* picked up the scent, solemnly quoting the state budget director on the tourism commission's "entitlement mentality" and adding, of course, that he could not make out "heads or tails" what the logo was meant to convey.

Connecticut has become a scandal-happy place as of late, with its embattled governor resigning earlier in 2004 amidst a firestorm of accusations of financial impropriety, including accepting thousands of dollars of free renovations on his summer house from favor-seeking state contractors. Indeed, when the executive director of the commission had the temerity to defend her design investment, she had her $118,451 annual salary published for her trouble, as well as the fact that she is married to the former state Senate minority leader. Logogate! Still, the $10,000 price tag—$415,000 less than the mayor of Bridgeport was accused of accepting in kickbacks several years ago—doesn't seem to warrant this level of fuss.

What ratchets up the excitement level is the emperor's-new-clothes element: a bunch of clever "artists" trying to put something over, once again, on the decent people. Here's a quote:

> The abstract total-design logo is the most marvelous fraud that the American graphic arts have ever perpetrated upon American business. Contrary to the conventional wisdom, these abstract logos, which a company (Chase Manhattan, Pan Am, Winston Sprocket, Kor Ban Chemical) is supposed to put on everything from memo pads to the side of its fifty-story building, make absolutely no impact—conscious or unconscious— upon its customers or the general public, except insofar as they create a feeling of vagueness or confusion.... Yet millions continue to be poured into the design of them. Why? Because the conversion to a total-design abstract logo format somehow makes it possible for the head of the corporation to tell himself: "I'm modern, up-to-date, with it, a man of the future. I've streamlined this old baby." Why else would they have their companies pour $30,000, $50,000, $100,000 into the concoction of symbols that any student at Pratt could, and would gladly, give him for $125 plus a couple of lunches at the Tratorria, or even the Zum-Zum? The answer: if the fee doesn't run into five figures, he doesn't feel streamlined. Logos are strictly a vanity industry, and all who enter the field should be merciless cynics if they wish to guarantee satisfaction.

That's Tom Wolfe, in his high *From Bauhaus to Our House* mode, quoted in 1972, the year he was a judge for the AIGA's Communication Graphics competition. He would no doubt agree with Kurt Vonnegut, Jr., who once accused abstract artists of conducting "a conspiracy with millionaires to make poor people feel stupid." And just to prove how far we haven't come in the last thirty years, the most popular remedy for the disaster has been that same old warhorse: let's have a contest! A professor at Housatonic Community College volunteered his school's graphic arts students, saying they "would have jumped at the chance to have some hands-on involvement in a real design project," adding that, after all, "art is about inclusion." And lest anyone feel excluded, others have gone the professor one better, suggesting that the contest be open to schoolchildren of all ages.

Despite the evidence of curvy check marks, dots-and-circles, and dozens of other successful abstract logos that have become part of our visual landscape since Wolfe issued his pronouncement, it's clear that we designers still risk being cast, despite our best intentions, as witchdoctors, trafficking in voodoo and incantations. What designer wouldn't sympathize with the embattled Peter Good, and his partner, Janet Cummings? "People see an end product and have no idea of the process," she told the *Times*, no doubt through gritted teeth. It's like any modern art. People say, well, I would have done that—after the fact.

Meanwhile, Connecticut's new governor, M. Jodi Rell, has scrambled to distance herself from the debacle: according to her spokesman, "The governor's office was not involved in this decision. But it certainly could have found better ways to use $10,000." If you're an elected official in Connecticut, you can get a perfectly decent little patio put in at your house in Litchfield for that much.

The Whole Damn Bus is Cheering

Stuck in horrible traffic on the New Jersey Turnpike last weekend, I didn't have much to look at other than the other slowly moving cars. Then I started noticing them, everywhere: those ribbon stickers.

While they come in different colors, the most popular is yellow. While they bear different messages, the most common is "Support Our Troops." And while the sentiments they espouse are noble, the design of these things is just plain awful.

The history of the yellow ribbon is sometimes traced back to a Civil War legend or a 1940s John Wayne movie, but for most of us it started with a 1973 pop song of excruciating banality: "Tie A Yellow Ribbon" by the ludicrous Tony Orlando and Dawn. Written by Irwin Levine and L. Russell Brown, the song combined a cloying, maddeningly unforgettable melody with lyrics no one would mistake for Cole Porter:

> I'm coming home, I've done my time
> And I have to know what is or isn't mine
> If you received my letter
> Telling you I'd soon be free
> Then you'd know just what to do
> If you still want me
> If you still want me

Oh, tie a yellow ribbon
'Round the old oak tree
It's been three long years
Do you still want me
If I don't see a yellow ribbon
'Round the old oak tree
I'll stay on the bus, forget about us
Put the blame on me
If I don't see a yellow ribbon
'Round the old oak tree

Note that the first two lines don't even rhyme. The concluding stanza brings it all home:

Now the whole damn bus is cheering
And I can't believe I see...
A hundred yellow ribbons 'round the old, the old oak tree!

Particularly unnerving to me, along with the cheesiness of the fermata before the climactic line, was the implication that the narrator managed to tell "the whole damn bus" about the pre-arranged signal. I mean, shut up already. I also thought, as did most of my friends, that the singer was a newly released prisoner, rather than a returning hero.

The 1980 capture of fifty-two American hostages in Iran provided the yellow ribbon with its first entree into mainstream culture. The ribbon, literally tied around trees, became a way of signaling support for the hostages and faith that they would be safely returned. The advent of the AIDS crisis in the mid-eighties enabled the next transition, from literal ribbon to symbolic ribbon. Folded back upon itself and pinned to a lapel, the simple red ribbon was a grass roots creation, a wearable symbol of concern for the AIDS/HIV crisis and of solidarity with its victims. There was no "official" version, so anyone could make one. Then the folded-over-ribbon form got a further boost, and its final codification, when jewelry designer Margo Manhattan created the "official" red enamel ribbon lapel pin for AmfAR in 1991.

This basic form is the progenitor for the dozens of bewildering variations that have sprung up in recent years. There are now ribbons for and against virtually everything. Often, one colored ribbon can stand for (or against) several things. Green, for example, is connected to bone marrow donation, childhood depression, regular depression, the environment, eye injury prevention, glaucoma, kidney cancer, kidney disease, kidney transplantation, leukemia, lyme disease, mental retardation, missing children, organ donation, tissue donation, and worker safety. Whew! If it helps, the alternate color for leukemia is orange, and the alternate color for missing children is yellow.

So comes, at last, the deluge: the transfiguration of the folded-over ribbon into ubiquitous bumper sticker, coming full circle to serve as a signal of support, a heartfelt one to be sure, for American servicemen and women in Iraq and Afghanistan. In my six-hour drive on Sunday (this was New York to Philly, with flooding on the Garden State and the NJ Turnpike closed south of Exit 4 due to "congestion," traffic fans) I saw dozens, if not hundreds, of them. There were a few pink ones (signifying concern about breast cancer, I hesitantly assume), more red, white, and blue ones (general patriotism). But of course the overwhelming majority were yellow, just like the song. And the most common design? A doggedly literal drawing of that crossed and folded-over ribbon, enhanced with some crappy Photoshop effects straight out of the Hallmark cardboard birthday-party decoration playbook, squashed as flat as a pancake on the fender of every other Honda Odyssey and Lincoln Navigator. A metaphor? A symbol? Exactly! But just to make sure, let's add "Support Our Troops" in case anyone misses the point. And in a world of nearly infinite choices, what typeface would be better to signal our steadfastness than . . . what is that, anyway? Nuptial Script?

Graphic designers used to know how to develop beautiful, simple, universal symbols capable of rallying millions of people to a cause. Regardless of how you feel about this war, or about war in general, the men and women who fight deserve our support. They also deserve a better symbol.

The Best Artist in the World

Chances are you've never heard of Alton S. Tobey, Jr., but when I was eight years old, I had no doubt about one thing: Alton Tobey was the best artist in the world.

We didn't have a lot of books in our house, so it was a big deal when my mother signed up for a special promotion at the local grocery store: each week, for a modest price, she would bring home a new volume of the *Golden Book History of the United States*. There were twelve volumes in all, from *The Explorers, 986 to 1701* to *The Age of the Atom, 1946 to the Present*. The present was 1963. The books were a little over my head, but I devoured them. They were simple, dramatic, and vivid. Best of all were the pictures. There were no photographs, even in the later volumes. Instead, each book was filled with what today I would call illustrations, but what then I thought of as paintings. These were no mere sketches, but epic canvases, rich in detail and magisterial in scope: the ambush of redcoats, the completion of the transcontinental railroad, the assassination of William McKinley, the battle of Gettysburg, hundreds of them, one more sweeping than the next. And each was signed with the same name: Alton S. Tobey.

I carried those books around with me all summer, and actually read them all the way through in order. By the time I was finished, those paintings were more familiar to me than the *Mona Lisa* or *The Last Supper*. I was just learning to draw, and I found a lot of subjects—people and animals, for instance—

frustratingly difficult. But this Tobey could do it all, and made it look effortless and exciting. My favorite painting in the Cleveland Museum of Art, J. M. W. Turner's *Burning of the Houses of Lords and Commons*, was pretty easy to copy. Tobey was impossible.

My tastes evolved, and I was soon seduced by the more profound ironies of Mort Drucker and Kelly Freas. Moreover, I was unnerved by the fact that no one else seemed to have heard of Alton Tobey. *My Golden Book History* set was consigned to the basement. So it was startling a few years later to encounter an enormous Tobey mural in the Smithsonian's National Museum of Natural History on a trip with my ninth grade class to Washington, D.C. Hey, it's Alton Tobey, I said, pointing at *Contemporary Cultural Mutilations in Pursuit of Beauty*. My classmates, of course, were sniggering at the master's lovingly detailed depictions of foot binding, face piercing, neck stretching, and other voyeuristic cultural anomalies. How depressing to see art on that level being used to divert a bunch of rowdy fourteen-year-olds.

Five years of design school and a move to New York later, I had nearly forgotten about the favorite artist of my childhood. My idea of a great historical image was more likely to be the concise metaphoric clarity of an Ivan Chermayeff poster for *Masterpiece Theatre* than an overwrought representational painting. I was doing a mechanical for a newsletter for the Hudson River Museum when a name leapt out at me from the type galleys, the chairman of the Museum's upcoming invitational art exhibit: Alton S. Tobey.

It was with trepidation that I trekked to Yonkers for the exhibit's opening, "Is Alton S. Tobey here?" I whispered to someone I knew at the Museum. "Who, Alton?" came the reply. "Sure, he's that guy over there." The guy looked like an artist. He actually had a goatee. I walked over, waited politely until he finished his conversation, and introduced myself.

Tobey was gracious and affable. When I told him about the effect that the *Golden Book History of the United States* had had on me, he laughed out loud. "I painted those for eighteen straight months," he said. "But the deal was that if I got them done on time, Golden would send Rosalyn and me on an all-expense-paid trip to Europe for the rest of the year." It wasn't until that moment that I realized what it must have taken to do all those paintings, more than three hundred fifty of them. As a working designer, I knew the kind of deadline-conscious calculations I made to cope with something as trivial as the paste-up of a thirty-two page brochure: one-fourth done, halfway done, ten more to go, five more.... To think of this guy working his way through American history with a paintbrush and a stack of blank canvases... my God. Was the trip to Europe worth it? He assured me it was. He and his wife were there for three months.

I was to see Alton Tobey one more time before his death on January 4, 2004, at the age of ninety. About a year and a half ago, he had a small exhibition of his paintings at the New Rochelle Library. I went with my son Andrew. And there they were, the originals from the *Golden Book* series: *Boarding the Mayflower, The Ambush of General Braddock, The Battle of Little Big Horn, Teddy Roosevelt Leading the Rough Riders.* Just a handful, but in real life they looked incredible. I hadn't seen most of them for over thirty years, but I saw now the reproductions hadn't done them justice, nowhere near.

Alton Tobey was there, silent in a wheelchair. Every now and then he would smile. Someone explained he hadn't been the same since Rosalyn had died the year before; they had been married for fifty-four years. I thought of that trip to Europe over forty years ago that had been subsidized by the paintings around us. I had brought a copy of the only volume of the *Golden Book* series I had managed to save, volume 7 (*The Age of Steel, 1889 to 1917*) in hopes of getting an autograph. But his hands were shaking, and it didn't seem right. I just waited my turn and shook his hand and congratulated him on the show. "Your paintings changed my life," I said. He grasped my hand in both of his and nodded. His hands weren't shaking any more.

The Supersized, Temporarily Impossible World of Bruce McCall

I was in Chicago last week and from a distance glimpsed something I thought at first was a hallucination. It got bigger as I got closer, and then finally, there it was: the most enormous McDonald's I have ever seen.

This was no mirage, but a newly opened restaurant built to celebrate the fiftieth anniversary of McDonald's. And this it does with a vengeance, deploying 24,000 square feet of space, two sixty-foot golden arches, seating for three hundred, two escalators, a (first ever!) double-lane drive-thru, and—lest anyone fear that Chicago's extraordinary design legacy is being ignored—a "living room" area with furniture by Mies van der Rohe.

Photographs and even the online animated fly-through fail to do it justice. This thing is just unbelievably big. And naturally, the design community has reacted with horror. But I find something funny and charming and peculiarly exuberant about the place—and something strangely familiar, too.

Although the Fiftieth Anniversary McDonald's is credited to Dan Wohlfeil, the McDonald's Director of Worldwide Architecture, it may as well have been created by our country's greatest unacknowledged design visionary, Bruce McCall.

Perhaps it's appropriate that McCall, the visual poet of American gigantism, the father of the Bulgemobile and the R.M.S. *Tyrannic* ("The Biggest Thing in All the World!"), was born and raised in Canada.

Growing up in Simcoe, Ontario, in the forties, he became suspicious of his inherited sense of Canadian superiority. "The few Canadian comic books were black-and-white, vapid, and hopelessly wholesome," he writes in his wonderful memoir, *Thin Ice*. The advertising in American comic books, on the other hand, painted a colorful world where kids "guzzled Royal Crown Cola, rode balloon-tired Schwinn bikes with sirens and headlights or deluxe coaster wagons or futuristic scooters. They shot pearl-handled cap guns drawn from tooled-leather holsters or Daisy air rifles, wore aviator goggles, flew gasoline-powered model airplanes."

"I was beginning to discern," he writes, "that this bounty showered down upon American boyhood was a mere by-product of a system so inconceivably rich and generous that it was almost carelessly throwing off wealth in every direction, nonstop."

Yearning for the glories of his homeland's inaccessible neighbor to the south and trapped in a house with a remote, mercurial father and an alcoholic mother, McCall withdrew into a "compulsive passion for drawing," eventually dropping out of high school to take a job as a commercial artist. Windsor Advertising Artists Ltd. must have seemed like heaven: "They'd even pay me—thirty-five dollars a week, plus all the art supplies I wanted, free! Sweeter still, they'd pay me to draw and paint cars!" The studio's sole account was Dodge, and McCall soon learned he was in an environment where "creativity had as much to do with commercial art—or car art—as it did with Martinizing shirts," learning illustration techniques that were "as formalized and unresponsive to improvisation as a Japanese tea ceremony." After it all came to a crashing halt in 1959 (the year Dodge "went photographic" and fired its army of illustrators), McCall remained in the car business as an artist and a writer, eventually working in an ad agency in New York where he headed up the firm's Mercedes account.

It was in 1970s New York that he finally synthesized his profoundly mixed feelings about the commercial behemoth that had so long haunted his dreams and began to produce feverish after-hours work for the *National Lampoon*: impeccably illustrated brochures for an imaginary line of fifties-era cars, the Bulgemobiles. Impossibly huge and encrusted with acres of chrome, the Bulgemobiles were always drawn with carefree aristocrats at the wheel who were invariably blowing past Dust Bowl refugees or forlorn chain gangs. With tragically plausible brand names (Fireblast, Flashbolt, Blastfire, Firewood) and complemented by pitch-perfect slogans ("So All-Fired New They Make Tomorrow Seem Like Yesterday!" and "Too Great Not To Be Changed! Too Changed Not To Be Great!"), the Bulgemobiles epitomized McCall's vision of America as Brobdingnag: enormous, energetic, and a little bit stupid.

It is this vision that in one way or another has informed all of McCall's best illustrations: commuter flights by zeppelin to Muncie, Indiana; private subway stations for the Fifth Avenue plutocracy; elegant alfresco dining on the wings of airborne planes; block-long limousines; jousting autogiros and polo played on vintage tanks; and my favorite, the R.M.S. *Tyrannic*, an ocean liner bigger than a mountain. Strictly speaking, the *Tyrannic* is a tribute to British, not American, imperial power, but it is classic McCall, with comically vast interior views that abuse one-point perspective in ways unimagined by Raphael or Carpaccio. His imagination ultimately landed him a coveted private office at *The New Yorker*, where his work as a writer and cover artist regularly appears.

In the nineteenth century, Albert Bierstadt's epic landscape paintings of the Rocky Mountains and the Yosemite Valley were met with suspicion by New York critics: surely the American West couldn't be...well, that big. Imagine their surprise when the paintings turned out to be accurate.

With Bruce McCall, the process works in reverse. He tries to imagine an America so supersized that it could never be possible. I wonder how he feels when places like McDonald's keep proving him wrong.

The Unbearable Lightness
of Fred Marcellino

Until I was in my early twenties, my library was dominated by paperbacks. Buying a new hardcover book was an extravagance I couldn't afford on a college student's budget. But after I settled into my first job, I started treating myself to the occasional visit to the new releases section of the bookstore. Fifteen to twenty bucks was still a lot of money, so I'd usually do a lot of careful research before entering the bookstore to buy, say, the latest Philip Roth or John Updike.

But every once in a while, in what for me was then an act of madcap daring, I'd make an impulse purchase and buy a hardcover book based on almost nothing more than the design of its dust jacket. When the gamble paid off, these were books I'd come to really treasure: usually novels, their authors unknown to me, the settings unfamiliar and exciting. I've saved them all, and I took an armful down from my shelf the other day. *Loving Little Egypt* by Thomas McMahon, *The Lost Language of Cranes* by David Leavitt, *The New Confessions* by William Boyd, *The Twenty-Seventh City* by Jonathan Franzen. Wildly different books, with one thing in common. Fred Marcellino was the designer of all their covers.

Fred Marcellino is not a designer whose name you hear much these days. Ned Drew and Paul Sternberger, the authors of *By Its Cover: Modern American Book Cover Design*, stop short—just barely, one senses—of consigning him to the dustbin of design history. Parked astride Chapter Four

("The Bland Breeding the Bland: American Book Cover Design Disoriented") and Chapter Five ("The Pillaged, Parodied, and Profound"), Marcellino is characterized in less than glowing terms: "Fred Marcellino fostered a vast spectrum of depersonalizing styles in the 1970s and 1980s in order to meet the needs of his clients," they write, quoting a contemporary critic who observed that he had "no desire to use his work as a vehicle for the expression of some compelling personal vision."

Strange, because I can always tell a Marcellino cover. Born in Brooklyn in 1939, Fred Marcellino always wanted to be an artist, and was admitted as a student to tuition-free Cooper Union, graduating in 1960. Then followed graduate studies in the School of Art at Yale and a Fulbright Scholarship to study painting in Italy. He returned to New York in 1964, a scene dominated by the dusk of abstract expressionism and the dawn of pop, no place for a young painter besotted by Titian, Giorgione, and Veronese. Marcellino retreated into commercial design, first editorial illustration and album covers, then books.

"I took to books immediately," Marcellino said. "With record covers I never had much to go on. I never even got to hear the music....With books, on the other hand, there was something that you could read, almost devour, really get your teeth into. There's a lot more to work with in a book; I found it much, much more exciting. I just like to read; I like books."
It's hard to remember now, after Chip Kidd, after Michael Ian Kaye, after Carin Goldberg, that there was a time when it was considered taboo to illustrate a novel with anything but plain type or an illustration: the fear was that people would wonder, if the subject was fictional, whom exactly the photograph was supposed to depict. So it fell upon Fred Marcellino, who combined the skill of a genre painter with the typographic sense of an upscale package designer, to create the look of quality fiction. A Marcellino cover was as loaded with allusion and metaphor as a della Francesca *Annunciation*.

Take the cover for Tom Wolfe's *The Bonfire of the Vanities*. It's an atypical Marcellino cover in that it bows to the "big book look" conventions established decades before, most notably by Paul Bacon. The rule was (and is) simple: the more famous the author, the bigger the name. But, upon examination, the cover's lovely illustration is anything but simple. It depicts a glass coffee table (referred to nowhere in the book) on a fancy Persian rug in a (presumably) upscale East Side penthouse, its fragile surface reflecting the towers of Manhattan, with all their preening ambition, neatly turned upside down, as would be the prospects of the protagonists in Wolfe's sprawling tale of 1980s-style class warfare. And, as is so common in Marcellino's work, in the pale reflection, a fleeting glimpse of sky. Tom Wolfe's turbocharged verbal acrobatics, with their mountainous piles of descriptive specificity, are completely ignored in favor of an image that seems to have no subject, no focus. How obscure, and how neat, the allegory is.

That sky would appear again and again on Marcellino covers. On *Birdy* by William Wharton, on *Hearts* by Hilma Wolitzer, glimpsed beyond high walls on The Handmaid's Tale by Margaret Atwood, as a backdrop for the iconic (and much imitated) floating bowler hat on The *Unbearable Lightness of Being* by Milan Kundera. Steven Heller called Marcellino "a master of sky" and noted how "many of his book jacket illustrations use rich, cloud-studded skyscrapers as backdrops and dramatic light sources for effect....The way in which he manipulated light on such subjects as walls, chairs, and doors enabled him to transform the commonplace into charged graphic symbols."

Even at his height, the end was near for Fred Marcellino's unique style of image-making. Louise Fili's 1983 cover for *The Lover* by Marguerite Duras is considered one of the first examples of a photograph being used successfully to sell a novel. At Knopf under Sonny Mehta, it became positively de rigueur. Gone were the days when an illustrator would devote God knows how many hours to painstakingly rendering chairs stacked on a restaurant table. The future would belong to designers like Chip Kidd: "I found the image for Amy Bloom's Come to Me in a dumpster on the street in the East Village in the late 1980s. Someone had thrown out a whole stack of 1930s-vintage product shots of stuffed furniture. Fabulous." Out with the garret-bound *artiste*, stinking of turpentine, toiling away over an easel. In with the flaneurs of Avenue B, plucking *objets trouvés* from obscurity like old-time movie producers discovering starlets at Schwab's.

I thought again of the power of book covers while opening presents this Christmas. My gifts were what they've been for years: books and CDs. As I was cleaning up in the aftermath, it occurred to me that, unlike everyone else in my family, my gifts are products that more or less remain in their packages for as long as I own them. I remembered encountering a Marcellino package almost twenty years ago, a first novel from a writer I'd never heard of, Jonathan Franzen. According to the flap copy, *The Twenty-Seventh City* is the story of what happens when St. Louis, Missouri, decides to install a young, charismatic émigré from Bombay as its first female chief of police. "No sooner has Jammu been installed, however," we learn, "than the city becomes embroiled in a bizarre and all-pervasive political conspiracy."

I don't remember exactly what I was shopping for that day eighteen years ago, but it wasn't a book about the intersection of feminism, British colonialism, Midwestern corruption, and teenage romance. Instead, years before *The Corrections*, and the National Book Award, and the notorious

Oprah contretemps, what attracted me to the work of Jonathan Franzen was a haunting image of an Indian woman's face, impossibly large, peering from beyond the Gateway Arch, inviting me into an unknown world. It was a recommendation I dared not ignore. I belonged to a book club that had only two members: me and a person I'd never met, Fred Marcellino.

In 1990, perhaps sensing that the tide was running against him, Marcellino quit book cover design and began creating children's books. He won a Caldecott Honor that year for his illustrations for *Puss in Boots*; his first original book, *I, Crocodile*, was named one of the 1999 *New York Times* Best Illustrated Children's Books. Fred Marcellino died two years later at the age of sixty-one.

The Comfort of Style

You probably got one emailed to you back in the fall of 2001. I bet I got at least ten. It was a brutally unsubtle joke, but in those early aching days when I first saw it, it gave me a little satisfaction: the World Trade Center rebuilt as a blunt, defiant gesture. Philip Nobel saw it too. "Within days of the attack, a crude Photoshop doctoring of the Twin Towers—cut, multiplied, and pasted back on the pre-eleventh skyline—was making the rounds on the nation's jangling e-mail nerves," he writes in the first pages of his book *Sixteen Acres: Architecture and the Outrageous Struggle for the Future of Ground Zero*. "This was the first scheme many people saw— FUCK YOU! —the first essay at making meaning through construction at Ground Zero."

In describing the labyrinthine battles to determine what would be built on the World Trade Center site, Nobel tells the story of an amazing moment in New York history. Never have more people cared more passionately about design—its communicative power, its transformative potential—and never have designers seemed more marginal.

In just a few years, the issues around the rebuilding of the World Trade Center site have generated a surprisingly broad range of books. These include Michael Sorkin's bracingly contentious Starting from Zero; the considerably more measured *Up From Zero* by Paul Goldberger; Daniel Libeskind's predictably personal but surprisingly moving *Breaking Ground*; and Suzanne Stephens's indispensable overview *Imagining Ground Zero: Official and Unofficial Proposals for the World Trade Center Site*. Nobel's book differs from all of these in one crucial respect. Like the others, it is a book about design. Unlike the others, it contains not a single picture.

One senses that this is no accident. For years, designers have complained that our work is too often reduced to eye candy, rewarded for its suitability in the forum of the coffee table book, rather than in the rough-and-tumble of the real world. Here at last is an account of the design process in context, surrounded by the all-too-real world of envy, anger, pride, greed, and nearly every other deadly and not-so-deadly sin. The result of all that context? In Nobel's telling, design is rendered nearly irrelevant.

This irrelevancy was somewhat oxymoronic. As Nobel said in an interview with *Metropolis*, "The demands on the site, the perception that it had to provide symbolic answers, were firmly ensconced in the public's imagination.... Everyone was talking from day one about architectural form. So the idea that you would take a step back and plan, discuss the context, and do simple space planning and then move onto architectural form—no one was ready for that." The public was looking for architecture as catharsis, as bold symbolic gesture, an image that could provide the jolt of that original crude Photoshop paste-up job.

But there were other factors at work, and as always in New York, power and profits were first among them. It was the interplay of those factors that drove the process in the end and will determine what gets built downtown. This tension remains not just here but everywhere. And in the face of these challenges, one wonders which designers can truly rise to the challenge. In my favorite passage from Sixteen Acres Nobel describes the dilemma of design in the real world:

> Every architecture project starts with an infinity of possibilities. And that has its own terror. On one side, there's the physical world in all its unruly grace—space, climate, the land—and the thorny trappings of human society—money, politics, use. Then there's history, weighing on this unformed thing, and taste, and clients, and time. Some of these factors can be listed neatly as fixed specifics in a program brief, but that does not strip them of their caprice. As an architect first faces a design, the competing forces arrange themselves into fleeting orders that collapse and collapse again as they are tested by an equally volatile set of priorities and goals. To commit this roiling mess to form is necessarily daunting....
>
> This is true of all building, everywhere. But there is usually a reprieve: when an architect commits to an exclusive ideological or formal strategy— be it Beaux Arts or blob—one path through the thicket is marked. That is a great relief, the comfort of style, and seeking it is one reason why, looking at the methods promoted by leading architects, we see so many fixed forms, universal ideas, and gimcrack gimmicks applied to widely differing architectural dilemmas.

The comfort of style, indeed. In the end, our cities are less the product of these protean visions, and more the wildly compromised outcome of interplay of factors beyond any one person's control. New York City in general, then, and the World Trade Center site in particular, may be the ultimate demonstration of this. In a forum at The Architectural League, Nobel had a good phrase for the result: "a circus that imprints itself on the skyline." Until designers develop the mastery that will earn them a place in the center ring, they will have to take their comforts where they can find them.

Authenticity: A User's Guide

I've always considered radio the most *vérité* of news sources, but a recent piece on the weekly National Public Radio show *On the Media*, "Pulling Back the Curtain," exposed how much work goes into making NPR's reporting sound so, well, real. "The public is far less aware of editing on radio than on television or in print," said reporter John Solomon. "For example, to eliminate words, a TV producer has to use more visible means, such as a cutaway shot or jump cut. Newspaper reporters by form must put a break between non-consecutive quotations, among other constraints." Solomon then demonstrated how a radio producer, in contrast, could digitally alter a recording to tighten awkward pauses, eliminate words, restructure sentences, all to create a new, improved, seamless, and utterly convincing version of reality.

The show's host, Brooke Gladstone, suggested in her introduction to the piece that some listeners might be shocked by these revelations. And perhaps some were. But I found it absolutely familiar. Faking it? It's what we designers do all the time.

No one loves authenticity like a graphic designer. And no one is quite as good at simulating it. On the designer blog Speak Up, Marian Bantjes described the professional pride she took in forging a parking permit for a friend. "And I have to say," she admitted, "that it is one of the most satisfying design tasks I have ever undertaken." This provoked an outpouring of confessions from other designers who gleefully described concocting driver's licenses, report cards, concert tickets, and even currency.

Every piece of graphic design is, in part or in whole, a forgery. I remember the first time I assembled a prototype for presentation to a client: a two-color business card, 10-point PMS Warm Red Univers on ivory Mohawk Superfine. The half-day process involved would be incomprehensible to a young designer working in a modern studio today; with its cutting, pasting, spraying, stirring, and rubbing, it was more like making a pineapple upside-down cake from scratch. But what satisfaction I took in the final result. It was like magic: it looked real. No wonder my favorite character in *The Great Escape* wasn't the incredibly cool Steve McQueen, but the bewhiskered and bespeckled Donald Pleasence, who couldn't ride a stolen motorcycle behind enemy lines but could make an imitation German passport capable of fooling the sharpest eyes in the Gestapo.

And the illusion works on yet another level. Consider: that business card was for a start-up business that until that moment had no existence outside of a three-page business plan and the rich fantasy life of its would-be founder. My prototype business card brought those fantasies to life. And reproduced en masse and handed with confidence to potential investors, it ultimately helped make the fantasy a reality. Graphic design is the fiction that anticipates the fact.

At Disney World, where as one might expect the artifice is raised to Wagnerian levels, the designer in me has always preferred the ingenuity of a motion simulation ride like Star Tours (where you seem to be flying through space but you're actually sitting in a tilting chair) to Space Mountain (where you seem to be going up and down steep hills and, um, you actually are going up and down steep hills). On another level of design experience, I remember arriving with a colleague for a stay at Disney's Wilderness Lodge, a staggeringly detailed evocation of the classic hotels built in the National Parks one hundred years ago by the Great Northern Railway, complete with pine trees, massive rock outcroppings, and piped-in wood smoke, all courtesy of modern-day Denver architect Peter Dominick. "To build something like this in the Rocky Mountains is nothing," said my friend. "But in the middle of a swamp in the center of Florida? That takes genius."

Designers have a love-hate relationship with our addiction to simulation. In the case of the late Tibor Kalman, it was mostly the latter. "What's going on here? Theft? Cheap shots?" he asked in a footnote to his legendary 1990 jeremiad "Good History/Bad History." "Parody?

Appropriation? Why do designers do this? Is it because the designers don't have new ideas? Is it glorification of the good old days of design? Is it a way to create a sense of old-time quality in a new-fangled product? Are the designers being lazy, just ripping off an idea to save time and make for an easier client sell?"

Maybe all of the above. Maybe we just can't resist. And maybe familiar cues are simply the means by which people navigate through a confusing world. Tibor was obsessed with, among other things, spaghetti sauce packaging. In the eighties, Joe Duffy's elegant work for Classico particularly irritated him. I found the packages not only beautiful but useful (in their original incarnation, the sturdy jars were great to reuse) but Tibor was bugged by their seductive beauty, the way they conjured a siren song of ersatz Venetian landscapes and rustic Tuscan hills. But what would the alternative be? What would a jar of pasta sauce look like if it were entirely original? Would you know what it was if you saw it on the grocery store shelf? Would you trust it enough to put its contents on your spaghetti? Is that level of originality even possible?

Simulation, evocation, contextualism: call it what you will, but this thing that we designers are so good at seems to serve a basic human need. Although we hunger for authenticity, it's a hard thing to invent overnight. But that doesn't stop us from trying.

Designing Under the Influence

The other day I was interviewing a young designer, just nine months out of school. The best piece in her portfolio was a packaging program for an imaginary CD release: packaging, advertising, posters. All of it was Futura Bold Italic, knocked out in white in bright red bands, set on top of black and white halftones. Naturally, it looked great. Naturally, I asked, "So, why were you going for a Barbara Kruger kind of thing here?"

And she said: "Who's Barbara Kruger?"

Okay, let's begin. My first response: "Um, Barbara Kruger is an artist who is...um, pretty well known for doing work that...well, looks exactly like this."

"Really? I've never heard of her."

At first I was speechless. Then, I started working out the possibilities. One: My twenty-three-year-old interviewee had never actually seen any of Barbara Kruger's work and had simply, by coincidence, decided to use the same typeface, color palette, and combinational strategy as the renowned artist. Two: One of her instructors, seeing the direction her work was taking, steered her, unknowingly or knowingly, in the direction of Kruger's work. Three: She was just plain lying. And, finally, four: Kruger's work, after having been so well established for so many years, has simply become part of the atmosphere, inhaled by legions of artists, typographers, and design students everywhere, and exhaled, occasionally, as a piece of work that looks like something Barbara Kruger would do.

Let's be generous and take option four. My visitor isn't alone, of course.

Kruger, who herself began as a graphic designer, has created a body of work that has served as a subtle or not-so-subtle touchpoint for many designers over the past two decades. Occasionally the reference is purposeful, as in my own partner Paula Scher's cover for From Suffragettes to She-Devils, which uses Kruger's trademark typeface for a book that surveys a century of graphics in support of women's rights, although in this case the Futura is turned sideways and printed in shocking pink. Similarly, the late Dan Friedman's square logo for Art Against AIDS deploys Futura (Extra Bold) and a red-and-white color scheme in a way that is both effective and evocative.

Farther afield, the brand identity for the Barbican Art Gallery uses the same typeface and, controversially, applies it (usually at an angle to render the italic strokes dead vertical) to every exhibition that appears there. Sometimes it seems appropriate: when the subject is the work of Daniel Libeskind, the onrushing italics seem to evoke his urgent, jagged forms. Other times, the connection is more remote, or downright nonexistent. But, of course, searching for any connection at all is purely a parlor game. The goal of the One Gallery, One Font philosophy is not to serve any particular exhibition, but to create a unified identity for the Barbican Art Gallery, which it certainly does. I wonder, however, what would happen if the Barbican ever mounted an exhibition on Barbara Kruger? Would the collision of typographic matter and anti-matter create some kind of giant vortex as the snake ate its own graphic tail?

We've debated imitation, influence, plagiarism, homage, and coincidence before, and every time, the question eventually comes up: is it possible for someone to "own" a graphic style? Legally, the answer is (mostly) no. And as we sit squarely in a culture intoxicated by sampling and appropriation, can we expect no less from graphic design? I remember my disorientation several years ago, when I first saw the new American Apparel store down in Greenwich Village. A banner bearing the store's resolutely hip logo hung out front: the name rendered (American Airlines–style) in cool Helvetica, paired with a stripey star symbol that effortlessly evoked the reverse hip of seventies American style. And no wonder: it was the very logo that Chermayeff and Geismar's Bruce Blackburn had designed for the American bicentennial back in 1976.

Today, Blackburn's logo is gone from the American Apparel identity. A lawsuit? Or, more likely, the great zeitgeist wheel has turned once again, rendering the 1976 logo too outré to bother plagiarizing? No matter. We've arrived at a moment where all that has preceded us provides an enormous mother lode of graphic reference points, endlessly tempting, endlessly confusing. Does Barbara Kruger own Futura Bold Italic in white and red? Does Bruce Blackburn own stripey five-pointed stars? How much design history does one have to know before he or she dares put pencil to paper? Picture a frantic land-grab, as one design pioneer after another lunges out into the diminishing frontier, staking out ever-shrinking plots of graphic territory, erecting Keep Out! signs at the borders: This is mine! This is mine!

I remember seeing an Esquire cover about ten years ago: the subject was radio personality Howard Stern. What a ripoff, I thought, seeing the all-too-familiar Futura Italic. To my surprise, it turned out to be a Barbara Kruger cover illustrating a Barbara Kruger article. Who would have thought: she's a Howard Stern fan. And the lesson? If anyone can rip you off, you may as well beat them to the punch.

Me and My Pyramid

The Department of Agriculture has unveiled a radical redesign of a beloved staple of American culinary life: the food pyramid. I feel sad.

I have fond memories of the old food pyramid, which was modified many times over the past years but maintained its basic configuration. Even as a child, I found it pretty easy to understand.

At the bottom sat the firm foundation: Grains. Six to eleven servings daily! That's a lot of Wonder Bread. Next tier up were two groups of things that were less fun to eat, Fruits and Vegetables. The idea of eating vegetables every day as a child seemed absolutely bizarre to me, particularly the three to five servings the pyramid suggested. That would mean eating vegetables for breakfast, for god's sake. I had never heard of that. Above that, two more categories, Dairy and Meat. I liked milk, so that was fine. The interesting thing about the meat group was that it included meat, fish, and beans. I often wondered what kinds of influence lowly beans had to exert to get elevated up there next to meat.

Finally, appropriately set at the very pinnacle of the pyramid, was the only thing that made eating any fun at all: Sweets. "Use sparingly," we were advised, subtly and appropriately casting us as "users."

While the principles of the old pyramid were graspable, it was sometimes hard to reconcile those principles with my actual diet. Where, for instance, would I fit in one of the foods I most enjoyed using, Oreos? The outside was cakey and crunchy, sort of like bread, so I guess they were partly Grain. The creamy white inside seemed like milk, so they must be Dairy as well. Obviously they were sweet, but not that much: I mean, I never actually put sugar on Oreos. Finally, I had never knowingly consumed oil or fat, both of which sounded disgusting. So I would count Oreos as two thirds Grain, one-third Dairy, with a little bit of Sweet thrown in. A serving was always hard to calculate, so I would simply estimate it as reasonably as possible: about half of one of the three rows in a full bag, or about eight Oreos.

The new pyramid has none of the bracing clarity of the old one. As a seasoned graphic designer, I find myself with the dismaying ability to look beyond any new design and see the interminable series of meetings that was its genesis. The brief the Department of Agriculture gave its consultant, Porter Novelli, must have been daunting.

First, it retained the beloved pyramid form, but eliminated its implied hierarchy to displace Sweets from its position as King of All Food. So now we have something that can only be described as a pie chart made from only one slice of (inverted) pie. The usefully vague "serving" unit has been replaced with specific measures like cups and ounces; this means that relative amounts can no longer be compared, rendering the barely visible differences between the various groups meaningless without a key. In the fancier version of the pyramid, the key is represented by an uneasy combination of drawings and photographs of food items carelessly piled at the structure's base.

Finally, someone has dictated that exercise must be represented as part of the equation. So one side of the pyramid has been turned into a staircase, mounted enthusiastically by one of those odd, neutered sprites that you see everywhere in public sector graphics: neither young nor old, male nor female, raceless and faceless, representing everyone and no one. (I understand why they never have breasts or penises. But why do they never have hands or feet?)

I can clearly imagine this last transformative addition to the pyramid. There must have been one person in all those meetings who kept asking the same question: but how can we integrate exercise into the Pyramid? Finally: "here, give me the pencil; what if you just did it like this? Can you just clean this up?" Porter Novelli, who supposedly charged 2.5 million bucks for all their work on this project, which includes an interactive element to render twelve customized versions and a pretty zippy website, earned every penny.

Graphic designers are often asked to reduce complicated ideas to simple diagrams. Sometimes it's possible, but often it's not. Here, what we're left with is something that is well-intentioned but dysfunctional. The new food pyramid is what you could call a cat's breakfast, except it has vegetables in it. And everyone knows that not even a cat would eat vegetables for breakfast.

On (Design) Bullshit

In *Concert of Wills*, the fascinating 1997 documentary on the building of the Getty Center in Los Angeles, architect Richard Meier is beset on all sides by critics and carpers: homeowners who don't want the Center's white buildings ruining their views, museum administrators who worry that the severe stone benches will be uncomfortable, curators who want traditional molding on the gallery walls. The magisterial Meier takes them all in stride, until one moment that is the hold-your-breath climax of the film.

The client, against Meier's advice, has brought in artist Robert Irwin to create the Center's central garden. The filmmakers are there to record the unveiling of Irwin's proposal, and Meier's distaste is evident. The artist's bias for whimsical organic forms, his disregard for the architecture's rigorous orthonography, and perhaps even his Detroit Tigers baseball hat all rub Richard Meier the wrong way, and he and his team of architects begin a reasoned, strongly felt critique of the proposed plan. Irwin, sensing (correctly, as it turns out) that he has the client in his pocket, listens patiently and then says, "You want my response?"

His response is the worst accusation you can lodge against a designer: "Bullshit."

This single word literally brings the film to a crashing halt: a very long fifteen seconds of dead silence follows, broken at last by an awkward offscreen suggestion that perhaps on this note the meeting should end, which it does.

What is the relationship of bullshit and design?

In asking this question, I am of course aware that bullshit has become a subject of legitimate inquiry these days with the popularity of Harry G. Frankfurt's slender volume, *On Bullshit*. Frankfurt, Professor of Philosophy Emeritus at Princeton, is careful to distinguish bullshit from lies, pointing out that bullshit is "not designed primarily to give its audience a false belief about whatever state of affairs may be the topic, but that its primary intention is rather to give its audience a false impression concerning what is going on in the mind of the speaker."

It follows that every design presentation is inevitably, at least in part, an exercise in bullshit. The design process always combines the pursuit of functional goals with countless intuitive, even irrational decisions. The functional requirements—the house needs a bathroom, the headlines have to be legible, the toothbrush has to fit in your mouth—are concrete and often measurable. The intuitive decisions, on the other hand, are more or less beyond honest explanation. These might be: I just like to set my headlines in Bodoni, or I just like to make my products blobby, or I just like to cover my buildings in gridded white porcelain panels. In discussing design work with their clients, designers are direct about the functional parts of their solutions and obfuscate like mad about the intuitive parts, having learned early on that telling the simple truth—"I don't know, I just like it that way"— simply won't do.

So into this vacuum rushes the bullshit: theories about the symbolic qualities of colors or typefaces; unprovable claims about the historical inevitability of certain shapes, fanciful forced marriages of arbitrary design elements to hard-headed business goals. As Frankfurt points out, it's beside the point whether bullshit is true or false: "It is impossible for someone to lie unless he thinks he knows the truth. Producing bullshit requires no such conviction." There must only be the desire to conceal one's private intentions in the service of a larger goal: getting your client to do it the way you like it.

Early in my life as a designer, I acquired a reputation as a good bullshitter. I remember a group assignment in design school where the roles were divided up. The team leader suggested that one student make the models, another take the photographs, and, finally, "Michael here will handle the bullshitting." This meant that I would do the talking at the final critique, which I did, and well. I think I mastered this facility early because I was always insecure about my intuitive skills, not to mention my then-questionable personal magnetism. Before I could commit to a design decision, I needed to have an intellectual rationale worked out in my mind. I discovered in short order that most clients seemed grateful for the rationale as well. It put aside arguments about taste; it helped them make the leap of faith that any design decision requires; it made the design understandable to wider audiences. If pressed, however, I'd still have to admit that even my most beautifully wrought, bulletproof rationales still fit Harry Frankfurt's definition of bullshit.

Calling bullshit on a designer, then, stings all the more because it contains an element of accuracy. In *Concert of Wills*, Richard Meier is shown privately seething after Robert Irwin drops the b-word. "For one person to say," he tells the camera, "I want my object, I want my piece, to be more important than the larger landscape of the city...that my individual artwork is the controlling determinant, makes me furious, just makes me angry beyond belief." Of course, that same accusation could be leveled against Meier himself, who out of necessity had been nothing if not single-minded and obstinate during the endless process of designing and building the Getty. The difference is that each of Meier's victories was hard-won, with endless acres of negotiating, reasoning, and you-know-what expended in the process of winning over the project's army of stakeholders. On the other hand, Robert Irwin, flaunting intuition and impulse as his first, last, and only argument, required no compensating bullshit: he's the artist, and that's the way the artist likes it. Can you blame Meier for finding this maddening?

Every once in a while, however, there is satisfaction to be had when design bullshit attains the level of art. I remember working years ago with a challenging client who kept rejecting brochure designs for a Francophile real estate development because they "weren't French enough." I had no idea what French graphic design was supposed to look like but came up with an approach using Empire, a typeface designed by Milwaukee-born Morris Fuller Benton in 1937, and showed it to my boss, Massimo Vignelli. "That will work," he said, his eyes narrowing.

At the presentation, Massimo unveiled the new font choice with a flourish. "As you see," he said, "in this new design, we're using a typeface called Ahm-peere."

I was about to correct him when I realized he was using the French pronunciation of Empire.

The client bought it.

Call Me Shithead, or, What's in a Name?

Economist Steven Levitt is interested in more than money. Instead, he wants to know how people make decisions: how they decide how much to pay for something, how they describe themselves to potential blind dates, why they decide to lead a life of crime or go into professional sports. And, of course, what to name the baby.

In their book, *Freakonomics: A Rogue Economist Explores the Hidden Side of Everything*, Levitt and coauthor Stephen Dubner devote a chapter to the economics of baby names. What names are statistically correlated with educated parents? What names are correlated to socioeconomic status? Why are some names popular and some not? And along the way, they tell a story, perhaps apocryphal, of a baby girl who had been given a name with an exotic pronunciation, shuh-TEED, but an unfortunate spelling, *Shithead*.

Naming things—companies, products, brands—is a service that a lot of design firms, from Landor to Interbrand to Addison, are well compensated for providing. As such, it's also the only design-related activity that virtually every person on earth feels fully qualified to undertake on their own, for free.

Most clients would be hesitant to offer informed opinions about typefaces. Only ones sure of their own taste provide direction on things like color or form. But everyone has experience with naming, whether a baby or even a goldfish. The fact that it's so easy is what makes it so hard.

The biggest problem, of course, is that new names seldom sound good at first. Advertising executive Ron Holland thought that "Xerox" was a horrible name for their client's up-and-coming duplicating company. "They'll call it Ex-Rox, the famous Japanese laxative," he told his partner, George Lois. Upon learning in 1986 that the merger of Burroughs and Sperry would result in a new entity called Unisys, Calvin Trillin predicted that the company "will do everything in its power to live up to what the public might expect of a company that sounds like a disease." Today both of those names sound quite natural.

Given that birthing a new name for a business concern is such a traumatic experience, its no surprise some companies decide that nomenclature midwives are worth every penny. Not that the nomenclaturists agree, of course, at least with each other. As Ruth Shalit wrote in a classic article on Salon.com, the experts at Landor who came up with the name Agilent couldn't have been prouder. "It's funny, because 'Agilent' isn't even a real word," said David Redhill, Landor's global executive director at the time. "So it's pretty hard to get positive and negative impressions with any real basis in experience. But I'm pleased to say that when we unveiled the name last month at an all-company meeting, a thousand employees stood up and gave the name a standing ovation. And we thought, 'We have a good thing here.' A thousand cheering employees can't be wrong!"

Yet Shalit soon discovered that Landor's competitors were less than impressed. "What a crummy name," said Steve Manning of A Hundred Monkeys, a naming specialist firm. "The most namby-pamby, phonetically weak, light-in-its-shoes name in the entire history of naming . . . It ought to be taken out back and shot," said Rick Bragdon, president of the naming firm Idiom. "Perhaps it would be best if Landor just closed up shop," said Naseem Javed, president of ABC Namebank. Of course, once you start thinking about names, they all start to sound . . . well . . . Idiom? ABC Namebank?
A Hundred Monkeys?

You'd think that naming a baby was simpler. Maybe it's only because parents are blissfully unaware of how charged a name can be. In their book, Levitt and Dubner describe a series of "audit studies" that sent out identical resumes to employers with only one difference: one resume would bear a "black" name (DeShawn Williams) and the other a "white" one (Jake Williams). As you might sadly guess, the Jakes always get more interviews than the DeShawns. As a visit to the addictive Baby Name Wizard's Name Voyager website will suggest, trends in baby names ebb and flow. But perhaps the trends are not quite as unpredictable as they seem at first glance. Levitt and Dubner, observing that the most popular names tend to start as "high-end" upper-income names (the once-tony "Madison" was the third most popular name for white girls in 2000), project that the most popular girl names in 2015 might be Annika, Clementine, and Philippa, and for boys, Asher, Finnigan, and Sumner. Agilent, a name I rather like, is nowhere to be found.

There is a rare occasion when naming the product and naming the baby come together. The poet Marianne Moore was once recruited by a pair of ambitious young executives at Ford to come up with a "colossal name" for the company's newest car. She set upon the project with enthusiasm, coming up with names that included the Silver Sword, the Aerundo, the Resilient Bullet, the Mongoose Civique, the Pastelogram, and the Utopian Turtletop. After considering Moore's suggestions and thousands of others, the company settled on a name that coincidentally was the same one that founder Henry Ford had picked for another one of his babies: Edsel. When the car flopped, the name was blamed. Although it could have been worse. Just ask Shithead.

Avoiding Poor, Lonely Obvious

Does anyone devote as much energy to avoiding simple, sensible solutions as the modern graphic designer?

Among the design professions, graphic design is an embarrassingly low-risk enterprise. Our colleagues in architecture, industrial design, and fashion design are tormented by nightmares of smoldering rubble, brutally hacked off fingers, and embarrassing wardrobe malfunctions. We graphic designers flirt with...paper cuts. Thus liberated from serious threats, we invent our own: skating on the edge of illegibility, daring readers to navigate indecipherable layouts, and concocting unlikely new ways to solve problems that don't actually exist.

Our daredevil ambitions are never so roused as when we're our own audience. A recent case can be found in the July/August 2005 issue of the otherwise exemplary publication *I.D.* There, faced with the seemingly simple challenge of faithfully reproducing the winners of their annual design competition, the magazine's creators opted to take the hard way out. Swerving wildly to avoid the obvious, they drove right off the cliff of coherence.

Let me say this straight out: I love *I.D*, I really do. Julie Lasky is a great editor who has produced some of the best issues ever in that estimable journal's long history.

But the visual presentation in *I.D*'s 51st Annual Design Review is just plain nuts. The issue is taken up by descriptions and photographs of winners

(Best of Category, Design Distinction, Honorable Mention) in eight categories (Consumer Products, Graphics, Packaging, Environments, Furniture, Equipment, Concepts, and Interactive). The descriptions make good reading. The photographs are, well, problematic. Most of the winners are pictured not in isolation but in situ, the situ in this case being the other winners. This means that the reader is faced with page after page of stuff piled all over the place, handsomely photographed in that flatly lit deadpan way that's been so popular for the last decade or so, each flea-market-style composition daring us to guess which of the things shown is actually the subject of the photograph.

As a graphic designer myself, I know how this happens. Every edition of the annual design review presents the same problem. Every year, dozens of products, packages, chairs, posters, books, and devices win *I.D* awards, and every year the readers want to know what the winners look like. Simple descriptive images: well, that's been done, right? So obvious! How about if we evoke the confusion, the ennui, the sensory overload of the judging process itself? A daring choice! Does it work? Not really, but as Dr. Johnson said of a dog walking on its hind legs, we're meant to be surprised not to find it necessarily done well, but simply done at all.

If this sounds familiar, it should. Rick Poynor lodged a similar complaint on Design Observer against *Recollected Work,* a monograph from graphic designers Armand Mevis and Linda van Deursen. The book consists largely of page after full-bleed page of piles of their work, cropped, partially obscured, more or less incomprehensible. To quote Rick: "Seventeen years of work blurs together, like grubby laundry turning over and over in a washing machine. Nothing has any space around it. Everything becomes flotsam. Any sense of development is erased." And that's putting it kindly. Of course, they could have just lined up all the images, foregoing the cropping, proper borders all around—insert sigh here—but that would have been...you know.

And then there was another incident back in pre-September 2001. In those more innocent days, the U.S. graphic design community was embroiled in a gigantic debate over Jennifer Sterling's design of the annual publication of the American Institute of Graphic Arts, *365: AIGA Year in Design.* Sterling's design approach had been reliably iconoclastic, cropping posters, showing fragments of books and packages, and generally rendering the work unintelligible. An astonishingly long (for those days) thread piled up on AIGA's website with complaints about Sterling's hubris: you would have thought she was blowing up Buddhas in Afghanistan.

I myself have been guilty of this same kind of straining for novelty. Asked to design a catalog for the AIGA Fifty Books of the Year show back in

1995, I was determined to do anything to avoid shooting the entries with a flatbed camera on a clean white background. Like laying out cadavers at the morgue, I remember sneering to a colleague. Instead, we brought in Victor Schrager, who lovingly photographed the books in unlikely, if beautifully lit, positions. I fondly remember one shot showing Paul Rand's *From Lascaux to Brooklyn* masterfully astride a supine copy of David Carson's *The End of Print*. Flipping through it today, I admire Schrager's beautiful pictures and wonder what those books actually looked like.

Graphic design is easy, of course, so we kill ourselves trying to make it hard. I should have remembered a lesson I received at one of my first jobs, a summer internship in the design department at WGBH-TV in Boston. I had been assigned a rare design project. Given my status—I was the most junior of three interns—it was probably something like a hallway flyer for the annual blood drive. I labored over this 8.5″ x 11″ opus all day, never forgetting what I then held as the twin tenets of responsible design practice (one, create something absolutely without precedent; and two, demonstrate to onlookers how clever I am). Given my predilections at that point in my nascent career, this probably involved merging the home-grown rigorous modernism of Lester Beall and Will Burtin with the formal experimentation of Wolfgang Weingart and April Greiman. My only inhibition was the lack of a Macintosh computer, which would not be invented for seven years.

Late in the day, the station's head of design, the legendary Chris Pullman, came by my desk. "What's this?" he asked. Breathlessly, I described the visionary thinking that informed the yet-unfinished masterpiece before me. Pullman stared at the mess for a moment, and then his face brightened. "Hey," he said, as if a great idea was just occurring to him. "Why avoid the obvious?" He then took away everything but the headline: GIVE BLOOD NOW. "Try that!" he said cheerfully, walking away.

Poor, poor Obvious. Come sit by me. I'll be your friend.

My Favorite Book is Not About Design (or Is It?)

It was a hot summer weekend more than twenty years ago when I first picked up what would become my favorite book. I was at a bed and breakfast with friends in Spring Lake, New Jersey. The house's bookshelf was filled with those kind of dented volumes you find in summer places: Reader's Digest Condensed Books, celebrity biographies, trashy romances. And one worn hardcover with a title that sounded vaguely familiar: *Act One*. I picked it up, started reading, and was basically out of commission for the rest of the weekend.

Act One by Moss Hart is not the best book I've ever read. But it is my favorite. Most people to whom I recommend it have never heard of it, or of its author. But on about my fifth rereading I realized why I like it so much: it's the best, funniest, and most inspiring description of the creative process ever put down on paper.

If you cared about show business in the middle of the twentieth century, you certainly knew who Moss Hart was. A fantastically successful playwright and director, Hart was at the peak of his fame in 1959, having just mounted, against considerable odds, what would become one of the most acclaimed musicals of all time, *My Fair Lady*. That was the year he published *Act One*, the story of his life, or—as the title implies—the first part of his life.

Hart was born and raised poor in the Bronx (as he puts it, "in an atmosphere of unrelieved poverty"), trapped in a love-starved, dysfunctional family, and desperate to escape. Salvation came at the hands of his Aunt

Kate, who introduced him to the theater. Broadway became his obsession, and his memoir maps his journey from the Bronx to Forty-second Street.

The structure of *Act One* is ingenious. The first part describes his slow, painful, funny climb from poverty to semi-poverty: from office boy for a theatrical agent, Augustus ("King of the One Night Stands") Pitou; to failed actor and budding director; to social director of a two-bit summer camp in the Catskills. The first part of the book ends with Hart, determined to make it to the big time, sitting down on the beach at Coney Island to write his first play.

Part Two opens in 1929, four years later, in the same spot. But Hart's circumstances are thrillingly transformed: he is now the most sought-after social director on the Catskills circuit, with a personal staff of more than two dozen people and a brand-new 1,500-seat theater at his disposal.By not dwelling on the events that brought him to this surprisingly esteemed position (the future head of MGM is his assistant, and the future head of Paramount is his biggest rival), Hart can continue to portray himself as green-gilled naif for the rest of the book.

And it's the rest of the book that is the real subject of *Act One*: the story of how Hart's first Broadway hit, *Once in a Lifetime* came to be. Describing the solitary process of writing a play doesn't sound particularly interesting, but Hart's producer agreed to mount his first effort on the condition that he collaborate with George S. Kaufman, then Broadway's unchallenged king of comedy. The interplay of the awestruck Hart and the sardonic, aloof Kaufman transform a lonesome activity into a tremendously engaging one.

It turns out that the art of writing a play, in Hart's description at least, is a process that will seem familiar to many designers. You start with a concept (the theme), develop a design (the plot), and then implement it (the script). Like design, doing it takes some inspiration and a little bit of genius, but mainly lots and lots of hard work. And although writing a play is considered an art, unlike painting or novel writing, the user feedback is brutally immediate in the form of out-of-town tryouts where the audiences leave no doubt about what's working and what's not.

And Kaufman and Hart soon learn their play isn't working. *Once in a Lifetime* is a frantic satirical comedy about the coming of talking pictures to Hollywood; if it sounds familiar, you probably recognize the plot from the movie musical version, *Singin' in the Rain*. The play's preview audiences love the first half, but midway through the second act, it begins to fall flat: "There were laughs, of course, during the rest of the act but they were scattered and thinnish and sounded as though the audience were forcing themselves to laugh at things they didn't quite find funny." The third act is a disaster, the audience reaction to which Hart describes in a fit of nearly rapturous masochism:

A deadly cough or two began to echo hollowly through the auditorium—that telltake tocsin that pierces the playwright's eardrums, those sounds that penetrate his heart like carefully aimed poison darts—and after the first few tentative coughs a sudden epidemic of respiratory ailments seemed to spread through every chest in the audience as though a long-awaited signal had been given. Great clearings of the throat, prodigious nose-blowings, Gargantuan sneezes came from all parts of the theatre both upstairs and down, all of them gradually blending until the odious sound emerged as one great and constant cough that drowned out every line that was being uttered on stage.

Then begins the grueling process by which Hart and Kaufman write and rewrite the play through its previews in Atlantic City and Philadelphia. It improves, but not quite enough. "Comedies usually have to be ninety-five percent airtight—at least that's been my experience," Kaufman tells his partner a week before opening night. "You can squeak by with ninety per cent once in a while, but not with eighty-five, and according to my figures, not to keep any secrets from you, this one just inches over the seventy mark. I don't know what son-of-a-bitch set up those figures, but there you are." Disconsolate, Hart goes out for a drink with his producer, Sam Harris, as they both try to forget the surefire flop they have on their hands. At the end of the evening, the producer says, almost as a parting thought, that he wishes they weren't doing such a "noisy" play: "Just think about it. Except for those two minutes at the beginning of the first act, there isn't another spot in this whole play where two people sit down and talk quietly to each other. Is that right, or isn't it?" Hart is puzzled, and then electrified, for his producer has just provided him with the key for resolving the play's last act.

I stared at him silently, my mind racing back and forth over what he had said, an odd excitement beginning to take possession of me.... Far from clutching at straws, it seemed to me that Sam Harris had in his own paradoxical fashion put his finger straight on that unfathomable fault in the third act that had defied all our efforts. The more I thought of it, the more certain I became that he was correct, though I could not define why...

I was much too stimulated now to think of going to sleep. It was a fine moonlit night and I kept walking. I tried to find my way toward the park, for the air in the streets was still stifling, but I stumbled instead upon a children's playground.... I walked to a swing and sat down on it. I swung back and forth, and higher and more wildly I made the swing go, the greater impression of coolness it created. I was a little apprehensive that a policeman might happen by and wonder what a grown man was doing in a child's swing at four o'clock in the morning. I became absorbed in threading my way through the labyrinth of that third act, and with a shock of recognition I thought I saw clearly where we had gone wrong, and then, in a sudden flash of improvisation, exactly the right way to resolve it. I let the swing come to a full stop and sat there transfixed by the rightness of the idea, but a little staggered at the audacity of it, or at what it might entail.

If you're a designer—indeed, if you're in any kind of creative enterprise—I'm guessing you can identify with that grown man in the swing at four in the morning, your heart racing with the thrill of finally solving a seemingly intractable problem. Do I have to add that the last minute rewrite—the addition of one intimate moment in the midst of what had been ceaseless mayhem—saves the day? ("The quiet scene Sam Harris had asked for was playing line after line to the biggest laughs in the play. Even some of the perfectly straight lines seemed to evoke laughter, and the laughter mounted until it became one continuous roar.") *Once in a Lifetime* becomes a huge hit, and the young playwright's future is secured.

In *Dazzler: The Life and Times of Moss Hart*, Steven Bach suggests that Hart took so many dramatic liberties in Act One that it was nearly a work of fiction. And when I finally saw *Once in a Lifetime* in a production at the Williamstown Theatre Festival (starring no less than Lauren Graham from Gilmore Girls), I found it anachronistic and, honestly, not as funny in the twenty-first century as it evidently was seventy years earlier.

But does it really matter? For Act One, in the end, is a parable: about childhood dreams, about the search for success, about the hard work of creativity. But more than anything else, it's about the conviction that so many of us hold that we're just one brilliant inspiration—and a few swings on a late-night playground—away from transforming our lives forever. If this is dramatic liberty, I'll take it. Isn't that what design is all about?

Rick Valicenti: This Time It's Personal

The more graphic design monographs are published, the less certain we seem to be about their purpose. Are they history? Inspiration? Self promotion? Self indulgence? This confusion often begins with the subjects themselves. Some emulate the authority of the art history book but add confessional captions suited to a tell-all memoir. Others lose themselves in experimental layouts that provide a live demonstration of creative virtuosity, but impede understanding by the uninitiated.

And then there's Rick Valicenti. In his newly published book *Emotion as Promotion: A Book of Thirst*, Valicenti does the seemingly impossible; he provides a glimpse into a designer's life that is at once accessibly seductive and brazenly idiosyncratic. It is a combination that few would attempt and even fewer would pull off. Valicenti does it.

Many designers find themselves trapped in situations far removed from the passions that led them to enter the field in the first place. Each of them can take comfort and inspiration from Valicenti's ability to reinvent himself. He started out as the consummate professional. An early triumph was the lurid and ubiquitous red Helvetica Bold logo for Chicago's Jewel supermarket chain; in the book he surrounds it with over four dozen similar logos, viewing his role as the Patient Zero of the gruesome Helvetica Bold epidemic with a mixture of pride and horror. Nearly a decade of buttoned-up success followed, and then he threw it all away.

"After eight years of operating a design-as-vendor-operation titled R. Valicenti Design," he writes, "I decided I would build a practice only for a discerning clientele. Cultural institutions were my first target." A typo (1st, 2nd…3st) suggested the studio's name: Thirst. *Emotion as Promotion* provides a comprehensive look at the nearly fifteen years of work that followed from this decision.

The studio's work is shown in a refreshingly intelligible, even obvious, manner, ranging from conventional assignments handled unconventionally (an annual report for the Chicago Board of Trade), to risky experiments that defy classification (a self-funded ad in *I.D.* that exuberantly embeds the slogan "Fuck Apathy" in an anti-Bush message). Valicenti calls on clients, co-workers and collaborators to provide the context in similarly inventive ways: reconstructed meeting transcripts, reproductions of email exchanges, and—for two particularly heartbreaking failed corporate identities—full-blown Elizabethan dramas.

Stories of clients gone bad are fun to tell, of course, and they've become a staple of the contemporary graphic design monograph. In contrast, Valicenti is unique in his unself-conscious passion for those clients that love him back: Herman Miller, Gary Fisher Mountain Bikes, and especially Thirst's most enthusiastic patron, Gilbert Paper. A recorded conference call between three Gilbert executives titled "The Client's on the Line" goes on too long (and, in true Valicenti heart-on-his-sleeve fashion, is almost downright mushy at times) but serves as an unvarnished demonstration of one of the book's aphorisms: "There are only two ways to secure design's opportunities: reputation and personal relationships." Valicenti has built the first through the second.

The creation of Thirst wasn't the last transformation in the restless career of Rick Valicenti. In 1995, the studio closed its downtown location and relocated to Valicenti's suburban home forty miles away. "My new desk faced the woods (beyond an open courtyard, beyond our pool). Right behind me was the kitchen door. Our cherry table, once reserved for meals and homework, made itself the hub of a Thirst boardroom." In a world where most of us carefully guard our hip profession's black-clad image, Valicenti cheerfully embraced all the trappings of Midwestern American suburbia, documenting the neighborhood McMansions and casting his soccer-mom neighbors as surreal heroines in Photoshopped fantasies. The raw material is anything but hip, which makes the resulting imagery especially arresting.

The change was temporary. "Our routine dissolved when another round of success came to Thirst, which soon outnumbered family in the residence," says Valicenti. "So ended the Good Life." It is telling that Valicenti spends so much time seeking a balance between two things—success and the good life—that most people find anything but mutually exclusive.

Toward the end of the book, Valicenti writes:

> The seduction of the big brand name is very real; the excitement of the phone call from New York or Frankfurt or Tokyo is quite attractive; the notion of designing a brand mascot or national advertising image is a thrill. But somewhere along the way the glitter would fade and it would be just me and the process. I never woke up with a real sense of purpose or a relationship I could value. So in the end, if I would not want to have a new client wake up in my house and share breakfast with my family, why should I give up my time for them?

Designers yearn to be provided opportunities for personal expression, but we labor under the illusion that business must be, in the end, an impersonal activity. But is it? Taking the work personally involves considerable risks: exposure, rejection, embarrassment. *Emotion as Promotion* is a valuable testament to how substantial the rewards can be.

Credit Line Goes Here

Who designs my work? Well, I do, of course. Basically. More or less.

Design is essentially a collaborative enterprise. That makes assigning credit for the products of our work a complicated issue. Take a poster called "Light Years," a pretty well-known poster for The Architectural League of New York. It's simple: the five letters of the two words "Light" and "Years" are superimposed on each other. The overlapping letters have a mysterious luminescent effect on the black background. There's a small line of type at the bottom. When it's published, it's often credited just to me. But its genesis is a little more complicated.

Like a lot of widely reproduced graphic artifacts, the poster has become separated from its original purpose; most people have no idea that it's an invitation for an annual benefit for The Architectural League of New York called the Beaux Arts Ball. I design one every year. Each one has a different theme. That year the theme was "Light Years." I recall my pleasure in discovering, after doing some sketching, the rather obvious fact that the two words have the same number of letters. I thought we could take advantage of that by somehow superimposing the letters of the two words. I took some sketches of this idea and others to Nicole Trice, a design student from the University of Cincinnati who was serving a three-month internship with us, and told her to try some variations to see what would work. There was one version I liked the best, and that was the one we sent to the printer. I asked her how she achieved the effect that made the letters seem to glow, and she told me, but I've forgotten. I never touched the Mac.

So, the formal attribution for the poster goes to me and Nicole. But I've done one of these every year, and seldom as successfully. This particular one works because that year's ball committee (Walter Chatham, Cristina Grajales, Frank Lupo, and Allen Prusis) picked a theme we could really work with (or at least that was mathematically convenient); the management of The Architectural League (Rosalie Genevro and Anne Rieselbach) approved the design and paid for its reproduction; and the printer (Rich Kaplan at Finlay Brothers) did a beautiful job printing it, with no one supervising on press (couldn't afford the trip to Hartford for a freebie). Also, what about the letterforms, which play such a large part in the design? Interstate, by Tobias Frere-Jones. Finally, I'm not sure this poster would have looked exactly like this without the influence—a complicated subject to be sure—of artists and designers I've admired like Ed Ruscha and Josef Muller-Brockmann. That's a lot of people, and I probably left someone out.

When a design artifact becomes more widely known, it grows ever distant from the complications surrounding its birth, and sometimes, as in the case of the poster above, even its context and meaning. Continually referencing endless lists of collaborators seldom serves the purposes of journalists, curators, and design historians, who want clarity and simplicity. I can't say I blame them: that long roll call of people that appears every time I open my copy of Adobe Photoshop must be significant, but to me the names are as unreal and fantastical as the people who attended parties at Jay Gatsby's house in the summer of 1922.

Lone authorship corresponds more neatly to the popular image of personal creativity, so even objects that could not possibly be the handiwork of a single person, like the iPod, nonetheless become associated with a single name, like Apple's Jonathan Ive. Likewise, although *Emotion as Promotion: A Book of Thirst* lists Rick Valicenti as editor rather than author, and a long list of collaborators appears on one of its early pages, it's hard to think of it as anything but a compendium of Rick Valicenti's work. This is even true in a book like *Tibor Kalman: Perverse Optimist,* in which efforts are made to bring in the voices of collaborators and to credit everyone involved in the design of every reproduced image: perhaps in the end the only picture that really matters is the big smiling face of Tibor on the cover.

Tibor is the classic example of a non-designer who managed to exert an influence on—and get credit for the work of—a generation of talented designers, without really doing any hands-on design himself. Another is the late Muriel Cooper from the legendary MIT Media Lab. I was talking the other day to my partner Lisa Strausfeld about the time she was a student there. "I used to wonder why Muriel got credit for so much of the work that came out of the Media Lab. But now it strikes me how pervasive she was," Lisa said. "She picked all the typefaces that we worked with. She set up the structure of the problems and guided the way we solved them." Like Kalman, Muriel Cooper authored a vast body of material just by force of intellect and personality, while all the while other people thought they were actually "doing the work."

And none of those people—some of whom have names you might recognize—are listed in the captions for the images that illustrate Cooper's biography on the website of the American Institute of Graphic Arts. It's not fair, of course, but what's an ambitious but anonymous young designer to do? The solution is almost too simple. Filling out the information forms for design competitions and publications is tedious work. Chances are good that whoever is stuck with doing it would love to be relieved of the responsibility. Volunteer for the job. That way, you can make sure that the credits are scrupulously accurate, with one exception: no matter what, make sure your boss gets listed as creative director.

That worked for me way back when. Come to think of it, it still does.

Every New Yorker is a Target

I have been a faithful subscriber to *The New Yorker* for over twenty years, but I have to admit that I had forgotten that the issue of August 22, 2005 was supposed be different. So I suspected nothing when I opened the front cover to find a full page, red-and-white illustration by Stina Persson featuring a woman's face, some vague neon signs, and a pattern made up of the dot-in-a-circle motif that is the logo of the Target Corporation: a typical image ad. On the opposite page, however, was more of the same: subway car, taxicab, skyline, boom box, Target logo, this time rendered by Linda Zacks. Turn the page, there's a single-column ad next to the magazine's table of contents (an illustration by Carlos Aponte featuring more than thirty Targets in various New York settings) facing still another full-page ad, this time a group of Target logos dropping over an art deco skyscraper rendered by none other than Milton Glaser.

For the first time in its eighty-year history, *The New Yorker* was giving itself up to a single advertiser.

I must confess, the effect is unnerving. In high school, I read a book called *Subliminal Seduction*, an early exposé of the psychological techniques used by advertisers to market to unwary consumers. The most thrilling passages described sinister exercises in which the word "sex" would be almost imperceptibly airbrushed onto the ice cubes in a photograph of a glass of whiskey. This effort was somehow meant to push the viewer one step closer to alcoholism. How exactly this process was intended to work (particularly in view of the fact that the glass, encoded ice cubes and all, was usually photographed in the hands of a woman with mammoth breasts and spectacular cleavage) was always unclear to me. But the idea that ad agencies were skillfully embedding secret messages in product photography had immense appeal to my inner fourteen-year-old conspiracy theorist; it also explained why I was always so darned horny.

The all-Target *New Yorker* is the product of more nakedly mercenary world where advertisers no longer need conceal their aims. There's nothing subliminal about it: I counted over two hundred Target logos in the first nineteen pages alone, and there were still eleven ads left to go when I gave up. The illustrators acquit themselves well: Robert Risko turns in a funny image of a substantial construction worker perched on a typically un-ergonomic modern cafe stool with a single logo on his back-pocket handkerchief; Yuko Shimizu turns in a spirited biker chick crossing the Brooklyn Bridge with the logo rising before her. Best of all is Me Company's vertiginous computer-generated cityscape, the last ad inside the magazine, which surely pushes the logo count well into four figures, if not five.

Although the publisher has publicly stated that the decision to go with a single advertiser had no effect on the magazine's editorial content—as editor David Remnick put it in the *New York Times*, "Ads are ads"—the inescapable world of Target creates a disorienting context. Every non-Target illustration in the issue looks a little... funny. Indeed, when I saw the large woodcut that Milton Glaser's former partner Seymour Chwast produced to illustrate Gina Ochsner's short story "Thicker Than Water" (two blackbirds with round eyes that sort of reminded me of...never mind), my first thought was: didn't Seymour get the memo? No, and he no doubt didn't get the paycheck, either. Even the cover drawing by Ian Falconer gives one pause: two boys, playing with a beach ball, a round beach ball, a round *red-and-white* beach ball.

Isn't it every advertiser's ultimate fantasy to implant a predisposition to see their logo everywhere you look? So Target's experiment—which may have cost a million dollars—must be rated a resounding success. But after my head cleared, I managed to actually read the issue, and came across a review by Ian Buruma of *Under the Loving Care of the Fatherly Leader: North Korea and the Kim*

Dynasty by Bradley Martin. The review is illustrated with a full-page comic by graphic novelist Guy Delisle that recounts his brief stint working in Pyongyang. "Everywhere you look, you look at one of the Kims," reads the caption. "At first I found it amusing. But after a while that omnipresence began to weigh on me. And at the end of my two month's stay it was driving me crazy. On my return flight, I saw North Korean apparatchiks taking their 'Dear Leader' badges off. So maybe I was not the only one who had that feeling."

After a while, it just seems like everything's about Target.

I am a Plagiarist

During much of 2006, the New York media world was obsessed with the story of Kaavya Viswanathan, a Harvard undergraduate who landed a two-book deal for $500,000 from Little, Brown and Company while still in high school. Within weeks of the publication of her first novel, *How Opal Mehta Got Kissed, Got Wild, and Got a Life*, allegations arose that she had copied passages from books by another young adult author. Soon schadenfreude-fueled investigators uncovered similarities to still other books. Confronted with the near-duplicate passages, Viswanathan first denied everything ("I have no idea what you are talking about"), then conceded inadvertent wrongdoing ("any phrasing similarities between her works and mine were completely unintentional and unconscious"), and finally admitted to the *New York Times* that the problem was her photographic memory ("I remember by reading. I never take notes... I really thought the words were my own").

Kurt Andersen, assessing the controversy in *New York* magazine, observed, "Plagiarists almost never simply confess. There are always mitigating circumstances."

Well, let me be the first to come clean: I am a plagiarist.

Or am I? About a year ago, I was asked by a longtime client, the Yale School of Architecture, to design a poster for a symposium they were organizing. The event had one of the most cumbersome names I'd ever been asked to handle: "Non-Standard Structures: An Organic Order of Irregular Geometries,

Hybrid Members, and Chaotic Assemblies." I was stumped. I described my interpretation of the symposium's theme—the strange forms that can result from computer-generated processes—to one of my partners, Abbott Miller, and he suggested I use a version of Hoefler & Frere-Jones's as-of-yet unreleased typeface Retina. This was a great idea. Designed for very small reproduction on newsprint, the letterforms were drawn with exaggerated interior forms to compensate for ink spread. Blown up to headline size, the font looked bizarrely distorted, but each oddity was a product of nothing more than technical requirements: an apt metaphor for the design work that the symposium would address.

Still, that was a long headline. It was hard to make the letterforms big enough to demonstrate the distortion. I tried a bunch of variations without success. Finally, with the deadline looming, out of nowhere a picture formed in my mind: big type at the top, reducing in size from line to line as it moved down the poster, almost a parody of that long symposium title. And one more finishing touch: thick bars underlining every word. This approach came together quickly. It was one of those solutions that, for me at least, had a mysterious sense of preordained rightness.

And for good reason. My solution was very similar to something I had seen almost thirty years ago, a piece by one of my favorite designers, Willi Kunz. There are differences, of course: Kunz's type goes from small to big, and mine goes the other way around; Kunz's horizontal lines change size, and mine do not; and, naturally, Kunz uses Akzidenz Grotesk, rather than a typeface that wouldn't be invented until 2002. But still, the black on white, the change in typographic scale, the underscores: all these add up to two solutions that look more alike than different.

I didn't realize this until a few weeks ago, when I was looking through the newly published fourth edition of Phil Meggs's *History of Graphic Design*. And there it was, on page 476, a reproduction of Willi Kunz's abstract letterpress exploration from 1975. I recognized it immediately as something I had seen in my design school days. More recently, it was reproduced in Kunz's *Typography: Macro- and Microaesthetics,* published in 2004, a copy of which I own.

Did I think of it consciously when I designed my poster? No, my excuse was the same as Kaavya Viswanathan's: I saw something, stored it in my memory, forgot where it came from, and pulled it out later—much later—when I needed it. Unlike some plagiarists, I didn't make changes to cover my tracks. (At various points, Viswanathan appears to have changed names like "Cinnabon" to "Mrs. Fields" and "Human Evolution" to "Psych," as one professor at Harvard observed, "in the hope of making the result less easily googleable.") My sin is more like that of George Harrison, who was successfully sued for cribbing his song "My Sweet Lord" from an earlier hit by the Chiffons, "He's So Fine." Just like me, Harrison claimed—more credibly than Viswanathan—that any similarities between his work and another's were unintended and unconscious. Nonetheless, the judge's ruling against him was unequivocal: "His subconscious knew it already had worked in a song his conscious did not remember...That is, under the law, infringement of copyright, and is no less so even though subconsciously accomplished."

I find all of this rather scary. I don't claim to have a photographic memory, but my mind is stuffed full of graphic design, graphic design done by other people. How can I be sure that any idea that comes out of that same mind is absolutely my own? Writing in *Slate*, Joshua Foer reports that after Helen Keller was accused of plagiarism, she was virtually paralyzed. "I have ever since been tortured by the fear that what I write is not my own," said Keller. "For a long time, when I wrote a letter, even to my mother, I was seized with a sudden feeling, and I would spell the sentences over and over, to make sure that I had not read them in a book." The challenge is even more pronounced in design, where we manipulate more generalized visual forms rather than specific sequences of words.

In the end, accusations of plagiarism are notoriously subjective, and some people who have seen my piece and Kunz's side by side have said they're quite different. You can judge for yourself. All I know for certain is that I felt a powerful sense of unease when I turned to page 476 in *History of Graphic Design*. That alone compels me to offer Willi Kunz an apology. I just wish for both our sakes that I had a $500,000 advance to offer him as well.

Looking for Celebration, Florida

After twenty years, Michael Eisner stepped down in September of 2005, as head of the Walt Disney Company. He left a substantial, if mixed, legacy. On his watch, Disney created a worldwide empire of theme parks, launched a cruise ship line, bought a television network, and joined the first ranks of Hollywood movie studios.

And, along the way, they built a town in central Florida called Celebration, where nearly 10,000 people live today, inspiring at least three books, dozens of websites, and—uniquely, to my knowledge, among American communities—one song by the leftist agitprop band Chumbawamba ("Social engineering/It gives you that fuzzy feeling/Down in Celebration, Florida").

I worked on the graphics for Celebration, Florida. To this day, it remains one of my favorite projects.

Celebration has its origins, some say, in Walt Disney's original vision for EPCOT, an acronym with a largely forgotten source: the Experimental Prototype Community of Tomorrow. Disney conceived it as a real, albeit futuristic, working town with actual citizens commuting by monorail to a town center housed under a geodesic dome. This vision proved more durable as theme park than working town, but the dream lived on. And when Disney's real estate experts decided that 10,000 acres of undeveloped swampland immediately south of Disney World might be worth more to the company as residential development, the time was right for Eisner to make Walt's fantasy real.

Celebration, however, was a fantasy more suited to Andy Hardy than Buck Rogers. The city was to be the most fully realized expression of the principles of New Urbanism, the planning theory that seeks to reinstate the virtues of early-twentieth-century American town life by making small, pedestrian-scaled communities that mix a variety of housing choices with retail and business. This is not a radical idea, but only seems so in a country single-mindedly dedicated to replicating the economically convenient tropes of suburban sprawl. A successful model already existed just to the north in the Florida panhandle town of Seaside, where New Urbanist pioneers Andrés Duany and Elizabeth Plater-Zyberk had first developed their town planning ideas. In Celebration, Disney was in effect mounting a major-studio remake of DPZ's surprisingly profitable indy feature, complete with serious budgets and big-name talent. Planned by Robert A. M. Stern and Jaquelin Robertson, Celebration would bring together many of Eisner's favored architects: In addition to buildings by Stern and Robertson, the town would feature a bank by Robert Venturi, a post office by Michael Graves, a movie theater by Cesar Pelli, and a town hall by Philip Johnson. Houses would be built according to an old-fashioned pattern book, with models for six different styles: Classical, Victorian, Colonial Revival, Coastal, Mediterranean, and French Normandy. (Notably missing: "Gehry-esque.")

Our job was to create the signage. It was a fascinating challenge, trying to create a coherent sense of place without overwhelming the residents with "branding." There were only a few useful models to go on. Forest Hills Gardens, in Queens, New York, was my favorite; there, anonymous signmakers had created a charming consistency without succumbing to sameness or cliche. We worked with so many different architects that the early choice of Cheltenham as the "town typeface" seemed prescient, since it too was designed by an architect, Bertram Goodhue. We ended up designing not only street signs and shop signs, but manhole covers, fountains, golf course graphics, park trail markers, the sales center, and even that pattern book for the houses. We resisted invitations to design a logo, arguing that towns didn't have logos; finally, an unused manhole cover design featuring a silhouetted girl on a Schwinn-style bicycle and a dog became the "town seal." Everyone was amazingly idealistic; the true believers managing the project would make many of the my non-profit clients look crass and cynical by comparison. We were building the future! It was one of those rare occasions when I felt like I got to design the whole world. It has not happened since.

Celebration turned ten years old in 2005, and it has worn well despite some bumps at the start. (Many of these involved the town's school, a well-funded progressive institution that was a powerful lure to homebuyers but which turned out to be a bit too experimental for many parents.) Real estate values there are far above the national average, and as Witold Rybczynski has observed, "While Celebration was artfully designed to return to small-town values, it has suffered the fate of many attractive small towns, such as Aspen or Nantucket: Its downtown has become a tourist destination." Yet when I lecture and describe projects I've worked on, nine times out of ten the first question is about Celebration, and the question is usually some version of: But isn't that Disney town sort of, you know, creepy?

Creepy. Well. For many, the relentlessly cheerful monoculture suggested by the Disney imprimatur provides an inescapably Orwellian aspect to the entire enterprise. Yet, as a place to live, particularly in central Florida, Celebration is relatively benign. Consider, instead, the kind of Floridian residential development where more than one of my close relatives make their homes; its archetype is familiar to any viewer of *Seinfeld*: Del Boca Vista Phase 3, where Jerry's parents spend their time golfing, fighting over the air conditioning and engaging in condominium-centered political intrigue. On the face of it, Celebration compares favorably. The community is not gated; the mixture of houses and apartments, of small yards and well-planned common park space, is lively and convincing; you can actually having a pleasant experience walking around. And of course, if Disney creeps you out, you can remember what Eisner said at a press conference before the town's ribbon cutting: "The first principle of Celebration is that no one is actually required to live here."

Of course, designers are always eager to talk about authenticity, or the lack thereof, at Celebration. Here I find myself confused. The styles proscribed in Celebration's pattern book—Classical, Victorian, Colonial Revival—are viewed with suspicion, if not outright contempt, a recipe for stagecraft and fakery. But authenticity is a slippery thing. I live in a 1909 house that the realtor said was Victorian but I'd more accurately call Craftsman Style. Far from "authentic," to me it looks like it was built by someone who had seen some pictures of Greene and Greene houses and thought one might look good in Westchester County. It's surrounded by equally inauthentic hundred-year-old houses, all of which look swell today because they're so old. New Urbanists often say that nostalgia is the Trojan horse in which they deliver their radical planning ideas: small lots, mixed use, limited parking. Jaquelin Robertson once said in Celebration's early days, "This will look great when all these trees grow in." I suspect he's right.

What unnerves me most about Celebration is actually what is not Celebration. Despite the increasing popularity of New Urbanist principles, the country's vast scale means that places like Celebration will remain anomalies, isolated Brigadoons dropped into bleak exurban landscapes. I remember an early planning meeting for the project, where, after hours of talk about picket fences, paving patterns and live oak trees, the discussion turned to the design of a "vertical entry feature," a tall landmark that would provide a target to guide people to the town. We were considering relocating a historic water tower to the site. Then someone said, "Wait: how tall would it be compared to the water slide?" Water slide? What water slide? Well, across the street from the town's entrance was a completely unquaint, moderately tawdry water park, populated by screaming kids and rowdy teens drinking Mountain Dews and eating twist cones. And we suddenly remembered what so much design was being deployed to help us forget: that real life, in all its uncontrolled, aggressive profusion, would be transpiring as usual right across the street from, and indeed all around, this carefully planned precinct.

In the cult novel *Time and Again* by Jack Finney, the modern-day protagonist is enlisted to serve in a secret time-travel experiment. But the experiment doesn't involve molecular transmutation, black holes, or oscillating tunnels. Instead, the hero (oddly enough, a commercial artist who happens to be obsessed with the past) is moved into the nineteenth-century New York City landmark the Dakota, and is gradually surrounded with all the details of 1882 day-to-day life, down to the daily delivery of facsimile newspapers. Finally, with the illusion seamless and complete, it becomes reality: one morning the hero simply wakes up in the real, unsimulated world of 1882, as easy as that. Celebration, speaks to that same yearning, that same science fiction fantasy, and the same promise that one day the fantasy will be made real.

Time travel is only science fiction when it happens suddenly, and compared with most places we like, Celebration happened suddenly. But we travel through time every day of our lives. It's simply at a pace too slow to notice. After only ten years, Celebration may still seem like a fantasy. But eventually, at a rate too slow to notice, those trees will grow in.

The Great Non-Amber-Colored Hope

Every design profession needs its iconic success story. Architects have the Guggenheim Museum in Bilbao. Product designers have the Apple iPod.

And now, at last, graphic designers have an icon to call their very own: a little pill bottle, about four inches tall.

Despite all the claims that designers make for the importance of what they do, it's hard to find examples of successful designs—especially graphic designs—that truly resonate with the general public. Editors face this problem every time they try to assemble a Special Design Issue for a non-design-specialized magazine. You can't make the case for design by showing a lot of esoteric stuff, things that normal people never see, wouldn't understand, or (worst of all) can't buy. So out come the Bilbaos and the iPods, the VW New Beetles and the Oxo Good Grips, accompanied by the usual suspects, Starck and Koolhaas, Ive and Gehry.

Poor graphic design seldom fits the specifications. Even the American Institute of Graphic Arts has a problem with it. Take a look at "What every business needs," a publication the AIGA has published that, in their words, "explains for your client, whether in-house or external, the role designers and designing can play in problem-solving." In it, the power of design is demonstrated with six examples. Three are products: a yellow Beetle, a slightly out-of-date looking iMac, and an Oxo Good Grips potato peeler. They all look vivid and dramatic, self-evident and even inarguable. Without requiring much explanation, the images alone, instantly familiar all, make a case for design as an important part of everyday life.

The other three are from the world of graphic design. They all look a little vague and mushy. There's the cheerful and messy Amazon.com home page, and the functional but hardly elegant FedEx order form: both are iconic because of their ubiquity rather than their questionable formal qualities. The third is the Nike swoosh, an indisputably monumental piece of graphic design that was commissioned from a Portland State art student for $35. The message to clients seems to be that where graphic design is concerned, take your pick: useful but dull or mysterious and cheap.

Then along came Deborah Adler, the designer of the ClearRx pill bottle.

In the tradition of Maya Lin, the design for the ClearRx package was a student project, conceived in the innovative MFA design program at New York's School of Visual Arts. A press release from SVA describes the project's genesis:

> Adler first had the idea to redesign the standard amber-colored prescription bottle when her grandmother accidentally swallowed pills meant for Deborah's grandfather. Adler quickly came to the conclusion that the prescription bottle was not just unattractive—it was actually dangerous. Motivated by a desire to make people's lives easier and safer, in 2002 she designed a comprehensive system for packaging prescription medicine as her Master's thesis. "I wanted to design the bottle so that when you open up your medicine cabinet, you instantly know which is your drug, what the name of the drug is, and how to take it," says Adler. The results are a redesigned prescription and communication system, which includes: the redesigned bottle, easy-to-read label, removable information card, color-coded rings and redesigned warning icons.

As someone who has tried for years to interest the general public in graphic design without much success, I can tell you straight out that this story has it all. The subject is a common object with which nearly everyone is familiar, and with which everyone is frustrated to boot. The problem to be solved is not mere ugliness (although an amber-colored prescription bottle *is* ugly) but literally a matter of life or death. Even the moment of inspiration is appealing: who can't relate to the story of those confused grandparents, and cheer when graphic design comes to the rescue?

And cheer they have. The story of Adler's bottle has been featured in nearly fifty publications, from *Business Week*, *Plastics News*, and *Pharmacy*

Today to the *Providence Sunday Journal,* the *Pittsburgh Tribune-Review,* the *Rocky Mountain Telegram* and the *Honolulu Advertiser. New York* magazine gave the humble package a lavishly illustrated feature story, "The Perfect Prescription," that provided the kind of step-by-step exegesis that magazines usually reserve for more important subjects like apartment renovations. Adler was interviewed on National Public Radio and spoke at the Cooper-Hewitt National Design Museum. The bottle was featured in the Museum of Modern Art's first major design exhibition in its new galleries, Safe: Design Takes on Risk followed by From Master's Thesis to Medicine Cabinet, an exhibition at SVA's Westside Gallery.

Much of this media frenzy has been due in large part to the project's receipt of the ultimate benediction in a market economy: the bottle will be used as the standard pharmacy package at, of all places, Target. The discount retailer is widely regarded as the corporate world's leading design advocate, assuming the halo worn previously by IBM, Apple, and Nike. (Surely in the next edition of the AIGA business design guide, the circle-and-dot will replace the swoosh, no doubt further baffling potential clients who wonder why anything that looks so easy is worth that much fuss.) Target, who Adler contacted through an AIGA connection, paired her with industrial designer Klaus Rosburg; Adler gratefully credits him with making the project a reality, along with Target Creative Director Minda Gralnek and a support team of over one hundred people.

I must confess I did not know Target even had a pharmacy. It's a bit buried on their homepage, down near the bottom in a box hyping their photo studio and grocery coupons. But evidently they do, and they are obviously staking a lot on the competitive advantage that ClearRx will provide. Once you find the pharmacy on the website, it's all about the bottle, and not just the design but the story behind it. We meet the designer, and note the use of the singular: Target knows from their experience with Graves, Starck, and Mizrahi that this is no time to dwell on the kind of large and complex team which brings any beautiful design to the marketplace. So it's in Adler's own voice that we get the now-familiar genesis story. And we also get some nice new touches, including the news that the grandparents have similar names—Helen and Herman—which further accounts for the inadvertant drug-swapping that started the whole thing. From such details are legends made.

Despite all the legend-making, however, there's no mistaking the bottom line: Target, to their credit, knew a superior design when they saw it, worked hard to bring it to market, and are banking on their conviction that it will get them customers. And if ClearRx is a success, you can be sure that no one will be happier than the graphic design community. Starved for years for persuasive proof that graphic design can make a difference, we finally have an icon to call our own. It looks good and it makes the world a better place. It's perfect. I predict we'll see a lot—a lot—of it in the years to come. I just hope we don't overdose.

The Mysterious Power of Context

A while ago, I was designing the identity for a large, fashion-oriented organization. It was time to decide which typeface we'd use for their name. Opinions were not hard to come by: this was the kind of place where people were not unused to exercising their visual connoisseurship. But a final decision was elusive.

We decided to recommend a straightforward sans serif font. Predictably, this recommendation was greeted by complaints. It was too generic, too mechanical, too unstylish, too unrefined. I had trouble responding until I added two more elements to the presentation. The first was a medium weight, completely bland, sans serif "C." "Does this look stylish to you?" I would ask. "Does it communicate anything about fashion or taste?" Naturally, the answer was no.

Then I would show the same letter as it usually appears as the first in a six-letter sequence: CHANEL. "Now what do you think?"

It worked every time. But how?

The answer, of course, is context. The lettering in the Chanel logo is neutral, blank, open-ended: what we see when we look at it is eight decades' worth of accumulated associations. In the world of identity design, very few designs mean anything when they're brand new. A good logo, according to Paul Rand, provides the "pleasure of recognition and the promise of meaning." The promise, of course, is only fulfilled over time. "It is only by association with a product, a service, a business, or a corporation that a logo takes on any real meaning," Rand wrote in 1991. "It derives its meaning and usefulness from the quality of that which it symbolizes."

Everyone seems to understand this intellectually. Yet each time I unveil a new logo proposal to a client, I sense the yearning for that some enchanted evening moment: love at first sight, getting swept off your feet by the never-before-seen stranger across the dance floor. Tell clients "Don't worry, you'll learn to love it," and they react like an unwilling bride getting hustled into an unsuitable arranged marriage. In fact, perhaps designers should spend less time reading Paul Rand and more time reading Jane Austen: after all, it is a truth universally acknowledged that a corporation in possession of a good fortune must be in want of a logo, isn't it? Finding that one perfect logo is worth its own romantic novel.

All of this is compounded by the fact that designers themselves have very little faith in context. We too want the quick hit, the clever idea that will sell itself in the meeting and, even better, jump off the table in design competitions. More than anything, we want to proffer the promise of control: the control of communication, the control of meaning. To admit the truth—that so much is out of our hands—marginalizes our power to the point where it seems positively self-destructive. This is especially true in graphic design, where much of our work's functional requirements are minimal on one hand and vague on the other. "The pleasure of recognition and the promise of meaning" is a nice two line performance specification, but one that's impossible to put to the test.

Yet all around us are demonstrations of how effective a blank slate can be. It's just hard to learn from them. I'd like to think, for instance, that I'd see the potential of a red dot in a red circle if I was designing a logo for a company named Target. But in truth I'd probably say, "What, that's all?" and not let it into the initial presentation. How, after all, could you guarantee that the client would invest forty years in transforming that blank slate into a vivid three-dimensional picture?

Appreciating the power of context takes patience, humility, and, perhaps in the end, a sense of resignation. You sense it in this account of designer Carolyn Davidson's disappointing presentation for her first big ($35) freelance project:

> After sifting through the stack of drawings, Knight and the other men in the room kept coming back—albeit with something less than enthusiasm—to the design that looked like a checkmark.
>
> "It doesn't do anything," Johnson complained. "It's just a decoration. Adidas' stripes support the arch. Puma's stripe supports the ball of the foot. Tiger's does both. This doesn't do either."
>
> "Oh, c'mon," Woodell said. "We've got to pick something. The three stripes are taken."
>
> That was the trouble, thought Davidson. They were all in love with the three stripes. They didn't want a new logo; they wanted an old logo, the one

that belonged to Adidas. Davidson liked [them] but found it disheartening to go out on her very first real job and get this kind of reception.

We all know the ending to this story: the client grudgingly accepted Carolyn Davidson's chubby checkmark, and the rest, as recounted in *Swoosh: The Unauthorized Story of Nike and the Men Who Played There*, is corporate identity history. The swoosh has proven durable enough to stand for the company's dedication to athletic achievement, its opponents' resistance to the forces of global capital, and a lot of things in between. Sometimes, the client is smarter than we think. Give Nike founder Phil Knight credit: he had the vision to admit, "I don't love it. But I think it'll grow on me."

Maybe he believed it. Or maybe he was just tired of trying to decide. Either way, context did the rest.

The Final Days of AT&T

From a press release dated October 27, 2005:

> SBC Communications Inc. today announced it will adopt AT&T, Inc. as its name following completion of its acquisition of AT&T, which is expected in late 2005.
>
> The decision is a milestone in the history of telecommunications, extending the reign of a global icon. AT&T is inextricably linked to the birth and growth of the communications industry, delivering groundbreaking innovations that enabled modern computers and electronic devices, wireless phones, and Voice over IP (VoIP). The brand also has represented quality service, integrity, and reliability for more than 120 years.
>
> At close, the new company will unveil a fresh, new logo. After completion of the merger, the transition to the new brand will be heavily promoted with the largest multimedia advertising and marketing campaign in either company's history, as well as through other promotional initiatives.

So take a long, last look at Saul Bass's finest moment. AT&T will live on, but its logo is about to disappear.

American Telephone & Telegraph was founded in 1885 as a subsidiary of Alexander Graham Bell's Bell Telephone Company to create a long-distance network for Bell's local operating companies. In 1915, AT&T opened transcontinental telephone service, essentially wiring the United States, and added service to Cuba, Great Britain, and Japan by 1934. Along the way, AT&T acquired the assets of the Bell Company and the operating companies of the Bell Telephone System, opened Bell Laboratories (birthplace of the transistor and UNIX), introduced the modem, launched the first commercial satellite, and, with a near monopoly on American telecommunications, became the largest corporation in the world.

From the start, there had been a perfect confluence between the inventor's name and the sound his product made. Best of all, unlike so many other brand names, it was a word that could be represented with a simple picture. The first Bell logo—a realistic drawing of a bell with "Long Distance Service" written on it, created by Bell manager Angus Hibbard—appeared in 1889. It would have this form for over 75 years, with more writing around the bell ("American Telephone & Telegraph Co./Bell System/And Associated Companies") and on it ("Local and Long Distance Service"), all enclosed, after 1900, in a circle. Revisions were made periodically and many of the nearly two dozen operating companies came up with their own variations.

In 1968, Saul Bass was hired to bring order to the system, and created a classic modern identity program. In Nixon-era America, Bass's simplified bell-in-circle logo, rigorous Helvetica-based typographic system, and ochre-and–process blue color scheme became as familiar as the Coca-Cola signature. It was the ideal graphic analog for a phone system that was hailed as the best in the world, a virtually indestructable monopoly posing as a public utility: Ma Bell, utterly reliable and as ubiquitous as air.

But nothing lasts forever, even notionally benevolent monopolies. So everything changed in 1982, when AT&T and the U.S. Justice Department agreed to settle an antitrust suit that had been filed against the company eight years before. AT&T agreed to divest itself of its local telephone operations, and seven independent "baby Bells" came into place. This was a gold rush for identity designers. Gone were the Bell logo, the ochre-and-blue stripes, and familiar names like Ohio Bell and Wisconsin Telephone, names as sturdy and plainspoken as the telephones that Henry Dreyfus had designed for Bell since 1930. On New Year's Day, 1984, Americans awoke to a world in which their telephone service would be provided by newly minted entities with fanciful monikers like Ameritech, USWest, and Pacific Telesis.

AT&T did not cease to exist. On the contrary, not only would it continue its traditional activities as a long-distance service provider, it was now at liberty to pursue business that had been off-limits in its quasi-monopolistic days.

Saul Bass was called back to design the identity that would represent AT&T in this post-divestiture new world order.

And Bass was ready. I've heard from more than one person that Bass had tried without success to sell a striped globe logo to several previous clients (or even "every client that came along" as one insider told me). This may not be true, but there is no doubt that Bass liked round logos with horizontal stripes: witness Continental Airlines and Minolta, to name two. But with the new AT&T, he had at last the big client ready for the big idea. Their logo would be nothing but a sphere, a circle crossed with lines modulated in width to create the illusion of dimensionality. And this client bought it, perhaps because like the bell, this new, seemingly abstract image had a reassuringly literal meaning; at AT&T's online brand center, the logo is described as "a world circled by electronic communications." It's not just a logo, it's a picture of a globe girded by wires and cables. Some people saw even more: in some circles, the sphere was nicknamed the "The Death Star."

Despite Bass's logo, after 1984, nothing was stable again in the telecom business. I have some first hand experience with the early days of AT&T's divestiture, since my wife Dorothy's first job in New York in 1980 was working for AT&T. Or rather, she was hired by AT&T, but actually went to work for one of the corporation's operating units, New York Telephone. Without changing desks or jobs, in the next few years she worked for something called American Bell, which in turn had its name changed to AT&T Advanced Information Systems, and then finally NYNEX. (If she had saved some of her American Bell business cards, she might be making a pretty penny on eBay today: the company lasted only a few months before the Justice Department ruled that no AT&T entity could use the Bell name; this makes an American Bell card the corporate design equivalent of an Inverted Jenny postage stamp.) After she left, NYNEX merged with Bell Atlantic to create Verizon, which some people say has the worst logo in the world.

And now, twenty years later, SBC Communications, Inc., a descendent of Southwestern Bell, has taken over its former parent company: the child becomes the father to Ma, as it were. Their brand strategy lets them have their cake and eat it too. By retaining the AT&T name ("an iconic name... amazing heritage...tremendous strength." —Alan Siegel, Siegel and Gale), they signal continuity. By replacing the Bass sphere with a "fresh, new logo," they signal vitality and change. Who's going to argue with that?

A moment of silence, please. On October 23, 1963, demolition began on New York City's Pennsylvania Station. The controversy over the destruction of this McKim, Mead & White masterpiece effectively launched the historic preservation movement in this country. Today, the proposed demolition of buildings of even questionable architectural merit provokes outcry.

Graphic design, unlike architecture, leaves no footprint. When one of the best-known logos in the world disappears overnight, the only hole created is in our collective consciousness. By New Year's Eve, Saul Bass's sphere will be no more. Will anyone mourn—or protest—its passing?

Designing Twyla Tharp's
Upper Room

In 1986, choreographer Twyla Tharp, coming off horrible reviews for her latest project, an over-elaborate Broadway revival of *Singin' in the Rain*, decided to get back to basics. Remembering the characteristics of one of her favorite pieces from twelve years before, *The Fugue*—"no costumes, no music, no lights, just committed and extraordinary souls doing a hard day's work with intelligence and love"—she decided her next piece would project the same simplicity.

This piece turned out to be *In the Upper Room*. Unlike *The Fugue*, this dance would have costumes (by Norma Kamali) and music (by Philip Glass) and lights (by Jennifer Tipton), but the goal would be a new kind of simplicity. She explained to Tipton and her set designer, Santo Loquasto, how the piece would begin. The lights would come up on two women standing on a bare stage, each striking the stage with one foot and withdrawing back into the space. And then, something amazing would happen: three men would suddenly materialize at the center of the stage. As Tharp puts it in her 1992 memoir, *Push Comes to Shove*, "All I said to Jenny and Santo was, 'I don't care how you do it, they must just appear out of nowhere.'"

And that's basically what happens.

When the subject is great experience design, some designers think of Starbucks. What a pity. I think of *In the Upper Room*.

Set to one of Philip Glass's best, most propulsive scores, *In the Upper Room* is forty continuous minutes of what one reviewer has called "the sheer exuberance of motion." I usually like contrast and dynamics; *In the Upper Room* has none. It starts with the dial set at ten and turns it north of eleven. In those days Tharp had been working with Teddy Atlas, a boxer who had helped train the young Mike Tyson, and it shows; she describes the piece as "a display of athletic prowess based on endurance, power, speed, and timing." It is just about as subtle as Chuck Yeager breaking the sound barrier, and as thrilling.

What is subtle is the way lighting designer Jennifer Tipton met Tharp's impossible challenge, to make the dancers "appear out of nowhere" on an empty stage. Here's how she did it. Thanks to smoke machines, *In the Upper Room* is staged in an even, featureless haze. The dancers are invisible until they are picked out by Tipton's precise, razor-sharp lighting. It's a simple effect, familiar to anyone who has driven a car on a foggy night, but in the hands of this brilliant designer the results are as mesmerizing as anything by James Turrell. As the piece reaches its climax, dancers materialize out of nowhere before your eyes every few seconds. Tipton's lighting is the kind of magic that delights you even when you know exactly how the trick works.

Because it plays such a major role in the production, the lighting for *In the Upper Room* has been much discussed and widely honored. This degree of attention is unusual. Like many designers, Tipton's work is frequently dismissed as that of a technician, a craft worker supporting the real artists. As she observes in "Light Unseen," an essay in the latest issue of *Esopus*,

> To be a lighting designer, one must accept the fact that few people will notice what you do. I have always said that 99 $^{44}/_{100}$ percent of the audience will not see the lighting, but 100 percent of the audience will be affected by it. I had hoped that my art would change that in some small way, but light seems to be too transparent, too ephemeral. We look through it to see the dance or the play, not really noting that there is a person who controls our perception by shaping it and giving it meaning and context.

But every once in a while, the artistry of the lighting designer materializes on stage right in front of you. "*In the Upper Room* is the only piece I've done," Tharp has said, "that generates a standing ovation at almost every performance." It did so again the last time I saw it, when the audience jumped to its feet on cue to applaud Twyla Tharp, Philip Glass, thirteen extraordinary American Ballet Theatre dancers, and—probably without knowing it—the evening's unheralded star, Jennifer Tipton.

Innovation is the New Black

Last month I was invited by Patrick Whitney, director of the Institute of Design at the Illinois Institute of Technology, to participate in a symposium on the "'creative corporation' and the adoption of design by business leaders."

It turned out that the operant word at the symposium wasn't *design* but *innovation*. Yes, innovation. Everyone wanted to know about it. Everyone wanted to talk about it. One of the panelists was *Business Week*'s legendary design advocate Bruce Nussbaum. "When I talk to my editors about design, I have trouble keeping them interested," he confessed. "But there's a tremendous interest in innovation." The lesson to me seemed clear. If we want the business world to pay attention to us, we need to purge the d-word from our vocabularies. That's right: we are all innovators now.

A recent email provides proof of the timeliness of this approach. "Empower Yourself to Innovate," the DMI urges me, sounding suspiciously like Stuart Smalley. A visit to the DMI's website for their upcoming conference, "Empowered Innovation," confirms that the organization has already gotten with the program in a big way. The word "design" is nowhere to be found in the main description of the conference. It finally makes its appearance halfway through a list of conference topics that include "Innovation within an Organizational Context," "Experimentation Matters: New Opportunities for Innovation," and "Culture-Driven Innovation." It turns out that Magdalena De Gasperi from Braun GmbH will be speaking on "The Impact of Innovation and Design on Brand Equity." Design, it appears, is welcome only when properly escorted...by Innovation! And it's no surprise that the organization officially known as the Design Management Institute is using its acronym more and more and letting its formal name wither quietly away, just like KFC did as it sought to distance itself from the greasy brand equity of the words Fried Chicken. I suppose I hardly need to add that the DMI has a blog called—care to guess?—that's right, the Innovation Blog.

This mania for innovation, or at least for endlessly repeating the word "innovation," is just the latest in a long line of fads that have swept the business world for years. In the mid-eighties, Motorola developed a seemingly effective quality management program based on a sophisticated statistical model called Six Sigma, which involved attempting to reduce the number of defects in their business processes to fewer than 3.4 per million. Within a few years, managers everywhere were demanding that their organizations begin "implementing Six Sigma principles." The mystical invocation of the Greek letter; the unnerving specificity of 3.4 per million (as opposed to the presumably unacceptable 3.5 per million); the talismanic power of the bell curve diagram that was often used to "illustrate" the theory: all of this arcana was meant to instill awe in employees who would shrug off a homelier directive like "measure twice, cut once."

It's not hard to see why innovation is becoming the design world's favorite euphemism. Design sounds cosmetic and ephemeral; innovation sounds energetic and essential. Design conjures images of androgynous figures in black turtlenecks wielding clove cigarettes; innovators are forthright fellows with their shirtsleeves rolled up, covering whiteboards with vigorous magic-markered diagrams, arrows pointing to words like "Results!" But best of all, the cult of innovation neatly sidesteps the problem that has befuddled the business case for design from the beginning. Thomas Watson Jr.'s famous dictum "good design is good business" implies that there's good design and there's bad design; what he doesn't reveal is how to reliably tell one from the other. Neither has anyone else. It's taken for granted that innovation, however, is always good.

Everyone wins on the innovation bandwagon. A recalcitrant client may cheerfully admit to having no taste, but no one wants to stand accused of opposing innovation. And a growing number of firms stand ready to lead the innovation charge; a much-talked-about August 2005 article in *Business Week*, "Get Creative! How to Build Innovative Companies," singled out Doblin, Design Continuum, Ziba, and IDEO. In fact, if anyone deserves the credit for inventing the don't-think-of-it-as-design-think-of-it-as-innovation meme, it's IDEO. "Innovation at IDEO," visitors are assured on their website, "is grounded in a collaborative methodology that simultaneously examines user desirability, technical feasibility, and business viability." No idle sitting around and waiting for inspiration to strike at IDEO! Skeptics requiring further persuasion will find it in *The Art of Innovation* and *The Ten Faces of Innovation,* two books that IDEO general manager Tom Kelley has written on the subject.

I was surprised to learn, however, that although innovation is always good, it isn't always effective. "We all know that reliable methods of innovation are becoming important to businesses as they realize that 96% of all innovation attempts fail to meet their financial goals," read the invitation to the Institute of Design symposium, a figure derived from research by Doblin. Now, I suppose you could do worse than failing twenty-four out of every twenty-five tries, but this sounds suspiciously like Albert Einstein's famous definition of insanity: doing the same thing over and over again but expecting a different result. But thank goodness, a solution is at hand: "Business leaders are increasingly looking to design to not just help, but lead their innovation processes." So we come full circle. Don't say design, say innovation, and when innovation doesn't work, make sure you saved some of that design stuff, because you're going to need it.

With this new vision of design-as-innovation identified—somewhat chillingly, if you ask me—in *Business Week* as "the Next Big Thing after Six Sigma" (the ironically intended capitalization is theirs), perhaps a new golden age of respect for designers—or innovators, or whatever you want to call us—is upon us at last. Or maybe it simply announces the availability of a turbo-charged version of the kind of frantic rationalizations that we've always deployed in our desperation to put our ideas across. Either way, I'm reminded of something Charles Eames used to say: innovate as a last resort. Have we run out of options at last?

Wilson Pickett, Design Theorist, 1942–2006

Anyone formulating a methodology for design practice must somehow reconcile two things: the need to address the objective practical requirements of design problems and the desire to create solutions that are original, aesthetically pleasurable, and somehow expressive of the designer's unique point of view. Through the ages, some of our most revered aphorists have attempted to sum it up, from "utilitas, firmitas et venustas," to "form follows function," to "graphic design which evokes the symmetria of Vitruvius, the dynamic symmetry of Hambidge, the asymmetry of Mondrian; which is a good gestalt, generated by intuition or by computer, by invention or by a system of coordinates is not good design if it does not communicate." All good attempts, but too Latin, too overused, too long. Also: they do not rhyme.

Ladies and gentlemen, I give you Mister Wilson Pickett.

When Wilson Pickett, The Wicked One, The Midnight Mover, was interviewed in Gerri Hirshey's wonderful 1984 book *Nowhere to Run: The Story of Soul Music*, he was forty-three, a good decade-plus beyond the years when he dominated the pop charts. Born in Prattville, Alabama, he moved in his early teens to Detroit and was plunged into a tumultuous milieu: Jackie Wilson, Little Willie Brown, Joe Stubbs, Eddie Floyd, dozens of singers and groups all looking for the next big hit. "Style, for soul music, would become paramount," wrote Hirshey. "In a music distinguished by the power and peculiarities of individual voices, the weight would rest on the singer, more than the song, much as it does in gospel." Where does style come from? What was Pickett's secret?

"You harmonize; then you customize."

There it is. You harmonize—you satisfy the basic requirements of the genre, some of which, in music, are as inarguable as mathematics—and then you customize. You fit it to the place you're coming from, to your own particular skills, to the moment you're in. "What kid doesn't want to own the latest model?" Pickett asked Hirshey. "You got no cash for music lessons, arrangers, uniforms, backup bands, guitars. No nothin'. So you look around for a good, solid used chassis. This is your twelve-bar blues. Then you look around for what else you got. And if you come up like most of us, that would be gospel." Pickett said it took "a lot of messin' around and singin' in Detroit alleys" to make it all come together. "Sure, you mixed it up. Customize, like I say."

Harmonize, then customize. I find this as good a model for making great design work as anything else I've ever heard. Design—graphic design at least—is mostly ephemeral. Graphic design artifacts could do worse than aspire to the condition of pop music, which, as Hirshey observes, is "born of infatuations, wave after wave of them, each so true to its era that a two-minute thirty-second song can be a perfectly wrought miniature of a place, a climate, a time."

Wilson Pickett, the man responsible for hits like "Mustang Sally," "Land of 1,000 Dances," and "In the Midnight Hour," and who, with artists and producers like Aretha Franklin, Steve Cropper, Jerry Wexler, and Ahmet Ertegun, helped create the legendary "Muscle Shoals" sound that ruled the airwaves throughout the 1960s, died January 19, 2006, in Ashburn, Virginia. He was sixty-four.

Design by Committee

Design by committee. No one likes it. No one wants it. Even clients disavow it: "We don't want to get you into a design-by-committee situation here," they'll tell you, usually just before they actually start forming a committee to help you design.But every once in a while it works. If you doubt this, look at the complex of buildings that rises on the East River in midtown Manhattan: the headquarters of the United Nations.

> To those outside who question us we can reply: we are united, we are a team: the World Team of the United Nations laying down the plans of a world architecture, world, not international, for therein we shall respect the human, natural and cosmic laws. . . . There are no names attached to this work. As in any human enterprise, there is simply discipline, which alone is capable of bringing order.—Le Corbusier, quoted in *The U.N. Building*

The U.N. Headquarters Building was designed in the spring and summer of 1947, in the rush of optimism that followed the end of World War II. The site was a seventeen-acre wasteland of slaughterhouses and slums at the eastern end of Forty-second Street, purchased for the U.N. for $8.5 million by the Rockefeller family. Le Corbusier, who had submitted a provocative design for the never-realized Palace of the League of Nations twenty years before, was determined to make the U.N. a demonstration of his ideas about architecture and urbanism, and he made sure he was part of the process, actively lobbying the international committee that was charged with planning the U.N.'s home. But the Rockefeller money shifted the balance of power; the project's executive architect and director of planning would be the family's favorite, Wallace K. Harrison, who had worked on Rockefeller Center and, before that, the 1939 World's Fair in Queens. The tug of war between these two architects—Corbu, the intransigent ideologue, and Harrison, the practical company man—would define the terms under which the committee would operate.

"A survey of the history of the U.N. Building's design does not give the reader a sense that anything great could emerge from that tortured and happenstance process," says Aaron Betsky in The U.N. Building, a new book of beautiful photographs by Ben Murphy, former art director of The Face, which has been published by Thames & Hudson in anticipation of the design's sixtieth anniversary. Le Corbusier suggested a list of leading modernist architects to collaborate on the project, but Harrison formed a team of less-well-known and perhaps more malleable designers who had been nominated by the U.N.'s member governments. In addition to Harrison and Corbusier, it included Nikolai Bassov (Soviet Union), Gaston Brunfaut (Belgium), Ernest Cormier (Canada), Liang Seu-Cheng (China), Sven Markelius (Sweden), Oscar Niemeyer (Brazil), Howard Robertson (United Kingdom), Guy Soilleux (Australia), and Julio Vilamajo (Uruguay). (Alvar Aalto, Mies van der Rohe, and Walter Gropius were excluded from the team because Finland and Germany were not then members of the U.N.)

The design process took four months. Harrison's assistant George Dudley kept a journal of the committee's forty-five meetings, eventually published as Workshop for Peace: Designing the United Nations Headquarters. This process, writes Betsky, "was unprecedented in the way it sought to produce a unified design out of the collective labors of a group of architects drawn from so wide a field, and such an idealistic way of working has not been tried since." It was quickly decided to separate out the functions of the institution into separate buildings. The debate, centered on the placement of these components: a general assembly building for delegates to meet; a conference building for meetings of committees and councils; and a secretariat building for the U.N.'s ongoing business. Le Corbusier had been long obsessed with an urban vision of "towers in a park," as opposed to a more modest grouping of smaller structures. Harrison's own, more populist, vision, shaped by the abstract structures of the World's Fair and the urban city-within-a-city at Rockefeller Center, was not entirely incompatible. The design committee generated proposals for every possible configuration of the complex's major elements, including one from Sweden's Sven Markelius, who proposed a curving bridge to connect the site with Queens to permit the U.N.'s future expansion.

In the end, it was not Le Corbusier or Harrison but a young Brazilian architect, Oscar Niemeyer, then not yet forty years old, who developed Corbusier's plan into the configuration that was the basis for the final design. As Betsky writes, "After much jockeying and arguments—Harrison claimed that at one of the meetings Le Corbusier tore all the drawings except his own off the wall and then stomped out (a claim that cannot be verified)—the committee unanimously agreed on a scheme." This arrangement—the low Conference Building on the East River, the bow tie–shaped General Assembly Building to the north, and, rising above it all, the slab of the Secretariat—is what was built, with some modifications, as the design team envisioned it.

More arguments were to follow, particularly over the cladding of the monumental Secretariat, where Le Corbusier demanded a *brise soleil* to provide shade, but lost, predictably, to the more practical Harrison, who suggested a brand-new product called Thermapane which had a distinctive green color and created the "glass wall" which has become indelibly associated with the United Nations. The detailing of the buildings, as well as the interiors, were overseen by Harrison and his firm. Interiors were created by designers as various as Denmark's Finn Juhl (the Trusteeship Council Chamber), Norway's Arnstein Arneberg (the Security Council Chamber), and the original design team's Sven Markelius (the Economic and Social Council Chamber).

"The initial reaction to the building upon its completion in 1952," writes Betsky, "was one of sometimes grudging and even surprised approval. Most critics had not expected this design by committee to work, but most were immediately struck by its effectiveness as image." Some, like Lewis Mumford, observed that the elegant Secretariat tower was still nothing more than an office building, signaling "that the managerial revolution had taken place and that bureaucracy rules the world," while nevertheless conceding that it was "one of the most perfect achievements of modern technics: as fragile as a spiderweb, as crystalline as a sheet of ice, as geometrical as a beehive."

In the half century since, critical opinion of the U.N. Headquarters has had its ups and downs. In 1978, Paul Goldberger called the glass box "a symbol not of progress but of conservatism," and said the U.N. looked "nothing if not old-fashioned, even a bit quaint." Inevitably, it is linked in the public mind to the disappointments that have followed the hopes of those early years. The buildings have not been well maintained, particularly the interiors, and their forlorn quality now project a kind of provincialism that makes the idea of world peace seem sentimental and naive. The U.N. is about to embark on an ambitious program of renovation, restoration, and expansion; one hopes that the physical renewal of the buildings might provoke a renewal of the collaborative ideals that caused them to be built in the first place.

But why be naive? We associate "design by committee" with compromise and acquiescence. Perhaps the secret of the U.N. design committee's success was not its mythic equanimity but rather the unremitting tension between Le Corbusier and Wallace Harrison, tension which continued after the project's completion as each disputed the other's contribution. Years later, Rem Koolhaas described the forced merger between Le Corbusier's "dry theoretical pretension" and Harrison's "polymorphously perverse professionalism" like this: "The U.N. was a building that an American could never have thought and a European could never have built. It was a collaboration, not only between two architects, but between cultures; a cross-fertilization between Europe and America produced a hybrid that could not have existed without their mating, however unenthusiastic."

In these pessimistic times, it's reassuring that enthusiasm is not a prerequisite to success and that conflict, not harmony, can be a source of greatness.

The Persistence of the Exotic Menial

It was September 1981 when design critic Ralph Caplan first unveiled the phrase. He was speaking at a Design Management Institute conference in Martha's Vineyard. His talk was titled "Once You Know Where Management Is Coming From, Where Do You Suggest They Go?"

"I want finally to address in some detail," Caplan said toward the end, "a role that I call 'the designer as exotic menial.' He is exotic because of the presumed mystery inherent in what he does, and menial because whatever he does is required only for relatively low-level objectives, to be considered only after the real business decisions are made. And although this is a horrendous misuse of the designer and of the design process, it is in my experience always done with the designer's collusion."

It's twenty-five years later. Has anything really changed?

Yearning for the spotlight—respect from the business community and attention from the general public—has been a ceaseless, all-consuming theme of ambitious designers for the last quarter century, and maybe long before that. W. A. Dwiggins, the American designer and typographer credited with introducing the term "graphic design," mocked this yearning in a 1941 essay, "A Technique for Dealing with Artists," that purported to advise clients on how they might get the most out of the design process: "If you like the work an artist shows you, do not try to express your approval in the form of apt technical comment. Confine yourself to the simple formula: 'I like that'; or grunt in an approving way." Sounds familiar.

Caplan expanded on his original speech in his 1982 book *By Design*, which was reissued with a new chapter aptly titled "The More Things Change, the More We Stay the Same." In it, he enumerates the ways that the awareness of design has increased among the general public. However, he adds, this increased awareness "cannot be equated with an understanding of design, which is still easily confused with styling."

The confusion is forgivable. Over the past quarter-century, designers have reacted to client disregard by upping the ante in exoticism, so that many of today's well-known professionals are as famous for their sartorial choices as their actual output. Capes and cigarette holders used to be reserved for a few iconic figures like Frank Lloyd Wright and Raymond Loewy, but now designers of all types are eager to cloak themselves in a suitable air of mystery. Eyeglasses, especially, have been a potent device with which to command public attention: witness Daniel Libeskind's square black frames (which provoke cries of "Hey, Mister Architect!" on the sidewalks of New York) or Karim Rashid's rose-colored aviators.

Graphic designers have had no more exciting proponent of this approach than Peter Saville. Greeting visitors to his Mayfair apartment in a silk dressing gown, voted the "most admired individual working within the creative industries," currently in possession of a sinecure at M&C Saatchi that seemingly requires no actual work, surely the indisputably talented Mr. Saville would seem to have it all. Yet even a character this charismatic seems unable to break through to the general public at broader levels. Much excitement in graphic design circles attended the release of *24 Hour Party People*, the story of Factory Records and the Manchester music scene of the 1980s, a scene as much associated with Saville's persona in the minds of designers as that of any of the actual musicians. What a disappointment it was to find the Saville character reduced to a bit part: in the credits, Enzo Cilenti, the actor who played Saville is listed twenty-seventh, right after Tracy Cunliffe, billed as "Other Girl in Nosh Van." And a running gag as well, since the character is usually shown arriving at the Hacienda with freshly-printed invitations to events that took place the night before. The exotic menial strikes again! If Peter Saville can't do it, what chance have we mere mortals?

For those who find that more exotic is not doing the trick, the other line of attack can only be less menial. And designers seem to have lost patience with halfway measures. Design in the service of low-level objectives? Forget about it! Rather than trying to inch up the totem pole, the favored strategy today is to declare that design is the totem pole itself, or perhaps even the whole reservation. Bruce Mau's Massive Change project started with exactly this kind of insight, a napkin sketch transposing design's role from something embedded, pearl-like, within concentric circles representing Nature, Culture, and Business, to something encompassing All of the Above. "No longer associated simply with objects and appearances, design is increasingly understood in a much wider sense as the human capacity to plan and produce desired outcomes," it says elsewhere on the Massive Change website. "Engineered as an international discursive project, Massive Change: The Future of Global Design, will map the new capacity, power, and promise of design. Massive Change explores paradigm-shifting events, ideas, and people, investigating the capacities and ethical dilemmas of design in manufacturing, transportation, urbanism, warfare, health, living, energy, markets, materials, the image, and information." Or, in other words, everything.

Similarly ambitious napkin-based impulses informed the founding of the Institute of Design at Stanford University. The D-School seeks to "tackle difficult, messy problems," the solutions to which are unlikely to be featured in the pages of *I.D.*'s Annual Design Review. These include drunk driving, oppressive commercial airline travel, and the boredom of waiting in line. In a world even more virtual, the NextDesign Leadership Workshop has no napkin but plenty of diagrams nonetheless, repositioning design practice from its tired focus on (menial) things like websites, chairs, buildings, and brands to more visionary, "unframed" problems. The scope of these problems is painted with a big brush: "Unlike traditional design, NextD focuses on building cross-disciplinary leadership skills and behaviors. NextD is designed to not only scale-up problem-solving skills but to make such ability applicable as the primary form of leadership navigation in any kind of problem solving situation. Unlike traditional design, NextD recognizes a multitude of possible value creating outcomes beyond the creation of objects." Tomorrow's designer, it appears, will settle for nothing less than a vast, limitless remit, and keep those goddamn objects out of it, thank you.

NextD, Stanford's D-School. . . a pattern starts to emerge, and it involves the fourth letter of the alphabet. What better way to transcend the earthbound chains of traditional design by abstracting it to a single letter? Indeed, language is an especially vexing problem for the graphic designer. "Most business people—the ones that hire us—think that we are at the table to create the 'look and feel,'" complain the proprietors of the website Beyond Graphic, in a nearly note-for-note reiteration of

Caplan's twenty-five-year-old speech that blames the word "graphic" for our travails. "They see our work as decoration, a nice-to-have after the strategic thinking is performed. This is why graphic designers remain at the bottom of the communications chain—below advertising profession-als, communication consultants, and marketing strategists." Below ad guys: ick. The recommended solution appears to be the substitution of "communication design" for "graphic design." Nice try, but a little behind the curve. More up-to-date is the American Institute of Graphic Arts, now officially known as "AIGA, the professional association for design," leaving generations to come wondering what those four letters once represented. Perhaps in the not-too-distant future we can achieve the perfection of "AIGA, the professional association for D" and final victory over the dreary inhibitions of specificity can be declared once and for all.

Whipsawed between the roles of unchallengably exotic stylemeis-ter and incomprehensibly non-menial solver-of-all-problems, what's a designer to do? As writer Virginia Postrel observed, "The first mistake is to justify design's importance by ignoring its unique contribution. Design-ers say We solve problems, and We can do strategy, and they forget that everyone else is also solving problems and contributing to strategy. The question is what problems can you uniquely solve?

"The second mistake is to swing in the opposite direction and push the style equivalent of basic research when the marketplace wants style's equivalent of applied engineering....Theoretical physics and engine mechanics are different, and both are valuable. So are cutting-edge design and less prestigious, more mundane design. It's important to remem-ber that 'good design' depends on context—good design for whom, for what purpose?"

Good design for whom? And good designers for whom? Thinking about the exotic menial brought Ralph Caplan back to the same point twenty-five years ago. "Making things nice is not making things right," he wrote in *By Design*. "And it is in the rightness of things that consumers have a stake. More than a stake, a role to play. For the designer's final collaborator is the end user." He concluded: "There is an implicit contrac-tual relationship between designer and user and—as with other contractual relationships—the contract may be betrayed."

In our quest for respect, designers spend a lot of time trying to muscle our way to center stage. Maybe we—and the world—would be better off if we spent less time worrying about the spotlight and more time worrying about all those people out there in the dark.

The Road to Hell: Now Paved with Innovation!

Designers don't have many advocates as enthusiastic and highly placed as Bruce Nussbaum. An assistant managing editor at *Business Week*, he's spearheaded the magazine's coverage of design and innovation for years and has become an important online voice for how business can use design as a strategic tool. That influence will only grow with the debut of *INside Innovation*, his new magazine that promises "a deep, deep dive into the innovation/design/creativity space."

I'm as intrigued as the next guy about what's to be found in the dark recesses of the "innovation/design/creativity space." But I suspect there's one fact about the genesis of this new magazine that will disturb many of my fellow innovation enthusiasts: the actual design of *INside Innovation* was created largely through an unpaid competition.

Designers, welcome to the brave new world of spec work.

Nussbaum has described the process of creating *INside Innovation* in real time on his blog with his customary ebullience. Here is his account of how they sought a designer:

> We broke lots of rules designing *IN*—and started changing culture at
> *BW* along the way. We opened the process by holding a contest and
> asking four players to pitch their concepts. You're not supposed to do
> this in mag design land. You're supposed to choose one brilliant design

shop first and work with that firm all the way through to the end. Our Art Director was kind of stunned when I first proposed the idea.

But I wanted to open the process and choose among many new ideas so I opened it up. And we asked three out of four to do it on spec (OK, we didn't have much money either to launch something new). The spec thing is a no-no in AIGA but it turned out it wasn't an issue—the three players who did it on spec said they were willing to do so because the process created new IP that they could use with their other clients.

I'm sure Nussbaum knows there's nothing innovative about the urge to get a lot of different talented people to work for you for free: it's the secret dream of every client I've ever met, each of whom could make a similar claim of poverty, particularly where design budgets are concerned. As for AIGA's attitude about spec work, dismissed here by Nussbaum as a vaguely prudish "no-no," the kind of backward thinking typical of squeamish strangers to the world of innovation, here's what it says in the AIGA code of ethics:

> A professional designer does not undertake speculative work or proposals (spec work) in which a client requests work without compensation and without developing a professional relationship that permits the designer sufficient access to the client to provide a responsible recommendation and without compensation.

Innovation: it's all about breaking the rules! Of course, a code of ethics isn't an "issue" for those change agents who simply decide not to abide by it, which was the decision made by three of the four competitors. Nussbaum doesn't make this clear on his site, but we can make a safe guess that it was the three large firms—IDEO, Stone Yamashita, and the eventual "winner," Modernista—that worked for free, and David Albertson, with a small three-person studio, who got paid. It's to Nussbaum and *Business Week*'s credit that anyone got paid at all, of course, but this does point out another troubling fact of life in spec world: it's a game that only the bigger firms can afford to play for long. The official rationale of how the big three transcended any qualms they may have had about the dusty old AIGA code of ethics—their interest in generating intellectual property that they might use for other clients—is plausible, I guess, if you consider a new way of handling the page numbers on the table of contents as portable "intellectual property." More likely their reasons were the obvious, more plainly self-serving ones: an eagerness to make a deposit in the favor bank of a well-connected journalist, the prospect of some good publicity (and Nussbaum, again to his credit, has been generous in providing it for all four), and the dream of a big score should the gamble pay off.

Ah, the big score. Unpaid competitions have been a way of life in other creative fields like architecture and advertising, but they've been resisted, barely, by graphic designers up until now. In those other cases, the potential prize is big: for architects, a chance to keep a studio busy for years on an important, visible project; for agencies, millions of dollars in commissions on advertising space. Still, it's amazing how often these competitions degenerate into debacles: witness the grinding entropy at Manhattan's World Trade Center site, or read the best book on advertising ever written, Randall Rothenberg's *Where the Suckers Moon*, which tells the story of a bloody (and ultimately fruitless) battle for the Subaru account back in the mid-nineties.

Spec competitions have been getting more popular in the context of digital communications, where working for free seems to get confused with the idealism of the open source movement. Indeed, the mothership of open sourcing, Wikipedia, is an unpaid contest to redesign their site. No one has nailed the ludicrousness of this practice as accurately as creative director Andy Rutledge, who has put forward the following hilarious analogy:

> I need a partner with whom to have a serious relationship but I don't want to invest any time or effort in finding the right woman; I shouldn't have to. I'm a great man and any woman should be proud to be with me, so I'm holding auditions. I'd like for all interested women to visit me and show me your "wares." I'm definitely looking for someone with a hot bod, and not afraid to show it off. Extra points for staying the night and letting me sample your attentions and enthusiasm.
>
> One lucky winner gets a $400 wedding ring and the prestige of having me for a partner ('cause I look good). The rest of you just get screwed. Awright, who's with me?

Tempting! Full disclosure time: I was approached about working on this project. I really like, and respect, Bruce Nussbaum, so I thought long and hard about it. Luckily, my position in a large firm permits me to work for free, and I regularly do so, for a large range of pro bono clients. Moreoever, if ethics were an issue, it was made clear to me (once again, to Nussbaum's credit) that I could suggest a fee, although I was told some of the others were working for free. In the end, to be perfectly honest, it wasn't the money (or lack thereof) that made the difference for me, but rather something I've learned the hard way: I stink at competitions.

Partly this is sheer egocentricism. I like that old-fashioned model that Nussbaum was eager to discard, the process by which you "choose one brilliant design shop first and work with that firm all the way through to the end." I like being that brilliant design shop. Moreover, if I'm doing a project, I devote myself to it single-mindedly. I expect the same kind of single-minded focus from the client.

In this specific case, I was baffled by how one was supposed to create something as intricate, as complicated as a magazine design in a blind competition. Were the players just supposed to go off and concoct layouts that said *innovation!* in a vacuum? I've found the success of every design project depends on a close give-and-take between the designer and client; this is especially true in editorial projects, which require an airtight fit between form and content. Hard enough to do with an editor at your elbow; impossible staring a blank piece of paper in an empty studio. Okay, I suppose it must be possible. Just not by me.

Finally, I'm both really busy on one hand, and secretly lazy on the other. What motivates me more than anything else is the conviction that my clients are depending on me: if we don't come through for them, there's no back up. The responsibility is mine and mine alone. Knowing that three or four other teams are toiling away at the same challenge, rather than whetting my competitive spirit, simply brings out the slacker in me. When the players are good—and IDEO, Stone Yamashita, Albertson, and Modernista are good—my attitude is knock yourself out, guys, I'm going home early tonight.

I'm not surprised Modernista won: as an ad agency, they're well familiar with the art of the unpaid pitch, and they're not just any agency, they're led by one of our best designers, Gary Koepke. Koepke is a great art director with the design of, among other things, *Vibe* magazine to his credit. And Bruce Nussbaum is even more excited than usual about the design that Modernista has created, calling it "modern, clean, elegant, perfect."

So my feelings about seeing *INside Innovation* this week couldn't be more mixed. On one hand, we desperately need a great magazine about design directed to a general audience, and I can't imagine anyone better than Bruce Nussbaum and *Business Week* to deliver it. On the other, the better it is, the better it will make the case for a design process that I feel is fundamentally wrong. If getting great work for free works for someone as smart and influential as Bruce Nussbaum, what's to stop every businessperson in the world from enthusiastically jumping on the bandwagon?

If this is innovation, I say to hell with it.

When Design is a Matter of Life or Death

You've taken on a design challenge and come up with a solution that's been widely admired and won you accolades. But a year or so later, you realize you made a mistake. There's something horribly wrong with your design. And it's not just something cosmetic—a badly resolved corner, some misspaced type—but a fundamental flaw that will almost certainly lead to catastrophic failure. And that failure will result not just in embarrassment, or professional ruin, but death, the death of thousands of people.

You are the only person that knows that something's wrong. What would you do?

This sounds like a hypothetical question. But it's not. It's the question that structural engineer William LeMessurier faced on a lonely July weekend almost thirty years ago.

LeMessurier was the structural engineer for Citicorp Center, arguably the most important skyscraper built in Manhattan in the years of the 1970s recession. Most people who know this landmark know it for two things: its distinctive, diagonal crown, and the four towering columns centered on each of its sides that seem to levitate it above Lexington Avenue. Architect Hugh Stubbins deliberately moved the columns from the corners in order to accomodate St. Peter's Church, which had long stood on the site's northwestern edge. William Le Messurier and his engineers had to figure out how to make sure the building would stand up on this unusual base. Their solution, a series of diagonal braces and a rooftop damper to limit the structure's sway, was acclaimed for its elegance and innovation.

A year after the building's opening, LeMessurier recieved a call from a student working on a paper, asking about the unusual position of the columns. LeMessurier answered the question, but something about the conversation started him thinking. He revisited his calculations and began to realize that under certain wind conditions, the bracing might not be sufficient to stabilize the building. A series of seemingly trivial mistakes and oversights, none significant alone, had combined to create a potentially dangerous situation. His concern mounting, he consulted a fellow engineer named Alan Davenport, an authority on the effect that winds have on tall buildings. Davenport reexamined the data and confirmed his worst fears: as it was currently designed, sufficiently high winds could indeed knock down the Citicorp building. Those wind conditions, LeMessurier was told, occur once every sixteen years.

The story of William LeMessurier and Citicorp Center was first told in a brilliant *New Yorker* article by Joe Morgenstern in 1995, "The Fifty-Nine-Story Crisis." In it, Morgenstern describes what LeMessurier faced as he realized that his greatest achievement was instead a disaster waiting to happen: "possible protracted litigation, probable bankruptcy, and professional disgrace." It was the last weekend in July. The height of hurricane season was approaching. He sat down in his summer house to try to figure out what to do. Morgenstern describes what happened next:

> LeMessurier considered his options. Silence was one of them; only Davenport knew the full implications of what he had found, and he would not disclose them on his own. Suicide was another: if LeMessurier drove along the Maine Turnpike at a hundred miles an hour and steered into a bridge abutment, that would be that. But keeping silent required betting other people's lives against the odds, while suicide struck him as a coward's way out and—although he was passionate about nineteenth-century classical music—unconvincingly melodramatic. What seized him an instant later was entirely convincing, because it was so unexpected: an almost giddy sense of power. "I had information that nobody else in the world had," LeMessurier recalls. "I had power in my hands to effect extraordinary events that only I could initiate. I mean, sixteen years to failure—that was very simple, very clear-cut. I almost said, thank you, dear Lord, for making this problem so sharply defined that there's no choice to make."

LeMessurier returned to Boston and told the building's architect, his friend Hugh Stubbins, what he had discovered, that Stubbins's masterpiece was fatally flawed. As LeMessurier told Morgenstern, "he winced," but understood immediately what needed to be done. The two men went to New York and told John Reed and Walter Wriston, respectively Citicorp's executive vice-president and chairman, everything. "I have a real problem for you, sir," LeMessurier began.

Remarkably, and perhaps disarmed by the engineer's forthrightness, the bankers didn't waste time assigning blame or brooding about how to spin the situation, but simply listened to LeMessurier's ideas about how the building could be fixed, and committed themselves to do whatever it took to set things right. With Leslie Robertson, the engineer of the World Trade Center, the team devised a plan to methodically reinforce all the bracing joints a floor at a time. The repairs would take the better part of three months, with work happening around the clock. Evacuation plans were put in place; three decades ago it was unimaginable that a building would fall down in Manhattan, and no one knew how extensive the damage might be. In the midst of it all, on Labor Day weekend, a hurricane began bearing down on the northeast. It veered out to sea before the building could be tested. All of these events were largely unknown until Morgenstern's *New Yorker* story, because of a bit of luck for LeMessurier and Citicorp: New York's newspapers went on strike the week the repairs began.

By mid-September, the building was fully secure and the crisis had passed. In the aftermath, Citicorp agreed to hold the architect, Hugh Stubbins, harmless. And, amazingly, although there were accounts that the repairs cost more than eight million dollars (the full amount has never been disclosed), the bank opted to settle with LeMessurier for two million, the limit of his professional liability insurance. The engineer was not ruined. In fact, as Morgenstern observes, LeMessurier "emerged with his reputation not merely unscathed but enhanced." His exemplary courage and candor set the tone. As Arthur Nusbaum, the building's project manager, put it, "It started with a guy who stood up and said, 'I got a problem, I made the problem, let's fix the problem.'" It almost seemed that as a result everyone involved behaved admirably.

We designers call ourselves problem solvers, but we tend to be picky about what problems we choose to solve. The hardest ones are the ones of our own making. They're seldom a matter of life or death, and maybe for that reason they're easier to evade, ignore, or leave to someone else. I face them all the time, and it's a testimony to one engineer's heroism that when I do, I often ask myself one question. It's one I recommend to everyone: what would William LeMessurier do?

In Praise of Slow Design

I got what I wanted for Christmas: *The Complete New Yorker*, which, as you probably know, is a digital archive of every issue of the weekly magazine since its first on February 21, 1925, on eight DVDs: every cover, every page, every story, every cartoon, every ad. I've been going through it compulsively ever since. I've read the work of Dorothy Parker, J. D. Salinger, Robert Benchley, Pauline Kael, Robert Caro, and Raymond Carver as subscribers first did; wallowed in the nightclub listings that conjure a lost world where "there's Billie Holiday to listen to" at the Downbeat on 52nd; and gaped at covers, funny and tragic, by Charles Addams, Saul Steinberg, Art Spiegelman, and Maira Kalman. From a journalistic, literary, and historical point of view, *The New Yorker* archive is endlessly fascinating.

And from a design point of view? Unbelievably boring. Or, I should say, unbelievably, wonderfully, perfectly, exquisitely boring. To a field that today seems to prize innovation above all else, *The New Yorker* makes a case for slow design: the patient, cautious, deliberate evolution of a nearly unchanging editoral format over decades. And the case they make is—let's admit it—pretty hard to argue with.

Incongruously, the magazine that set the standard for sophisticated urbanity for much of the twentieth century was founded by (in the words of playwright Ben Hecht) "a man who looked like a resident of the Ozarks and talked like a saloon brawler." Harold Ross was a Colorado miner's son and high school dropout who worked as a journeyman reporter and editor of the U.S. Army's newspaper before arriving in New York in 1923. There he fell in with a group of writers and artists, many of whom, like George S. Kaufman, Alexander Woollcott, and Dorothy Parker, already had established reputations in the city, and who would become the core contributors of a magazine he started two years later. "*The New Yorker* will be a reflection in word and picture of metropolitan life," Ross wrote in his prospectus for potential investors, adding that it "will be the magazine which is not edited for the old lady in Dubuque." He would be its editor for the next twenty-six years.

Rea Irvin was a member of Ross's original circle, and more than anyone else, was responsible for the way *The New Yorker*'s first issue looked and, to a remarkable degree, for the way it looks today. An artist and art director most recently of *Life* magazine, Irvin established the visual conventions that would endure through the publication's history, including the logo, set in a handdrawn font used throughout the magazine and still referred to today as "Irvin type," and the first cover, which introduced the monocled dandy "Eustace Tilly" as the magazine's de facto mascot. It also created the basic format for all the covers to come: a full-bleed illustration, the subject of which seldom if ever had any relationship to the issue's contents, with a band of color down the left hand side.

Many of the magazine's most idiosyncratic conventions bespoke an almost neurotic reticence. For forty-five years, *The New Yorker* had no table of contents. Ross's successor William Shawn introduced them without comment in 1969. Until the October 5, 1992 issue, bylines were placed unobtrusively at the end of articles, when they appeared at all, almost as an afterthought. "Regular readers of *The New Yorker* will note in this issue a number of changes in the magazine's format and design," warned the magazine's fourth editor, Tina Brown, and beginning with that issue, bylines finally appeared beneath the headlines. In the following months, *le deluge*: Brown would introduce brief article summaries (a.k.a. "decks") and photography to the interior, bringing in Richard Avedon, Gilles Peress, and Robert Polidori as regulars. The incorporation of these features—a table of contents, bylines, photographs—utterly commonplace in nearly every other general-interest magazine on earth, were each regarded as a revolutionary, even shocking, innovation within the pages of *The New Yorker*. Nonetheless, a comparision of that first issue to the one that arrived in my mailbox last week reveals more similarities than differences.

Publication design is a field addicted to ceaseless reinvention. Sometimes a magazine's redesign is generated by a change in editorial direction. More often, the motivation is commercial: the publisher needs to get the attention of fickle ad agency media buyers, and a new format—usually characterized as ever more "scannable" and "reader-friendly"—is just the thing. In contrast, one senses that each of the changes in *The New Yorker* was arrived at almost grudgingly. Designers are used to lecturing timid clients that change requires bravery. But after a certain point—eighty years?—*not* changing begins to seem like the bravest thing of all.

There is a slow design movement out there. "Daily life has become a cacophony of experiences that disable our senses, disconnect us from one another and damage the environment," say the designers of the not-for-profit slowLab. "But deep experience of the world—meaningful and revealing relationships with the people, places, and things we interact with—requires many speeds of engagement, and especially the slower ones." Inspired by other global "slow" movements in food and city planning, slow design is not just about duration or speed, but about thoughtfulness, deliberation, and—how else to put it?—tender loving care.

I imagine there are designers who would find *The New Yorker* exasperating. And certainly its timelessness can be interpreted as an attempt to hold on to a fantasy, an idea of the way life should be lived, against all odds. As musician and writer Momus observes on his site in a discussion about slow magazines, for their readers, "magazines, as well as representing lived lifestyles, also represent aspirations, dreams, and compensations for lifestyles they don't show." Or, to quote a letter the magazine received in 1956, after Ross had rerun—for the twenty-fifth time—the same illustration of Eustace Tilly to celebrate *The New Yorker*'s anniversary: "Since we have been subscribing since 1926 or '27, I feel I can address you as a close friend. I just want to thank you for the February 25th cover. The sight of Eustace Tilley [sic] cheered me, so unchanged in a chaotic world (from a doctor's wife in Albany to a widow in Nebraska....Please don't change, ever."

But *The New Yorker* has changed, and will keep changing. The latest update happened in 2000, when current editor David Remnick decided, among other things, to restructure the typography of the theater and movie listings and commissioned—are you ready?—the ultimate modernist, Massimo Vignelli. To his credit, Vignelli fully understood the delicacy of the situation and acted (unnoticed by nearly everyone) with the precision of a surgeon.

That delicacy has seldom been demonstrated as effectively as in the magazine's issue of August 31, 1946. Like many others, I read John Hersey's book *Hiroshima* in high school. I only found out much later that this account of the dropping of the first atomic bomb had been commissioned by *The New Yorker,* and that upon its receipt William Shawn convinced his boss Harold Ross to run the entire piece in a single issue. I was curious to see the article as it first ran, and it was the first thing I looked up once I had *The Complete New Yorker* loaded on my computer. On the opening page is the following note: "*The New Yorker* this week devotes its entire editorial space to an article on the almost complete obliteration of a city by one atomic bomb, and what happened to the people of that city. It does so in the conviction that few of us have yet comprehended the all but incredible destructive power of this weapon, and that everyone might well take time to consider the terrible implications of its use." At the top of the page sits Eustace Tilly in his customary spot. The story continues through the customary cartoons and ads for luxury goods. Any other magazine, I'm convinced, would have broken with convention and run a huge SPECIAL ISSUE! banner on the front. Instead, the cover is a pleasant summer picnic scene by Charles Martin.

Shawn and Ross urged Hersey to make the devastation as immediate as possible to their magazine's readers. It begins: "At exactly fifteen minutes past eight in the morning, on August 6, 1945, Japanese time, at the moment when the atomic bomb flashed above Hiroshima, Miss Toshiko Sasaki, a clerk in the personnel department of the East Asia Tin Works, had just sat down at her place in the plant office and was turning her head to speak to the girl at the next desk." In effect, it was an everyday moment, no more significant than the moment depicted on the cover. And, presented between the covers of a seemingly changeless magazine to creatures of habit expecting comfort, a devastating reminder of how quickly everything can change.

Massimo Vignelli's Pencil

Nothing could ever quite prepare you for your first visit to Massimo Vignelli's office on Manhattan's far west side.

475 Tenth Avenue is a lone white building in a curiously desolate part of New York City. At fourteen stories, it looms over the parking lots, garages, train yards, and vacant lots that surround it. Boarding the elevator, you might be reassured by some of the stops on your way to the penthouse floor. You'd pass Gwathmey Siegel & Associates on three, Richard Meier on six. As the door opened and closed, you might glimpse architectural models in glass vitrines, pristine drawings in simple frames and wonder: might this unprepossessing address actually be a design mecca?

But the last stop on the fourteenth floor was different. White doors in a mammoth frame would swing wide to admit you to a reception area that had no models under glass, no drawings on the wall. Instead, a featureless, utterly uniform gray floor and white, white walls. A spray of apple blossoms in a cylindrical vase on a round steel table. Nearly a block away, four matching chairs. And, directly before you, a cruciform metal enclosure into which, somehow, a receptionist had been inserted.

There were many potential clients who at this moment would realize that Vignelli Associates was not for them. They would make their visit as short as politely possible. But there were always a few who stepped over that threshold and felt as if they were home at last. They would linger over every detail in their tour of the 15,000-square-foot space: the Donald Judd–like cubic wooden workstations, the block-long wall of corrugated galvanized steel, the cubic volume of the intimate library, the James Bond effect of the pyramid-shaped skylight that could be silently closed with the touch of an invisible button.

If you were there to see Massimo, your tour would end in his office. Sitting before the giant steel plate that served as his desk, with walls clad in beeswax-rubbed lead panels to your right and a staggering view of the Empire State Building to your left, your gaze would come to rest, inevitably, on the only things on the table: a single black mechanical pencil resting upon a stack of blank, white paper.

I worked for Massimo Vignelli for ten years. Like everyone else in the office, I had my own copy of that pencil, even down to the mandatory thick 6B lead. Massimo wouldn't have had it any other way. Unlike many designers, he didn't mind being imitated. On the contrary, he prided himself on creating solutions that could be replicated, systems that were so foolproof that anyone could do them. I sometimes suspected that he had a secret (or not so secret) desire to design everything in the world. Since that was impossible even for a man of his substantial energy, he decided instead to enlist an army of disciples to design the world in his own image.

There were days when it almost seemed possible. You could fly into New York on American Airlines, find your way to the New York City subway, shop at Bloomingdale's, dine at Palio, and even worship at St. Peter's Church and never be out of touch with a Vignelli-designed logo, signage system, shopping bag, table setting, or pipe organ. With his wife, Lella, some longtime collaborators like David Law and Rebecca Rose, and an ever-changing but surprisingly small group of designers, interns, and acolytes, Massimo managed an output that would put offices ten times the size to shame.

Always optimistic, never cynical, Massimo had a hunger for new design challenges and approached every job as if he had never done such a thing before. Even creating something as simple as a business card (and a Vignelli-designed business card was nothing if not simple) would require sketch after sketch as Massimo tried to coax a few trusted elements and a famously limited palette of typefaces into some surprising new form. And when the pieces finally came together, inevitably no one would be as genuinely delighted as Massimo.

And what form of salesmanship is as effective as genuine enthusiasm? Massimo's presentation technique was as legendary as it was impossible to duplicate. With a client team in rapt attention, he would neatly straighten a stack of 19-inch square mounted drawings face down on the table before him. He would rest his fingertips on the top board, look around the room and pause as if to control an almost uncontainable excitement. Then, unable to wait a second longer, Massimo would burst out, "Wait until you see what we have for you today. It's...fantastic!" A carefully wrought presentation would follow, but for much of the audience the sale was already rung up. My God, you could see them thinking, if this guy is so sure, who are we to argue?

That passion is what many of Vignelli's critics miss when they group him with a generation of designers dedicated to a sterile brand of modernism. To be sure, he has always argued for functionalism and clarity. But the rationalism of modernism requires absolute self control, and in fact makes a fetish of a certain kind of self denial. Instead, Massimo's signature gestures—the expressionistic black stripes in the print work, the surreal contrasts of scale in the architecture, the inevitable intrusion of sensuality in the product design—were utterly intuitive, almost indulgent, and clearly as impossible for him to resist as breathing.

Later in his career, Massimo had begun designing clothes, simple ensembles in black and neutrals that someone once said made him look like "a Marxist priest at a pajama party." I repeated the quip for years until I realized what a perfect description it was of his singular combination of doctrinal rigor, religious fervor, and joy.

The lease on that space at 475 Tenth Avenue finally ran out and the rent increase was impossible to support. Massimo and Lella decided the time had come at last to close the office and to work out of their home. I was summoned last October to collect some things I had forgotten when I left Vignelli Associates ten years before. Stepping into that office was—as it always was for me—a homecoming. The packing up had been underway for weeks, and the office was almost empty, although the difference between empty and full would have been hard for many to detect.

The Vignellis were already gone, busy making their home office into a place that could inspire awe in another generation of clients and acolytes. Massimo's office was empty, but the black pencil and white pad of paper were in their customary place. I picked up the pencil to leave a note and the familiarity of the sensation shocked me: I had switched to easier to find (and easier to lose) cheap black pens a long time ago. And when I looked at what I had written, I noticed something funny about the handwriting. It looked just like Massimo's.

On Falling Off a Treadmill

Falling off a treadmill is an interesting experience. I turned forty and my wife bought me a membership to a health club. I had been a dutiful, if not doleful, jogger for years. My regular schedule was to run three miles five mornings a week, but of course it was hard to keep to this schedule, especially in the winter. I don't like to get up in the morning in general, especially when it's cold, and especially when I have to go outside and run for thirty minutes.

Then, of course, even when I could bring myself to run outside it was not without its considerable perils. Uneven terrain, sharp rocks, enormous wild geese. I also had a tendency to throw out my back, which could provide me with an excuse to not run again for weeks on end. There were other 6 a.m. excuses that I don't remember as clearly. One of them had to do with the Hale-Bopp comet.

The membership to the health club was supposed to change all this. I would now be able to exercise in a custom-designed, climate-controlled, year-round, goose- and comet-free environment. As a designer, I think I also felt compelled to favor the manmade over the natural.

I had never even set foot in a gym before. Several years ago, my partner Jim had designed a very cool-looking one full of cunning stair details, which I knew well from slides. Also, there was the 1988 movie *Perfect*, featuring Jamie Lee Curtis ("They call her the Pied Piper of aerobics") and a pre-comeback John Travolta. It was meant to be a sort of *Urban Cowboy* set in the world of health clubs, and I had seen it many times, mostly because of my enthusiasm for Travolta's delivery of a line to Jamie Lee that went something like, "You know, health clubs are like a modern expression of Emersonian transcendentalism. You are so hot."

The day of my first visit to the gym was ideal: bleak, cold, and drizzly, the kind of morning I would have definitely avoided in bed had I not had a modern expression of Emersonian transcendentalism to repair to. I knew at first glance from the conspicuous lack of cunning stair details that my new health club had not been designed by my partner Jim or anyone else with much imagination. It was an anonymous, functional space. The big design idea seemed to be the color blue, which had been deployed with a relentlessness that was mirrored by the floor plan: row after row of well-used machines.

A trainer gave me a tour of the equipment. Where the space was anonymous and unmemorable, the machines were well-designed dramatizations of form following function. There were devices that simulated things I did every day, like climbing stairs. There were also devices that simulated things I had never done and had no intention of doing, like rowing and cross-country skiing. The only device I was interested in was the treadmill, which I understood would simulate running three miles in ideal weather over perfectly even terrain.

If you've ever tried running on a treadmill, you know it takes some getting used to. It took me several weeks to master that peculiar sort of concentration that after time settles into a kind of dazed self-hypnosis. In the artificial world, there are no natural distractions like geese or comets. Instead, there are the similarly hypnotized people around you. There were also three television sets: one tuned to CNN, one tuned to MTV or VH-1, and another that, interestingly, always seemed to be showing golf. I never wore the headphones that could be tuned to pick up the sound, so while I ran I was treated to an ever-changing array of large-screen images: In those days, it was usually O. J. Simpson's house, Joan Osborne's nose ring, some guy swinging a Big Bertha while keeping his head down. There were also the controls on the machine itself. The numbing dullness of the routine made watching the time counter pass, say, 19.57 (the year of my birth) as exciting a landmark as making the last turn around the big tree used to be in the old days when I used to risk running outside.

That made falling off the treadmill all the more jarring. I had been running for about a month when I did something I later learned you should never do: I turned my head and looked behind me. I later told my wife that I had heard a "funny noise," but I later admitted that I thought I had spotted a Jamie Lee Curtis lookalike passing by on a balcony over the equipment floor. The wayward glance goes unpunished on the sidewalk but not on the treadmill. I became disoriented, lost my footing and fell down. I am practiced at falling on everything from asphalt tracks to gravel paths, but falling off a moving treadmill was something new. First you fall, then you sort of bounce off the moving belt, try unsuccessfully to gain purchase on it, bounce again, and finally are flung off the machine like a conveyor belt spitting out a hunk of scrap metal.

Around me, people shouted: Was I okay? Did I need help? I was bruised and embarrassed, but basically fine. The worst part was the trauma of the abrupt intrusion of hard reality to the waking dream of synthetic exercise. I had to sit on the floor for a few moments before I quite knew what had hit me. All around me, my fellow exercisers had determined that I was okay, and retreated into their own private realities. No one had gotten off their machines.

I went outside and it was an unseasonably warm, sunny day. The next day I went back to the gravel path I used to run on, the one with the geese. It was undesigned, at least not by human beings. Maybe some things should be left that way.

Appendix

1 **Warning: May Contain Non-Design Content**
Set in Absara, designed by Xavier Dupré, 2004
First appeared in a slightly different form on *Design Observer*, March 18, 2006.
To my embarrassment, my first $1,000 project is still available: Robert Stearns, *Robert Wilson: From a Theater of Images* (Cincinnati: Contemporary Arts Center, 1980).

2 **Why Designers Can't Think**
Set in Atma Serif, designed by Alan Greene, 2001.
First appeared in *Statements: The American Center for Design*, Spring 1988.
The division between "process" and "portfolio" schools is not as pronounced now as it was in the late eighties; nor are design students as sheltered from culture and politics. Nonetheless, there is still a division between schools that stress theory versus vocational training, and most designers enter the field without much exposure to issues outside of design.

3 **Waiting for Permission**
Set in Avance, designed by Evert Bloemsma, 2001.
First appeared in a slightly different form in *Rethinking Design*, Mohawk Paper Mills, 1992.
The quote from Milgram comes from his account of the experiments, originally published in 1974 and available in an anniversary edition: Stanley Milgram, *Obedience to Authority: An Experimental View* (New York: Harper Perennial Modern Classics, 2004). A vivid description of the obedience experiments and their aftermath can also be found in Lauren Slater's *Opening Skinner's Box: Great Psychological Experiments of the Twentieth Century* (New York: W.W. Norton & Company, 2004.) Finally, to come full circle, Chip Kidd's upcoming sequel to *The Cheese Monkeys* is reportedly set in the New Haven milieu that Milgram shared with Paul Rand and Bradbury Thompson.

4 **How to Become Famous**
Set in TheSans, designed by Lucas de Groot, 1994.
First appeared in *Communication Arts*, 1995.
The dated advice about slide projectors is preserved here as a historical curiosity.

5 **In Search of the Perfect Client**
Set in Baskerville, based on a design by John Baskerville, c.1760.
First appeared as "Three Little Words" in *I.D.*, 1995.
Watson's description of his encounter with the Olivetti showroom is in his autobiography: Thomas J. Watson, Jr., *Father, Son & Company: My Life at IBM and Beyond* (New York: Bantam Books, 1990). Peter Lawrence's quote is in his column in the January/February 1994 issue of *I.D.* Paul Rand's opinion piece is reprinted as "Failure by Design" in his collection *From Lascaux to Brooklyn* (New Haven: Yale University Press, 1996).

6 Histories in the Making

Set in Avenir, designed by Adrian Frutiger, 1988.

First appeared in *Eye*, no. 17, Summer 1995.

A review of three special issues of *Visible Language*: Andrew Blauvelt, editor, *New Perspectives: Critical Histories of Graphic Design, Part 1: Critique*, Volume 28.3 (1994); *New Perspectives: Critical Histories of Graphic Design, Part 2: Practices*, Volume 28.4 (1994); *New Perspectives: Critical Histories of Graphic Design, Part 3: Interpretations*, Volume 29.1 (1995).

7 Playing by Mr. Rand's Rules

Set in Bembo, based on a design by Francesco Griffo, 1495.

First appeared in *Eye*, no. 18, Autumn 1995.

A review of Paul Rand, *Design, Form, and Chaos* (New Haven: Yale University Press, 1993). I mention Rand's book, *A Designer's Art* (New Haven: Yale University Press, 1985).

8 David Carson and the End of Print

Set in Bulmer, designed by Morris Fuller Benton, 1927.

First appeared in *Eye*, no. 20, Spring 1996.

A review of David Carson, *The End of Print* (San Francisco: Chronicle Books, 1995).

9 Rob Roy Kelly's Old, Weird America

Set in Knockout, designed by Jonathan Hoefler, 1999.

First appeared on *Design Observer*, February 2, 2004.

Everyone should own Kelly's *American Wood Type, 1828–1900: Notes on the Evolution of Decorated and Large Types and Comments and Related Trades of the Period*, available most easily in its new edition (Cambridge: Da Capo Press, 1977). Griel Marcus's essay on Harry Smith appears in *The Old, Weird America: The World of Bob Dylan's Basement Tapes* (New York: Picador, 1997). *The Anthology of American Folk Music* was reissued by Smithsonian Folkways in 1997.

10 My Phone Call to Arnold Newman

Set in Celeste, designed by Christopher Burke, 1995.

First appeared on *Design Observer*, June 14, 2006.

11 Howard Roark Lives

Set in Century Expanded, designed by Morris Fuller Benton, 1900.

First appeared as " A Textbook Case" in *Interiors* (July 1996),

Ayn Rand's *The Fountainhead*, originally published in 1943, is available in a paperback anniversary edition (New York: Signet, 2003). Rand also wrote the screenplay for the 1949 movie version starring Gary Cooper and directed by King Vidor. The seminal anti-heroic view of design can be found in Robert Venturi, *Complexity and Contradiction in Modern Architecture* (New York: Museum of Modern Art, 2002), first published in 1966.

12 The Real and the Fake

Set in Arial, designed by Robin Nicholas and Patricia Saunders, 1982.

First appeared as "That's Entertainment" in *Interiors* (June 1997),

This essay was provoked by reading Ada Louise Huxtable, *The Unreal America: Architecture and Illusion* (New York: New Press, 1999). The scathing assessment of my beloved Sixth Avenue appears in Paul Goldberger, *The City Observed: New York* (New York: Random House, 1979).

13   Ten Footnotes to a Manifesto

Set in Danubia, designed by Victor Solt-Bittner, 2002.

First appeared in *I.D.*, 2000.

The "First Things First 2000" manifesto was published in the autumn 1999 issue of *Adbusters*, and reprinted in *Emigre* and the *AIGA Journal* in North America, in *Eye* and *Blueprint* in Britain, in *Items* in the Netherlands, and *Form* in Germany. Ken Garland's original 1963 manifesto can be found in Michael Bierut, Jessica Helfand, Steven Heller, Rick Poynor, editors, *Looking Closer 3: Classic Writings on Graphic Design* (New York: Allworth Press, 1999). Alexey Brodovitch's 1930 quote is from "What Pleases the Modern Man," reprinted in *Looking Closer 3*. The quote from Susan Nigra Snyder and Steven Izenour is from a letter to the *New York Times*, "Conde Nast Building: American's Square," October 17, 1999. Tibor Kalman's "Designers: stay away from corporations that want you to lie for them"appeared on a billboard designed by Jonathan Barnbrook and installed on the strip for the 1999 AIGA Biennial Conference in Las Vegas. Bill Golden's twenty-one-word-manifesto is from an address to the Ninth International Design Conference in Aspen in 1959 entitled "The Visual Environment of Advertising." It is reprinted in *The Visual Craft of William Golden* (New York: George Braziller, 1962). Ken Garland's quote "What I'm suggesting. . ." appears in his 1967 essay "Here Are Some Things We Must Do,"which appears in *Looking Closer 3*.

14   The *New York Times:* Apocalypse Now, Page A1

Set in News Gothic, designed by Morris Fuller Benton, 1908.

First appeared on *Design Observer*, October 28, 2003.

The unbylined article on the Times redesign was titled "A Face-Lift for the Times, Typographically, That Is" (21 October 2003, Section C, Page 9). The pro and con responses appeared on October 23 on the letters page under the headline "The *Times*'s New Look."

15   Graphic Design and the New Certainties

Set in Eureka, designed by Peter Bilak, 2001.

First appeared on *Design Observer*, November 10, 2003.

The online guide to the 2003 AIGA conference is at http://powerofdesign.aiga.org/ content.cfm/homecategory. For more on the sustainable design issues discussed at the conference, see Michael Braungart and William McDonough, *Cradle to Cradle: Remaking the Way We Make Things* (New York: North Point Press, 2002). J. Robert Oppenheimer's "I am become death..." is a quote from the Hindu scripture *The Bhagavad-Gita*. For more, see James A. Hijiya, "The Gita of Robert Oppenheimer," *Proceedings of the American Philosophical Society*, 144:2 (June 2000).

16   Mark Lombardi and the Ecstasy of Conspiracy

Set in Fedra Serif A Std, designed by Peter Bilak, 2003.

First appeared on *Design Observer*, November 24, 2003.

All references in the essay are from Robert Carleton Hobbs, Mark Lombardi and Judith Richards, *Mark Lombardi: Global Networks* (New York: Independent Curators Incorporated, 2003).

17 George Kennan and the Cold War Between Form and Content
Set in Courier, designed by Howard "Bud" Kettler, 1956.
First appeared on *Design Observer*, March 13, 2004.
All references in the essay are from George Frost Kennan, *Memoirs, 1925–1950* (New York: Little, Brown & Co., 1967). Kennan died in 2005.

18 Errol Morris Blows Up Spreadsheet, Thousands Killed
Set in DIN, designed by Albert-Jan Pool, 1995.
First appeared on *Design Observer*, March 13, 2004.
A great introduction to Errol Morris can be found in Mark Singer, *Mr. Personality: Profiles and Talk Pieces from The New Yorker* (New York: Mariner Books, 2005). See also Morris's website, http://www.errolmorris.com.

19 Catharsis, Salesmanship, and the Limits of Empire
Set in Clifford, designed by Akira Kobayashi, 1999.
First appeared on *Design Observer*, April 22, 2004.
See Nicholas Blechman, et al, *Empire (Nozone No. 9)* (New York: Princeton Architectural Press, 2004). Dan Hedel's assessment is in "Back Into Battle," *Eye*, no. 51, Spring 2004. Marlene McArty is quoted in a 1994 interview with Ellen Lupton for *Mixing Messages: Graphic Design in Contemporary Culture* (New York: Princeton Architectural Press, 1996) found at http://www.designwritingresearch.org/essays/bureau.html. Air America's founder describes his radio network's genesis in Sheldon Drobny, *The Road to Air America: Breaking the Right Wing Stranglehold on Our Nation's Airwaves* (New York: Select Books, 2004.)

20 Better Nation-Building Through Design
Set in JohnSans, designed by Frantisek Storm, 2001
First appeared on *Design Observer*, April 28, 2004.
The controversy over the "new" Iraqi flag was reported in "Iraqis Say Council-Approved National Flag Won't Fly," *Washington Post*, April 23, 2003. Al Jazeera's report is at http://english.aljazeera.net/NR/exeres/94E338BA-2CAF-4267-A9FC-5C425A108CE1.htm. About a month after the new Iraqi flag was unveiled, the Governing Council reverted to a slightly modified version of the flag that had been in use since 1991. The account of the 19th century rebranding of India is from Wally Olins, *Corporate Identity: Making Business Strategy Visible Through Design* (Boston: Harvard Business School Press, 1992.)

21 The T-shirt Competition Republicans Fear Most
Set in Times New Roman, designed by Stanley Morrison, 1931.
First appeared on *Design Observer*, May 9, 2004.
The Designs on the White House website is now down. The screenplay for *Manhattan* (1979) is by Woody Allen and Marshall Brickman. Muzafer Sherif's 1954 "Robbers Cave Experiment," which demonstrated the role that superordinate goals play in conflict resolution, is described in *In Common Predicament: The Social*

Psychology of Intergroup Conflict and Resolution (Boston: Houghton Mifflin Co., 1966).
See also Taylor Branch, *Parting the Waters: America in the King Years, 1954–63*
(New York: Simon and Schuster, 1988).

22   India Switches Brands
Set in Georgia, designed by Matthew Carter and Tom Rickner, 1996.
First appeared on *Design Observer*, May 17, 2004.
See Amy Waldman, "In Huge Upset, Gandhi's Party Wins Election in India," *New York
Times*, 13 May 2004.

23   Graphic Designers: Flush Left?
Set in Geometric, designed by William Addison Dwiggins, 1929.
First appeared on *Design Observer*, May 9, 2004.
See David Brooks, "Ruling Class War," *New York Times*, September 11, 2004. Adrian
Hanft's blog is Be A Design Group, at http://www.beadesigngroup.com.
Tom Lehrer's song "Werner von Braun" appeared on his 1965 album *That Was The
Year That Was.*

24   Just Say Yes
Set in Frutiger, designed by Adrian Frutiger, 1968.
First appeared on *Design Observer*, May 17, 2004.
Firsthand accounts of pranks staged by The Yes Men can be found at their website,
http://www.theyesmen.org. The press release quoted is from an email sent to the
author. Mainstream media reports on the Bhopal hoax can be found in Sean O'Neill,
"Cruel $12 billion hoax on Bhopal victims and BBC," *Times*, December 4, 2004, and
Alan Cowell, "BBC Falls Prey to Hoax on Anniversary of Bhopal Disaster," December
4, 2004. Ralph Caplan describes the sit-in as "the most elegant design solution of the
fifties" in *By Design: Why There are No Locks on the Bathroom Doors of the Hotel Louis
XIV and Other Object Lessons* (New York: St. Martin's Press, 1982). Then-Governor
George W. Bush's quote "There ought to be limits to freedom" was reported by Wayne
Slater, "Bush Criticizes Web Site as Malicious," *Dallas Morning News*, 22 May 1999.

25   Regrets Only
Set in Rockwell, designed by Lucian Bernhard, 1934.
First appeared on *Design Observer*, July 10, 2006.
The National Design Awards are described on the Cooper-Hewitt website at http://www.
cooperhewitt.org/NDA. The letter from Michael Rock, Susan Sellers, Georgie Stout,
Paula Scher, and Stefan Sagmeister, and the email from Chip Kidd are quoted with
permission of their authors. Laura Bush's remarks from the 2002 brunch can be
found at http://www.whitehouse.gov/news/releases/2002/07/20020710-14.html.
Nixon's quote, and more information about federal support for design, can be found
at http://www.idsa.org/whatsnew/sections/dh/special_awards/1979_NEA.html, as
well as at http://www.nea.gov/about/40th/fdip.html.

26   The Forgotten Design Legacy of the *National Lampoon*
Set in Cooper, designed by Oswald Cooper, 1921.
First appeared on *Design Observer*, January 5, 2004.
See Doug Kenny and P. J. O'Rourke, *National Lampoon's 1964 High School Yearbook,*

39th Reunion Edition (New York: Rugged Land, 2003). Tony Hendra writes about the *Lampoon*'s design philosophy in *Going Too Far* (New York: Doubleday, 1987).

27 *McSweeney's* No. 13 and the Revenge of the Nerds
Set in Garamond 3, designed by Morris Fuller Benton and T.M. Cleland, 1917, after Jean Jannon, 1615
First appeared on *Design Observer*, 29 May 2004.
A review of Chris Ware, editor, *McSweeney's Quarterly Concern No. 13* (New York: McSweeney's Books, 2004). Andrew Blauvelt identified *McSweeney's* as an example of a new trend in graphic design in "Toward a Complex Simplicity," *Eye*, no. 35, Spring 2000.

28 The Book (Cover) That Changed My Life
Set in ITC Bookman, designed by Edward Benguiat, 1975.
First appeared on *Design Observer*, March 19, 2004.
See, of course, J. D. Salinger, *The Catcher in the Rye* (New York: Bantam Books, 1964). Rachel Toor —a college admissions officer who has read many tributes to "CITR"— wrote *Admissions Confidential: An Insider's Account of the Elite College Admissions Process* (New York: St. Martin's Griffin, 2002). I am still waiting for the designer of the maroon cover to come forward.

29 Vladimir Nabokov: Father of Hypertext
Set in Janson, based on a design by Nicholas Kis, c.1690.
First appeared on *Design Observer*, January 11, 2004.
Hell, why settle for anything less than the first edition? Vladimir Nabokov, *Pale Fire*, (New York: G.P. Putnam's Sons, 1962). See also Brian Boyd, *Nabokov's Pale Fire: The Magic of Artistic Discovery* (Princeton, N.J.: Princeton University Press, 1999). Theodor Nelson proposed a demonstration of hyperlinks using *Pale Fire* for the IBM booth at the 1969 Joint Computer Conference; an amazing facsimile of the presentation script can be found at http://xanadu.com/XUarchive.

30 The Final Decline and Total Collapse of the American Magazine Cover
Set in HTF Didot, designed by Jonathan Hoefler, 1992, based on a design by Fermin Didot, 1784.
First appeared on *Design Observer*, February 18, 2004.
The indispensable survey is George Lois, *Covering the Sixties: The Esquire Era* (New York: Monacelli Press, 1996). For additional background, see, Carol Polsgrove, *It Wasn't Pretty Folks, But Didn't We Have Fun? Esquire in the Sixties* (New York: W. W. Norton & Co., 1995). An audio file of Lois's interview with Kurt Andersen can be found at http://www.studio360.org/show011704.html.

31 Information Design and the Placebo Effect
Set in MorganAvec, designed by Mario Feliciano 2003.
First appeared on *Design Observer*, February 28, 2004.
See Michael Luo, "For Exercise in New York Futility, Push Button," *New York Times*, February 27, 2004.

32 Stanley Kubrick and the Future of Graphic Design
Set in Futura, designed by Paul Renner, 1927.

First appeared on *Design Observer*, April 2, 2004.

See Jon Ronson, "Citizen Kubrick," *Guardian*, March 27, 2004. Stanley Kubrick's 1968 movie *2001: A Space Odyssey* was directed by Kubrick, and written by Kubrick and Arthur C. Clarke; the production design was by Ernest Archer, Harry Lange, and Tony Masters, set decoration by Robert Cartwright, and special effects by Con Pederson and Douglas Trumbull. *Dr. Strangelove, or: How I Learned to Stop Worrying and Love the Bomb* (1964) was written by Stanley Kubrick, Terry Southern, and Peter George; the quote from Keenan Wynn was my father's favorite line in the movie. Finally, if you love *2001*, track down a copy of Jerome Agel's *The Making of Kubrick's 2001* (New York: Signet Books, 1970).

33 I Hear You've Got Script Trouble: The Designer as Auteur

Set in American Typewriter, designed by Joel Kaden and Tony Stan, 1974.

First appeared on *Design Observer*, April 17, 2004.

William Goldman's books on screenwriting are *Adventures in the Screen Trade* (New York: Warner Books, 1989) and *Which Lie Did I Tell?* (New York: Vintage Books, 2001). Lorraine Wild's essay "Sand Castles" appears in *Emigre No. 66: Nudging Graphic Design* (New York: Princeton Architectural Press, 2004).

34 The Idealistic Corporation

Set in Filosofia, designed by Zuzana Licko, 1996.

First appeared on *Design Observer*, June 16, 2004.

Thomas J. Watson's essay "Good Design is Good Business" appears in Michael Bierut, Jessica Helfand, Steven Heller, Rick Poynor, editors, *Looking Closer 3: Classic Writings on Graphic Design* (New York: Allworth Press, 1999). Walter Paepcke's 1946 quote is from "Art in Industry," also in *Looking Closer 3*. I quote Paepcke's foreword to Herbert Bayer's *World Geo-Graphic Atlas* (Chicago: Container Corporation of America, 1953). Tibor Kalman is quoted from his introduction to Michael Bierut and Peter Hall, editors, *Tibor Kalman: Perverse Optimist* (New York: Princeton Architectural Press, 1998).

35 Barthes on the Ballpoint

Set in Adobe Jenson Pro, designed by Robert Slimbach, 1996.

First appeared on *Design Observer*, June 19, 2004

Barthes is quoted in "An Almost Obsessive Relation to Writing Instruments" in Roland Barthes, *The Grain of the Voice: Interviews 1962–1980*, trans. Linda Coverdale (Berkeley: University of California Press, 1991). The quote from Dan Hedley is from an email to the author.

36 The Tyranny of the Tagline

Set in Abadi, designed by Ong ChongWah, 1987.

First appeared on *Design Observer*, June 29, 2004.

The YWCA's website is http://www.ywca.org. David Oglivy's views on slogans are from *Ogilvy on Advertising* (New York: Vintage Books, 1985).

37 Ed Ruscha: When Art Rises to the Level of Graphic Design

Set in Stymie, designed by Morris Fuller Benton, 1931.

First appeared on *Design Observer*, July 12, 2004.

Ruscha's quote on making books is from the exhibition catalog by Cornelia Butler and

Margit Rowell, *Cotton Puffs, Q-Tips ®, Smoke and Mirrors: The Drawings of Ed Ruscha* (New York: Whitney Museum of Art, 2004). See also Karen Rosenberg, "L.A. Story: Ed Ruscha Gets a Double Feature at the Whitney,"in *New York*, June 28–July 5, 2004.

38   To Hell with the Simple Paper Clip
Set in Meta, designed by Erik Spiekermann, 1991-1998.
First appeared on *Design Observer*, July 14, 2004.
See Paola Antonelli, *Humble Masterpieces: Everyday Marvels of Design* (New York: Regan Books, 2005). I joined seventeen other "artists, designers, thinkers, and taste makers," including Martha Stewart and Joseph Holzman, in "Desire: My Favorite Thing" for *New York Times Magazine*, December 13, 1988.

39   The Man Who Saved Jackson Pollock
Set in Clarendon, designed by Edouard Hoffman, 1953, after Hermann Eidenbenz, 1845.
First appeared on *Design Observer*, June 6, 2005.
Herbert Matter failed to get the proper credit in Jack Kadden, "Commuter's Journal: A Bit of New Haven Line is Resurrected," *New York Times*, 7 December 2003. (I was not alone in writing to complain to Kadden; he replied to me that he had been taken aback by the ferocity of Matter's fans.) Paul Rand's poem for Matter is quoted in Steven Heller and David R. Brown, "Herbert Matter," *AIGA Graphic Design 5: The Annual of the American Institute of Graphic Arts* (New York: Watson Guptill Publications, 1983). As of this writing, the controversy about the legitimacy of the thirty-two paintings tentatively attributed to Jackson Pollock is still unresolved.

40   Homage to the Squares
Set in Swiss 721 BT, designed by Max Miedinger, 1982.
First appeared on *Design Observer*, April 3, 2005.
See Martin Filler and Nicholas Fox Weber, *Josef and Anni Albers: Designs for Living* (London and New York: Merrell, 2004). See also Barbara Bloemink, *Design is not Art: Functional Objects from Judd to Whiteread* (London and New York: Merrell, 2004). The quotes from Hockney, Burton, and Judd are in the latter. Tom Wolfe's sarcastic quote on Albers is from *The Painted Word* (Farrar, Strauss & Giroux, 1975).

41   Eero Saarinen's Forty-Year Layover
Set in Eurostile, designed by Aldo Novarese, 1962.
First appeared on *Design Observer,* August 4, 2004.
Director Michael Mayer's comments appeared in "Fall Rising," an interview with Randy Gener for the Roundabout Theater Company's publication *Front & Center*, Summer 2004. JetBlue's plan for renovating the terminal was approved and is now underway.

42   The Rendering and the Reality
Set in Monticello, designed by Matthew Carter, 2002, after C.H. Griffith, 1950.
First appeared on *Design Observer*, August 14, 2004.

43   What We Talk About When We Talk About Architecture
Set in Joanna, designed by Eric Gill, 1930.
First appeared on *Design Observer*, October 21, 2004.
All quoted dialog is from Jason Van Nest, Yen-Rong Chen, and Mathew Ford, editors,

Retrospecta (New Haven: Yale University School of Architecture, 2004). Oren Safdie's play "Private Jokes, Public Places" was reviewed in D. J. R. Bruckner, "Constructing a Comedy from Architects' Foibles," *New York Times*, 23 November 2003.

44 Colorama
Set in Flama, designed by Mario Feliciano, 2006.
First appeared on *Design Observer*, November 1, 2004.
See Alison Nordstrom, *Colorama: The World's Largest Photographs* (New York: Aperture, 2004). To fully appreciate suburban ennui and terror, try John Cheever, *The Stories of John Cheever* (New York: Random House, 1978).

45 Mr. Vignelli's Map
Set in Akzidenz Grotesk, designed by Günter Gerhard Lange, 1896.
First appeared on *Design Observer*, October 28, 2004.
The Vignelli map is described as "colorful and handsome" as well as "incomprehensible" in Clyde Haberman, "From Here to There, Please, With Clarity," *New York Times*, October 26, 2004. For a remarkable history of the London Underground map, see Ken Garland, *Mr. Beck's Underground Map* (London: Capital Transport Publications, 1994).

46 I Hate ITC Garamond
Set in ITC Garamond, designed by Tony Stan, 1975.
First appeared on *Design Observer*, October 1, 2004.
The Paula Scher / Roger Black debate was first reported by Karrie Jacobs in "An Existential Guide to Type," *Metropolis*, April 1988. Paul Goldberger's quote about accepting old buildings is in *Up From Zero* (New York: Random House, 2004). Finally, the text of J. Robert Moskin's *Mr. Truman's War: The Final Victories of WWII and the Birth of the Postwar World* (New York: Random House, 1996) is set entirely in ITC Garamond.

47 1989: Roots of Revolution
Set in Gotham, designed by Tobias Frere-Jones, 2000.
First appeared in a slightly different form on *Design Observer*, March 6, 2004.
The two polemics discussed here, Neville Brody and Stuart Ewen, "Design Insurgency," and Karrie Jacobs and Tibor Kalman, "We're Here to Be Bad," were published in the January/February 1990 issue of *Print*. John Emerson is quoted from an email to the author.

48 The World in Two Footnotes
Set in Palatino, designed by Hermann Zapf, 1948.
First appeared on *Design Observer*, November 18, 2004.
See John L. Walters, "Editorial"; Terry Eagleton, "Reading On Brand"; and Nick Bell, "The Steamroller of Branding": all in *Eye*, no. 53, Autumn 2004.

49 Logogate in Connecticut
Set in Helvetica, designed by Max Miedinger, 1957.
First appeared on *Design Observer*, November 21, 2004.
See Marian Gail Brown, "$10,000 Logo Provokes Head-Scratching,"*Connecticut Post*, November 8, 2004; the unsigned editorial "New Tourism Logo Raises Questions," *Connecticut Post*, November 16, 2004; and Alison Leigh Cowan, "$10,000 Logo for State Culture Agency Draws Angry Complaints," *New York Times*, November 18, 2004.

Tom Wolfe is quoted in *Communication Graphics 1972* (New York: American Institute of Graphic Arts, 1972). The Kurt Vonnegut quote is from *Breakfast of Champions* (New York: Delecorte Press, 1972).

50   The Whole Damn Bus is Cheering
Set in Trade Gothic, designed by Jackson Burke, 1948.
First appeared on *Design Observer*, December 1, 2004.
"Tie a Yellow Ribbon," words and music by Irwin Levine and L. Russell Brown, © 1972 Irwin Levine Music, BMI / Peer Music, BMI. Thanks to Chester for the inventory of colored ribbon symbolism.

51   The Best Artist in the World
Set in Scala Sans, designed by Martin Majoor, 1993.
First appeared on *Design Observer*, January 19, 2005.
Alton Tobey's masterpiece is the twelve-volume *Golden Book History of the United States* (New York: Golden Press, 1963). The best overview of his work is at www.altontobey.com.

52   The Supersized, Temporarily Impossible World of Bruce McCall
Set in Chaparral Pro, designed by Carol Twombly, 2000.
First appeared on *Design Observer*, April 18, 2005.
See Bruce McCall, *Thin Ice* (New York: Random House Value Publishing, 1999). McCall's best early work is collected in *Zany Afternoons* (New York: Alfred A. Knopf, 1982). A newer collection is *All Meat Looks Like South America: The World of Bruce McCall* (New York: Crown Publishing Group, 2003).

53   The Unbearable Lightness of Fred Marcellino
Set in Perpetua, designed by Eric Gill, 1928
First appeared on *Design Observer*, December 29, 2005.
See Ned Drew and Paul Sternberger, *By Its Cover: Modern American Book Cover Design* (New York: Princeton Architectural Press, 2005). Marcellino's biographical information, and the quote from Steven Heller, is from Nicholas Falletta, editor, *The Art of Fred Marcellino* (New York: Pulcinella Press, 2003). One of my favorite Marcellino covers is on Jonathan Franzen's *The Twenty-Seventh City* (New York: Farrar, Straus & Giroux, 1988).

54   The Comfort of Style
Set in Nobel, designed by Tobias Frere-Jones, 1993.
First appeared on *Design Observer*, February 3, 2005.
A review of Philip Nobel, *Sixteen Acres: Architecture and the Outrageous Struggle for the Future of Ground Zero* (New York: Metropolitan Books, 2004). Nobel was interviewed by Martin C. Pedersen in "Book Casts WTC Development as Modern Epic," *Metropolis*, December 2004. Nobel spoke at the Urban Center in New York on January 11; 2004, and the quote is from a transcript provided by The Architectural League.

55   Authenticity: A User's Guide
Set in Univers, designed by Adrian Frutiger, 1954.
First appeared on *Design Observer*, February 8, 2005.
A transcript and audio file of John Solomon's report "Pulling Back the Curtain" for

National Public Radio's *On the Media* can be found at http://www.onthemedia.org/ transcripts/transcripts_123104_curtain.html. Marian Bantjes's article for Speak Up, "True Confessions," can be found at http://www.underconsideration.com/speakup/ archives/002186.html#002186. "Good History/Bad History" by Tibor Kalman, J. Abbott Miller, and Karrie Jacobs is collected in Michael Bierut, William Drenttel, Steven Heller, and DK Holland, editors, *Looking Closer: Critical Writings on Graphic Design* (New York: Allworth Press, 1994).

56 Designing Under the Influence
Set in Futura Italic, designed by Paul Renner, 1927.
First appeared on *Design Observer*, February 26, 2005.
Of the many books on the artist, one of the best is the Lorraine Wild-designed *Barbara Kruger* (Cambridge, Mass.: MIT Press, 1999). Liz McQuiston, *From Suffragettes to She Devils* (London: Phaidon Press, 1997) not only includes useful information on Kruger, but also bears Paula Scher's cover as an homage. Kruger's *Esquire* cover was for the May 1992 issue on Howard Stern. This article received 270 comments, more than any other to date in the history of *Design Observer*, totaling over 60,000 words.

57 Me and My Pyramid
Set in Adobe Caslon, designed by Carol Twombly, 1990, after William Caslon, 1725.
First appeared on *Design Observer*, April 22, 2005.The United States Department of Agriculture's Food Pyramid currently resides at http://www.mypyramid.gov.

58 On (Design) Bullshit
Set in ITC Officina Sans, designed by Erik Spiekermann, 1990.
First appeared on *Design Observer*, May 9, 2005.
See Harry G. Frankfurt, *On Bullshit* (Princeton: Princeton University Press, 2005). All quoted dialog is from the documentary *Concert of Wills: Making the Getty Center*, written and directed by Susan Froemke, Bob Eisenhardt, and Albert Maysles (1998).

59 Call Me Shithead, or, What's in a Name?
Set in Thonburi, designer unknown.
First appeared on *Design Observer*, June 19, 2005.
For the economics of baby names, see Steven D. Levitt and Stephen J. Dubner, *Freakonomics: A Rogue Economist Explores the Hidden Side of Almost Everything* (New York: William Morrow, 2005). "Ex-Rox, the famous Japanese laxative" is from one of my favorite books, George Lois with Bill Pitts, *George, Be Careful: A Greek Florist's Kid in the Roughhouse World of Advertising* (New York: Saturday Review Press, 1972). Ruth Shalit's piece on naming firms, "The Name Game" appeared on Salon.com at http://salon.com/media/col/shal/1999/11/30/naming/print.html (November 30, 1999). The letters that provide the priceless account of Marianne Moore's attempts to provide a name for the Edsel have been widely reprinted, including Marianne Moore, "Correspondence with David Wallace" in Mordicai Richter, editor, *The Best of Modern Humor* (New York: Alfred A. Knopf, 1984). Finally, the fantastic Baby Name Wizard's NameVoyager can be found at http://babynamewizard.com/namevoyager/lnvo105.html.

60 Avoiding Poor, Lonely Obvious
Set in Hoefler Text, designed by Jonathan Hoefler, 1991.

First appeared on *Design Observer*, June 28, 2005."

The issue of *I.D.* in question is July/August 2005. See also Paul Elliman, *Mevis and Van Deursen: Recollected Work* (Rotterdam: Artimo Foundation Breda, 2005) and Rick Poynor's review, "*Mevis and Van Deursen: Rueful Recollections, Recycled Design*," at http://www.designobserver.com/archives/003288.html (June 3, 2005).

61 My Favorite Book is Not About Design (or Is It?)
Set in Scotch, designed by David Berlow, 1993.
First appeared on *Design Observer*, July 12, 2005.
All quoted passages are from Moss Hart, *Act One* (New York: Random House, 1959). See also Steven Bach, *Dazzler: The Life and Times of Moss Hart* (New York: Alfred A. Knopf, 2001).

62 Rick Valicenti: This Time It's Personal
Set in Galaxie Polaris, designed by Tracey Jenkins and Chester, 2005.
First appeared on *Design Observer*, July 14, 2005.
A review of Rick Valicenti, *Emotion as Promotion: A Book of Thirst* (New York: The Monacelli Press, 2005).

63 Credit Line Goes Here
Set in Interstate, designed by Tobias Frere-Jones, 1993.
First appeared in a slightly different form on *Design Observer*, July 22, 2005.

64 Every New Yorker is a Target
Set in Egyptian 505, designed by André Gürtler, 1966.
First appeared on *Design Observer*, August 16, 2005.
The issue of the *The New Yorker* discussed here is August 22, 2005. It also contains the comic about North Korea by Guy Delisle that I quote from. See also the ludicrous but exciting Wilson Bryan Key, *Subliminal Seduction* (New York: Signet Books, 1974). Editor David Remnick is quoted in Stuart Elliott, "And What Would Thurber Say? A Single-Sponsor *New York Times*" August 12, 2006.

65 I Am a Plagiarist
Set in Retina, designed by Jonathan Hoefler and Tobias Frere-Jones, 2003.
First appeared on *Design Observer*, May 11, 2006.
Accounts of Kaavya Viswanathan's travails appear in David Zhou, "Student's Novel Faces Plagiarism Controversy," *Harvard Crimson*, April 23, 2006; Paras D. Bhayani and David Zhou, "Soph Says She's Sorry for Overlap," *Harvard Crimson*, April 25, 2006; and Dinita Smith, "Novelist Said She Read Copied Books Several Times," *New York Times*, April 27, 2006. Kurt Andersen's assessment appears in "Generation Xerox," *New York*, May 15, 2006. See also Philip B. Meggs and Alston W. Purvis, *Meggs' History of Graphic Design, 4th Edition* (Hoboken, N.J.: John Wiley & Sons, 2006) and Willi Kunz, *Typography: Micro- and Macroaesthetics* (Sulgen: Arthur Niggli Ltd., 2004)

66 Looking for Celebration, Florida
Set in Cheltenham, designed by Bertram Goodhue, 1896.
First appeared on *Design Observer*, October 13, 2005.
Books on Celebration include Douglas Frantz and Catherine Collins, *Celebration, U.S.A.: Living in Disney's Brave New Town* (New York: Henry Holt and Company, 1999);

Andrew Ross, *The Celebration Chronicles: Life, Liberty, and the Pursuit of Property Value in Disney's New Town* (New York: Ballantine Books, 1999); and Michael Lassell, *Celebration: The Story of a Town* (New York: Roundtable Press, 2004). (Ross's is my favorite: informed, cynical, and funny.) Witold Rybczynski's "Celebration in Action: Disney's Controversial Town, a Decade On," is on Slate.com at http://www.slate.com/id/2113107. For Celebration's immediate antecedent, see Keller Easterling and David Mohney, *Seaside: Building a Town in America* (New York: Princeton Architectural Press, 1996). See also the beloved Jack Finney, *Time and Again* (New York: Scribner Paperback Fiction, 1995). Finally, Chumbawamba's song "Celebration, Florida" appears on their 2000 release *What You See Is What You Get*.

67 The Great Non-Amber-Colored Hope
Set in Warnock Pro, designed by Robert Slimbach, 2000.
First appeared on *Design Observer*, October 24, 2005.
The AIGA brochure "What Every Business Needs" is available at http://www.aiga.org/resources/teaser/2/4/8/documents/AIGAfinal-1.pdf. The story of the bottle's design appeared in, among other places, Sarah Bernard, "The Perfect Prescription," *New York*, April 18, 2005.

68 The Mysterious Power of Context
Set in ITC Stone Sans, designed by Sumner Stone, 1987.
First appeared on *Design Observer*, October 24, 2005.
See J. B. Strasser and Laurie Becklund, *Swoosh: The Unauthorized Story of Nike and the Men Who Played There* (New York: Harcourt Brace Jovanovich, 1991).

69 The Final Days of AT&T
Set in Bell Gothic, designed by C. H. Griffith, 1938.
First appeared on Design Observer, October 29, 2005.
The press release "SBC Communications to Adopt AT&T Name" can be found on SBC's website at http://www.sbc.com/gen/press-room?pid=7368. The history of the AT&T logo, including the description of the Bass logo as "a world circled by electronic communications," can be found at the company's online brand center at http://www.att.com/brand/history. As of this writing, it has not been updated to include the most recent transformation. Alan Siegel is quoted in Riva Richmond, "Will SBC Take Family Name? Ma Bell Exerts Brand Power," *Wall Street Journal*, January 31, 2005.

70 Designing Twyla Tharp's Upper Room
Set in Mrs. Eaves, designed by Zuzana Licko, 1996.
First appeared on *Design Observer*, November 6, 2005.
The quotes from Tharp are from Twyla Tharp, *Push Comes to Shove* (New York: Bantam Books, 1993). The quote from Jennifer Tipton is from her essay "Light Unseen," *Esopus* 5 (Fall 2005). "Sheer exuberance of motion" is from Nancy Gardner, "Music of Philip Glass Finds an Ideal Partner in Tharp,"*Philadelphia Inquirer*, January 8, 1987.

71 Innovation is the New Black
Set in Dante, designed by Giovanni Mardersteig, 1954.
First appeared on *Design Observer*, November 20, 2005.
The invitation to the Institute of Design innovation symposium can be found at http://

www.id.iit.edu/events/strategy_symposium_nyc.html. The website of the DMI (née the Design Management Institute) is http://www.dmi.org. See also Bruce Nussbaum, "Get Creative! How to Build Innovative Companies," Business Week, August 1, 2005. Tom Kelly's books are *The Art of Innovation* (New York: Currency Books, 2001) and *The Ten Faces of Innovation: IDEO's Strategies for Defeating the Devil's Advocate and Driving Creativity Throughout Your Organization* (New York: Currency Books, 2005). IDEO's website is http://www.ideo.com..

72 Wilson Pickett, Design Theorist, 1942-2006

Set in Bliss, designed by Jeremy Tankard, 1996.

First appeared on *Design Observer*, January 22, 2006.

"Utilitas, firmitas et venustas" ("Commodity, firmness and delight") is from *De Architectura* by Marcus Vitruvius Pollio (c. 80/70 B.C.-25 B.C.), widely available in English editions including Ingrid D. Rowland and Thomas Noble Howe, editors, *Ten Books on Architecture* (Cambridge: Cambridge University Press, 2001). "Form follows function" is attributed to Louis Sullivan (1856-1924). "Graphic design which evokes..." is from Paul Rand, *A Designer's Art* (New Haven: Yale University Press, 1985). All quotes on and by Pickett are from Gerri Hershey, *Nowhere to Run: The Story of Soul Music* (New York: Times Books, 1984).

73 Design by Committee

Set in Quadraat, designed by Fred Smeijers, 1992.

First appeared on *Design Observer*, February 12, 2006.

A review of Aaron Betsky, *The U.N. Building* (London: Thames & Hudson, 2006). See also George Dudley, *A Workshop for Peace* (Cambridge, Mass.: MIT Press, 1994). Paul Goldberger's quote is from *The City Observed: New York* (New York: Random House, 1979). Rem Koolhaas's quote is from *Delirious New York* (New York: Oxford University Press, 1978).

74 The Persistence of the Exotic Menial

Set in Bryant Pro, designed by Eric Olson, 2002.

First appeared on *Design Observer*, February 26, 2006.

Ralph Caplan is quoted from a transcript of his 1981 speech, later adapted as "The More Things Change, the More We Stay the Same," in *By Design: Why There are No Locks on the Bathroom Doors of the Hotel Louis XIV and Other Object Lessons* (New York: St. Martin's Press, 1982). See also W. A. Dwiggins, "A Technique for Dealing with Artists," Michael Bierut, Jessica Helfand, Steven Heller, Rick Poynor, editors, *Looking Closer 3: Classic Writings on Graphic Design* (New York: Allworth Press, 1999). Peter Saville was voted "more admired individual working with the creative industries" by the readers of *Creative Review*, as reported in Chris Hall, "Graphic Sex," *Icon*, July/August 2004. *24 Hour Party People* (2004) was directed by Michael Winterbottom and written by Frank Cotrell Boyce. The Massive Change website is at http://www.massivechange.com. The Institute of Design at Stanford University website is at http://www.stanford.edu/group/dschool; the napkin sketch that initiated its conception can be viewed at http://www.stanford.edu/group/dschool/ manifesto.html. The NextDesign Leadership Workshop website is at http://www. nextd.org. The Beyond Graphic website is at http://www.beyondgraphic.org. Virginia

Postrel was interviewed by Steve MacLaughlin for the website Boxes and Arrows at http://www.boxesandarrows.com/view/talking_with_virginia_postrel; Her book on design is *The Substance of Style: How the Rise of Aesthetic Value is Remaking Culture, Commerce, and Consciousness* (New York: Harper Perennial, 2004).

75 The Road to Hell: Now Paved with Innovation!
Set in Fournier, based on a design by Pierre Simon Fornier, c.1742.
First appeared on *Design Observer*, June 4, 2006.
Bruce Nussbaum's quotes are from his "Nussbaum on Design" blog at http://www. businessweek.com/innovate/NussbaumOnDesign, including "Backstory: How We Designed the New *INside Innovation* Magazine" at http://www.businessweek. com/innovate/NussbaumOnDesign/archives/2006/05/how_we_designed.html. AIGA's "Business and Ethical Expectations for Professional Designers" is at http:// www.aiga.org/resources/content/4/6/0/documents/AIGA_1ethics_.pdf. Blogger Andy Rutledge writes about spec work in "Redesign Competitions: Looking for a Commitment or just a Roll in the Hay?" at http://www.andyrutledge.com/redesign-contest.php. See also Randall Rothenberg, *Where the Suckers Moon: The Life and Death of an Advertising Campaign* (New York: Vintage Books, 1995). This article received one hundred fifty comments, including thoughtful defenses from Bruce Nussbaum and Keith Yamashita.

76 When Design is a Matter of Life or Death
Set in Vendetta, designed by John Downer, 1999.
First appeared on *Design Observer*, June 6, 2006.
See Joe Morgenstern, "The Fifty-Nine-Story Crisis," *New Yorker*, May 29, 1995.

77 In Praise of Slow Design
Set in Schneidler, designed by Friedrich Hermann Ernst Schneidler, 1936.
First appeared on *Design Observer*, January 15, 2006.
See David Remnick, introduction, *The Complete New Yorker* (New York: Random House, 2005). Also see Thomas Kunkel, *Genius in Disguise: Harold Ross of the New Yorker* (New York: Carrol & Graf Publishers, 1996). Ben Hecht is quoted in Piers Brendon, "Smart and Smarter," Columbia Journalism Review, May/June 1995. SlowLab's website is at http://www.slowlab.net. Momus discusses slow magazines on his blog at http://imomus.livejournal.com/164536.html. John Hersey's article, "Hiroshima," appeared in *The New Yorker's* August 6, 1945 issue, which is where the quoted editor's note also appears. For the entire article, see John Hersey, *Hiroshima* (New York: Alfred A. Knopf, 1946). The letter quoted is from Trysh Travis, "What We Talk About; When We Talk About: *The New Yorker,*" *Book History*, Volume 3, 2000.

78 Massimo Vignelli's Pencil
Set in Bodoni, based on a design by Giambattista Bodoni, 1788.
First appeared in *Domus*, 2001.

79 On Falling Off a Treadmill
Set in Gill Sans, designed by Eric Gill, 1928.
First appeared in *Interiors*, September 1997.
Perfect (1985) was directed by James Bridges and written by Aaron Latham.

Index

About the Author

Michael Bierut is a partner in the New York office of the international design consultancy Pentagram. He is coeditor of *Tibor Kalman: Perverse Optimist* and the five-edition *Looking Closer* series of design criticism anthologies, as well as cofounder of the online publication DesignObserver.com. A Senior Critic in Graphic Design at the Yale School of Art, he was also the recipient of the 2006 Medal of the American Institute of Graphic Arts, the profession's highest honor. He lives in Sleepy Hollow, New York, with his high school sweetheart Dorothy Kresz and their three children.